Adjusting to EU Enlargement

Adjusting to EU Enlargement

Recurring Issues in a New Setting

Edited by

Constantine A. Stephanou,
Jean Monnet Chair in European Organisation,
Panteion University, Athens, Greece;
Vice-President of ECSA-Europe.

Edward Elgar
Cheltenham, UK • Northampton, MA, USA

Published by
Edward Elgar Publishing Limited
Glensanda House
Montpellier Parade
Cheltenham
Glos GL50 1UA
UK

Edward Elgar Publishing, Inc.
136 West Street
Suite 202
Northampton
Massachusetts 01060
USA

A catalogue record for this book
is available from the British Library

Library of Congress Cataloguing in Publication Data
Adjusting to EU Enlargement : recurring issues in a new setting / edited
by Constantine A. Stephanou
     p   cm.
Includes bibliographical references and index.
1. Europe—Economic integration—Europe, Eastern. 2. Europe—Politics and
government—1989– 3. Europe—Foreign economic relations. I. Title:
Adjusting to EU Enlargement. II. Stephanou, Constantine A. III. Title.

HC241.25.E852A35 2006
337.1'42–dc22   2005031645

ISBN-13: 978 1 84542 604 0
ISBN-10: 1 84542 604 5

Printed and bound in Great Britain by MPG Books Ltd, Bodmin, Cornwall

Contents

Part I: The New Economic Setting

Part II: Governance and Cohesion of the Enlarged Union

Contributors

Nicholas C. BALTAS is Professor of Economics at the Athens University of Economics and Business and former Chairman of the Department of Economics. He also holds the Jean Monnet Chair on EU Institutions and Economic Policy, and is a former President of the Hellenic ECSA association. He studied economics at the Athens School of Economics and Business and obtained his MSocSc and PhD. in Economics from the University of Birminhgam (England). He has taught at the University of Thessaloniki. He has also occupied the position of Senior Economist at the Research and Planning Division of the Agricultural Bank of Greece. He has also been a member of the Independent Committee of Experts for the 2002 Monitoring Report in Non-Nuclear Energy of the European Commission and a member of the Independent Scientific Committee of Experts for the Ministry of Agriculture of Greece and has served as an expert to the Economic and Social Committee of Greece. He is currently the President of the Board of Directors of the Hellenic Railways Organization SA. His research interests cover several areas including micro-economic theory and applied economic topics related to agricultural economics, the economics of European integration, and environmental economics. He is the author of a number of books, research monographs and articles.

Carol COSGROVE-SACKS is Professor at the College of Europe, Bruges, and a consultant on international trade and economic integration, based in Geneva, Switzerland. From 1994 to 2005 she was the Director of Trade in the United Nations Economic Commission for Europe (UNECE), Geneva. In that capacity she was responsible for the UN's Wider Europe programme, supporting the integration of countries with economies in transition into the wider European and global economy. She advised governments throughout Eastern, Central and Southern Europe on their trade strategies. From 1981 to 1994 she was an international business development consultant, advising major companies, trade associations and governments on international trade and financing issues, especially regarding the EU. She is a Visiting Professor at the Europa Institute, Basel University, Switzerland, and the Centre for Euro-Asian Studies at the University of Reading, England.

Educated at the London School of Economics, she is the author / editor of several books on international economic relations, including *Trade Facilitation – the Challenges for Growth and Development* (Geneva: the United Nations, 2003), *Europe, Diplomacy & Development* (London: Palgrave, 2001) and *The EU & Developing Countries: Challenges of Globalization* (London: Macmillan, 1999).

Victoria CURZON PRICE is Professor of Economics at the University of Geneva. Current positions include: President of the Mont Pèlerin Society, member of the *Conseil de l'Université de Genève*, member of the Academic Advisory Council of the Institute of Economic Affairs, London and of the Centre for the New Europe, Brussels. Previous positions include: Membership of the Board and Vice President of the Mont Pèlerin Society (1996–2002), Director of the European Institute of the University of Geneva (1994–1998), faculty member of the International Management Institute, Geneva (1972–1990) and visiting professor at the University of Amsterdam during the 1980s. Professor Curzon Price is the author of many books and articles on international trade policy and European integration. Her current research interests include taxation and fiscal competition.

Christian FRANCK is Professor Ordinarius and President of the Institute of European Studies at the Université Catholique de Louvain (Belgium). He is Professor Chaire Jean Monnet in Political Sciences and Secretary General of the TransEuropean Policy Studies Association (TEPSA). He has been Advisor to the Belgian Minister for Development and to the Belgian Minister of External Trade. He has lectured in many foreign universities, such as Universidad Alcala de Henarès (Madrid), Universitad Pontificale de Lima, Ecole de Droit de Ouagadougou, Université Hassan II de Casablanca, Université de Paris X (Nanterre), Institut d'études politiques de Lille, Ecole internationale des sciences politiques de Katowice and Università di Roma III. He has written articles and books on topics referring mainly to the external policy of the European Union, the EU political system and Belgium's European policy.

Miroslav N. JOVANOVIC is Economic Affairs Officer at the UN Economic Commission for Europe in Geneva. He studied in Serbia, the Netherlands and Canada. His principal interests are in the areas of international economic integration; European Union and its enlargement; transnational corporations and foreign direct investment; competition, trade and industrial policies; as well as in geography of production: location of firms, clusters and industries. He is the author and editor of 15 books that include: *The Economics of International Integration* (2006), Cheltenham:

Edward Elgar; *The Economics of European Integration* (2005), Cheltenham: Edward Elgar (also published in Serbian and forthcoming in Greek); *Geography of Production and Economic Integration* (2001), London: Routledge; *International Economic Integration: Limits and Prospects* (1998), London: Routledge (also published in Greek); *European Economic Integration: Limits and Prospects* (1997), London: Routledge. He also published articles, served as a referee to publishers and lectured in Austria, Germany, Greece, Italy, Serbia, Switzerland and the United States.

Yelena KALYUZHNOVA is the Director of the Centre for Euro-Asian Studies at the University of Reading, and Senior Lecturer in the Economics Department at the University of Reading. Dr Kalyuzhnova is the author of the first major study of the Kazakhstani economy (1998). She has contributed to a wide variety of economic studies for international organisations and at present is programme leader of one of the current research projects at the Centre for Euro-Asian Studies.

Panagiotis LIARGOVAS received his BA degree from the University of Athens and his MA and PhD degrees in Economics from Clark University, Worcester MA as a Fulbright Scholar (1991). He has worked as a Director at the National School of Public Administration as well as a Special Advisor to the Mayor of Athens and to the Deputy Minister of Finance. He has taught in many universities including Clark University, the Universities of Bologna, Athens, Thessaly, Patras and Crete and the Athens University of Economics and Business. He is currently Associate Professor at the Department of Economics, University of Peloponnese, teaching International and European Economics. He is the author of three books (in Greek) and the editor of three books (two of them in English). He has written more than 60 articles in academic journals and in collected volumes. His research is focused on Economic Policy, International and European Economics.

Neill NUGENT is Professor of Politics and Jean Monnet Professor of European Integration at Manchester Metropolitan University, United Kingdom. His books include *European Union Enlargement* (editor), Palgrave-Macmillan, 2004; *The Government and Politics of the European Union*, Palgrave-Macmillan, 5th edition, 2003; *The European Commission,* Palgrave-Macmillan, 2001; *At the Heart of the Union: Studies of the European Commission* (editor), Macmillan, 2nd edn, 2000; and *Developments in the European Union* (co-editor) Macmillan, 1999. He has taught widely in Europe and the United States.

Franco PRAUSSELLO is full professor of International Economics, holder of Jean Monnet chairs in Economics of the EU since 1995, and co-ordinator of the PhD school in Economics and Finance of the EU at the University of Genoa. Associate Professor at the Université de Nice Sophia Antipolis and co-ordinator of the Jean Monnet European Centre of Excellence located in Genoa University, he has been visiting professor in the Universities of Moscow, Sfax (Tunisia), Istanbul, Baku, Odessa, Bratislava, Kisinev (Moldova). Member of the Scientific Board of the European Union Review and of the Association of the Italian Economists SIE. He is also general contractor of a number of Tempus-Tacis Joint European Projects with the Odessa National Maritime University and the National University Mechnikov in Odessa, and former expert of the Italian government and of the Italian Ministry of Education at OCDE and the Council of Europe. His main areas of expertise are International Finance and Economics, with particular emphasis on the issues concerning the European integration. Among his most recent publications: Praussello, F. (ed.) (2002) *Euro Circulation and the Economic and Monetary Union* (Milan: Franco Angeli); Praussello, F. (ed.) (2003) *The Economics of EU Enlargement* (Milan: Franco Angeli).

René SCHWOK is since 1992 Associate Professor at the European Graduate Institute and the Department of Political Science of the University of Geneva, Switzerland. He is the author of dozens of articles about European integration. He is also the author of the following books: *Théories de l'intégration européenne, Approches, concepts et débats*, Paris, Montchrestien, 2005. *Conséquences des accords bilatéraux entre la Suisse et l'Union européenne pour les cantons frontaliers de la France*, Genève, Institut européen de l'Université de Genève, 2000. *U.S.—EC Relations in the Post Cold War Era. Conflict or Partnership?* Boulder, Westview Press, 1991. *Suisse-Europe. Le choix historique*, Genève, Georg & L'Hebdo, 1992. *Switzerland and the European Common Market*, New York, Praeger, 1991. *Interprétations de la politique étrangère de Hitler*, Paris, Presses universitaires de France, 1987.

Constantine A. STEPHANOU has studied law and international relations at the University of Geneva. Since 1992 he has been Jean Monnet Professor of European Organisation at the Department of International & European Studies of the Panteion University of Social & Political Sciences, Athens, where he is also the Director of the Post-Graduate Programme of the Department. He is currently the President of the Hellenic ECSA association and Vice-President of ECSA-Europe. He has served as visiting Professor in France (Nice, Grenoble, Bordeaux and currently at Paris II), as well as at the Hebrew University of Jerusalem and the Universities of Utah (USA), Madrid

(Alcala de Henarès) and Tunis. He has acted as technical advisor to the Greek government during the IGCs for the revision of the EC/EU Treaties and has written extensively on issues related to the governance and citizenship of the European Union, including the book *Réformes et mutations de l'Union européenne*; Brussels, Bruylant, 1997.

Maria VAGLIASINDI is Senior Economist at the Office of the Chief Economist at the European Bank. Previously, she was Assistant Professor in Economics at the University of Edinburgh, where she was lecturing and undertaking research in the area of infrastructure regulation. She has a BA in Economics from the University of Pisa, an MPhil in Economics from the University of Oxford and a PhD in Economics from the University of Warwick. She also held teaching and research positions at the University of Pisa and Warwick. She has been involved in several projects on the interactions between regulation and competition and she is author of several publications in these areas.

Dimitris K. XENAKIS is advisor to the Hellenic Parliament. He has also taught at the Department of Political Science, University of Crete and the National School of Public Administration. In the past he has served as strategic analyst at the Defence Analysis Institute, as well as an advisor at the Genereral Secretariat for Financial Planning and Defence Investment, both at the Hellenic Ministry of Defence. He has authored *The Politics of Order Building in Europe and the Mediterranean* (DAI, 2004), *The Emerging Euro-Mediterranean System* (Manchester University Press, 2001) and has published in various journals, such as, *The Review of International Affairs*, *Mediterranean Quarterly*, *Cambridge Review of International Affairs*, *Perceptions*, and *Hellenic Studies*.

Acknowledgements

The present volume is the outcome of a research project carried out with the support of the European Commission in the framework of the Jean Monnet Project. Moreover, during my appointment as representative of the Greek Presidency of the EU (1st semester 2003)to the United Nations Economic Commission for Europe (UNECE), I benefited from extensive discussions regarding, in particular, the impact of EU enlargement on the non-acceding countries of the so-called 'wider Europe'. In this respect I would like express my warmest thanks to Dr. Carol Cosgrove-Sacks, former Director of the Trade Division, for her advice and her contribution to the present volume, as well as to her husband Jeff Sacks for the revision of the texts and his insightful remarks. Another source of inspiration has been Dr Miroslav Jovanovic, a well-known specialist of international and European integration, also working with UNECE. Finally, I would like to thank my assistant Sophia Ziakou for her loyalty and her involvement in the production of the book.

The Editor

Acknowledgements

Introduction

The EU enlargement process has generally been perceived as an opportunity for the EU to expand its market, enhance its competitiveness, stabilise its periphery and increase its say in the world. A related – and more controversial issue – has been the impact of widening on deepening. These issues have been raised in respect of previous enlargements and are likely to dominate political and academic debate in respect of the latest enlargement which took place on 1 May 2004. European public opinion remains sceptical about this enlargement which has coincided with economic recession and insecurity.

This collection of essays, presented in draft form at the 12th annual session of the Spetses European Summer Academy in July 2004, aims at evaluating the new setting and the adjustments to EU policy-making brought about by the recent EU enlargement. Some new Member States may actually be in a better position to benefit than old members from the new economic environment. Their policy preferences may also differ from those of the 'old Europe'. Are they likely to change the current policy-mix?

Part I deals with the new economic setting. It presents a fresh assessment of the impact of enlargement on trade, investment and competitiveness. In respect of agriculture, the budgetary implications are examined in the light of the recent CAP reform. Moreover, the functioning of EMU is examined in the light of increased economic heterogeneity. Part II deals with governance and cohesion of the Union. It focuses on the preferences of the new Member States, the coalitions that they may entail and their impact on policy-making and policy output. Such output may, in some cases, be curtailed and, in others, it may reflect a new balance between economic liberalism and state interventionism. Part III deals with the external relations of the Union. The central issue in this respect is to what extent the EU will be able to ensure stability in its periphery and bridge the gap between the new Member States and their neighbours. Policy adjustments are examined on the basis of proposals for new institutional and financial instruments. The final chapters aim at ascertaining to what extent the varying perceptions of old and new Member States in respect of energy and security dependence are likely to affect EU relations with its neighbours and the United States.

Before the latest enlargement most studies had predicted substantial changes in the integration process and, in some cases, cataclysmic consequences as a result of the accession of 10 new Members. The present volume provides evidence to the contrary. Research on these matters is a continuous process and I would like to thank the contributors for providing us with their most recent assessments of the latest enlargement.

The Editor

PART I

The New Economic Setting

1. Trade and Investment Patterns in an Enlarged Union

Victoria Curzon Price

THE EUROPEAN COMMUNITY IN A GLOBAL PERSPECTIVE

The EC was always an important factor in world trade and successive enlargements have made it ever more so. At its inception, EC-6 accounted for 24 per cent of world exports. By 1980, EC-9 accounted for 33 per cent. Today, EC-25 accounts for a massive 42 per cent of world trade (see Table 1.1). In the meantime, intra-area trade jumped from 8 per cent to 28 per cent of world exports.

The growth of the EC's overall share of world trade is largely the result of the mechanical fact of successive enlargements, because for all this period, older developed countries (such as EC members) on the whole lost trade shares to Japan, Asia and Latin America.

The growth of intra-EC trade, as we have seen, has been much faster and shows the significance of the trade preferences generated by the customs union: over a quarter of world trade now takes place on strongly preferential terms within the EC. How much of this is to be attributed to trade creation and how much to trade diversion, is not a question which will detain us here, because this static calculation would get lost in the dynamics of economic growth, successive enlargements and eight GATT Rounds of multilateral trade liberalization. Thus, over the period from 1960 to 2002, EC trade with the rest of the world (ROW) (mainly North America, Japan, Australasia and developing countries) rose in absolute terms from $20 billion to $863 billion and in share remained remarkably stable, in the range of 14–15 per cent of world trade. Although ROW has undoubtedly suffered some trade diversion over this period, it has been largely compensated by the sheer growth of the EU's economy and freer multilateral trade in general (over 40 times, see last column of Table 1.1).

Table 1.1
World perspective on enlargement, EC-6, EC-12, EC-15, EC-25 exports and intra-area exports as % world exports

	1960 $bn	1960 %	1980 $bn	1980 %	1992 $bn	1992 %	1999 $bn	1999 %	2002 $bn	2002 %	Change 1992=100	change 1960=100
	(EC-6)		(EC-9)		(EC-12)		(EC-15)		(EC-25)			
World X	126	100	2.034	100	3.655	100	5.644	100	6.272	100	172	4.978
total EC X	30	24	662	33	1.457	40	2.130	38	2.450	39	**168**	8.167
total CEEC X	-	-	-	-	51	1	108	2	153	2	**300**	-
total EC-25	-	-	-	-	1.508	41	2.239	40	2.603	42	173	-
intra EC X (as specified)	10	**8**	355	**17**	888	24	1.372	**24**	1.509	24	**170**	14.650
Trade with EFTA	7	6	78	4	137	4	75	1	141	2	**103**	2.014
Trade with Russia & CEECs	1	1	26	1	45	1	45	**1**	32	1	**71**	3.200
intra EC-25	-	-	-	-	-	-	-	-	1.740	**28**	-	-
EC trade with ROW**	20	16	307	15	569	16	759	13	941	14	**152**	4.381

Source: derived from IMF, Direction of Trade Statistics, 2000 and GATT, International Trade, 1965 & 1988–89.
* sum of intra EC-15 + intra-NM+ EC-15 exports to NM + NM exports to EC-15
** Total EC X – intra EC

This can be seen more clearly from Table 1.2, which takes the same figures, but relates them to EC trade instead of world trade. Thus intra-EC trade doubled from 33 per cent of EC-6 exports in 1960 to 67 per cent of EC-25 exports in 2002, while trade with ROW as a ratio of EC exports halved from 66 per cent in 1960 to 33 per cent in 2002. But this was 33 per cent of a much larger absolute figure than in 1960, which means that trade with ROW, as we saw, increased despite being discriminated against. Hence the difficulty of untangling trade creation from trade diversion in a dynamic context.

The growth of intra-EC trade has been slowing down for some time and has stabilized among the older members. Each new wave of economic integration, however, sets off a new phase of trade concentration between old and new and can change trade patterns between the older members as well.

Table 1.2
EC perspective on evolution of trade shares

	EC-6 (1960)		EC-9 (1980)		EC-12 (1990)		EC-15 (1992)		EC-25 (2002)	
	$bn	%	$bn	%	$bn	%	$bn	%	$bn	%
EC exports to world	30	100	662	100	1457	99.9	2450	100	2603	100
Of which: intra-area trade	10	33	355	54	888	61	1509	62	1740	67
trade with EFTA	7	23	78	12	137	9	141	6	141	5
Rest of World (ROW) (A-B)	19.7	66	307	46	569	39	941	38	863	33

Source: Same as Table 1.1.

PATTERNS OF TRADE SEEN FROM THE PERSPECTIVE OF NEW OR POTENTIAL MEMBERS AND NEIGHBOURS

The first and probably most important trend to note is the historic shift in trade patterns of Central and Eastern Europe since Soviet times (see Table 1.3). In less than twenty years, the CEECs have re-oriented their trade from East to West. In 1980, the USSR (CIS today) took 27 per cent of their exports, in 2002 the CIS took a mere 4.6 per cent. In 1980, developed market economies took 36 per cent of their exports, in 2002 73 per cent. Behind this geographic shift of course lies a qualitative leap. It is one thing to supply according to plan, without having to

account for costs, let alone cover them; it is quite another to sell to demanding
markets at competitive prices – and still make a living.

Table 1.3
Historic shift in trade patterns, 1980–2002 (%), CEECs

Exports to:	1980	1990	2002
World	100	100	100
CEECs	21.4	15.8	16.7
CIS	27.1	22.3	4.6
Developed market economies	35.7	49.5	72.7
of which to EC	-	-	67
Developing economies	15.8	12.4	6

Source: UNECE, Economic Survey of Europe, 2004, No. 1,Table B.14
and IMF, Direction of Trade Statistics, latest issue.

Intra CEEC trade hardly shifted at all geographically (falling from 21 per cent
in 1980 to 17 per cent in 2002), but its nature changed, from plan to market,
going through a collapse, then recovery.

The second point to note is how important the EC-15 has become for the new
CEEC members (see Table 1.4). On average, the EC-15 takes 68 per cent of
CEEC exports (up from 61 per cent in 1993) and supplies 58 per cent (down
from 65 per cent in 1993) of CEEC imports. Part of the reason for this
asymmetry may be the fact that the Europe Agreements allowed CEECs to open
their markets more slowly than the EC. For the moment we simply note the high
trade dependency ratio, due to the sheer size of the EC-15, its geographic
propinquity and the negotiation of relatively free trade arrangements.

Cyprus and Malta used to be much more trade-dependent on the EC in 1993
than they were ten years later. In 1993, over 70 per cent of their exports went to
the EC-15 and 86 per cent of the imports came from there. But by 2002, these
ratios had fallen drastically to 42 per cent and 48 per cent respectively.

In the meantime, potential members and neighbours (Turkey, Bulgaria,
Croatia, Romania, Russia and Ukraine) show lower dependency ratios with the
EC-15 (40 per cent on average for exports, 44 per cent for imports), due to
distance, much slower transitions to the market economy and weaker preferential
trade arrangements.

Turkey is a special case. It has enjoyed full customs union status with the EC-
15 since 1995 (and non-reciprocal access to EC manufactured goods markets for
many years before that), but this scarcely shows up in the statistics since 1993,
since dependency ratios with the EC-15 have, if anything, fallen slightly.

Table 1.4

Trade patterns with EU-15 seen from new or potential members and neighbours

	Exports to EU as total % trade			Imports from EU as total % trade		
	1993	2002	1993=100	1993	2002	1993=100
	%	%	Change	%	%	Change
Cyprus	71	49	69	79	42	53
Malta	77	39	51	95	56	58
NEW MED	**74**	**42**	**57**	**86**	**48**	**56**
Czech Republic	56	69	122	65	61	93
Hungary	67	75	112	61	56	92
Poland	71	69	97	91	62	68
Slovakia	30	61	201	29	50	171
Slovenia	60	59	99	61	68	111
Estonia	44	57	129	64	54	84
Latvia	84	60	71	50	53	105
Lithuania	74	48	65	46	43	93
CEECs	**61**	**68**	**111**	**65**	**58**	**89**
TOTAL NM	**61**	**67**	**110**	**67**	**58**	**87**
Turkey	53	52	97	49	46	93
Bulgaria	53	56	107	46	51	109
Croatia	53	52	99	57	56	98
Romania	42	67	159	49	59	119
Russia	45	35	78	42	40	95
Ukraine	31	20	64	46	24	53
PMN	**46**	**40**	**87**	**47**	**44**	**94**

Source: IMF, Direction of Trade Statistics, various issues.

What we are presumably seeing is the effect of preferential status being extended to the CEECs in the 1990s on Mediterranean countries with similar patterns of comparative advantage (light manufactures, processed food – i.e. labour intensive products). Thus Cyprus, Malta and Turkey must now compete with Slovenia, Slovakia and all the rest.

Does this hypothesis hold for other Mediterranean countries? It has often been suggested, for instance, that enlargement would be detrimental to Greece, Spain and Portugal not only through a reduction in EC regional aid transfers, but also from a form of reverse trade creation, in other words, that these countries would have to compete with the CEECs in labour-intensive manufactured goods on EC markets. EC trade dependency ratios for Greece, Spain and Portugal suggest that Greece may well have suffered from this effect, but not Spain or Portugal (see Table 1.5).

Table 1.5
Trade patterns seen from Greece, Spain and Portugal 1993–2002

	Exports to EU-15 as % total trade			Imports from EU-15 as % total trade		
	1993	1999	2002	1993	1999	2002
Greece	62	49	38	60	66	52
Spain	70	71	69	64	68	65
Portugal	80	82	80	74	77	77

Source: IMF, Direction of Trade Statistics, various issues.

Thus Greece's export trade dependency ratio on the EU-15 fell from 62 per cent in 1993 to 49 per cent in 1999 and again to 38 per cent in 2002. On the import side, the Greek ratio fell from 60 per cent to 52 per cent from 1993 to 2002. Like Cyprus and Malta, Greece 'disintegrated' from the EC-15 during this period. However, Spain and Portugal were generally unaffected.

Germany provides a representative market to test the extent to which CEECs replaced traditional low-labour cost Mediterranean suppliers during the 1990s. Tables 1.6 and 1.7 show that Greece and Cyprus, in particular, lost market share (– per cent and – 46 per cent respectively), while the CEECs and potential new members and neighbours gained substantially over the same period (+216 per cent and + 80 per cent respectively). It is difficult not to conclude that these trends are linked. The Eastern Mediterranean countries – closer to the CEECs geographically and culturally – were more affected than Spain and Portugal but even the latter experienced much slower growth in the German market than the CEECs (+72 per cent and +59 per cent respectively). We conclude, therefore, that 'reverse trade creation' has already taken place. How much enlargement, in itself, will add is anybody's guess.

Let us reflect for a moment on the meaning of this 'reverse trade creation'. When a customs union expands to take in new members which were previously discriminated against, it undoes the trade-diversion harm previously caused and generates new trade-creation benefits (a less efficient supplier is replaced by a more efficient one). The beneficiaries of the old trade-diversion effects (producers in Greece, Spain and Portugal selling on the German market) must now reallocate resources and find new products and new markets in a more competitive environment. Even in these countries, however, consumers benefit, as do producers in the long run, since the sooner they face up to competitive realities the stronger they will become.

Table 1.6

CEECs, new MED, old MED and PMN battle it out on the German market? 1993–2002

GERMAN IMPORTS FROM:			Change
	1993 $mn	1999 $mn	2002 $mn	1993=100
Cyprus	121	58	54	45
Malta	214	265	249	116
New Med	**335**	**323**	**303**	**90**
Czech Republic	3.880	10.789	15.146	390
Estonia	99	227	349	353
Hungary	2.726	9.520	11.241	412
Latvia	178	311	408	229
Lithuania	193	559	651	337
Poland	5.189	9.831	13.208	255
Slovakia	897	3.407	4.594	512
Slovenia	1.809	2.557	2.425	134
Total CEECs	**14.971**	**37.201**	**48.022**	**321**
Total NM	**15.306**	**37.524**	**48.325**	**316**
Turkey	4.025	6.010	6.383	159
Bulgaria	341	525	690	202
Croatia	829	685	575	69
Romania	824	1.894	2.299	279
Russia	6.478	8.868	12.268	189
Ukraine	247	611	710	287
PMN	**12.744**	**18.593**	**22.925**	**180**
Greece	1.855	1.809	1.463	79
Spain	8.485	15.160	14.590	172
Portugal	2.983	5.081	4.734	159
OLD MED	**13.323**	**22.050**	**20.787**	**156**

Source: IMF, Direction of Trade Statistics, various issues.

Of course this is not the only effect. An expanding customs union will also generate trade-diversion effects as new members displace third-country suppliers in the old customs union and as old customs union members displace third-country suppliers in the new members. The EC minimizes these negative effects on its immediate neighbours by negotiating bilateral free trade areas with them (note how most PMNs increased their exports to Germany almost as fast as the CEECs, with the exception of Croatia). For the remainder, especially for more distant Asia and Latin America, investment in the WTO represents the only alternative strategy, since the EU is unlikely to negotiate free trade areas with every third country suffering from trade diversion.

Table 1.7
CEECs, new MED, old MED, PMN battle it out on the German Market?

GERMAN EXPORTS TO:			Change
	1993 $mn	1999 $mn	2002 $mn	1993=100
Cyprus	517	413	406	79
Malta	274	266	238	87
New Med	**791**	**679**	**644**	**81**
Czech Republic	4.625	10.676	14.862	321
Estonia	103	328	576	559
Hungary	3.117	9.034	10.364	332
Latvia	211	471	821	389
Lithuania	303	795	1.429	472
Poland	5.867	13.176	15.014	256
Slovakia	1.489	3.025	3.745	252
Slovenia	1.489	2.204	2.185	147
Total CEECs	**17.204**	**39.709**	**48.996**	**285**
Total NM	**17.995**	**40.388**	**49.640**	**276**
Turkey	5.089	6.270	6.788	133
Bulgaria	546	766	1.074	197
Croatia	1.070	1.307	1.677	157
Romania	1.090	2.115	3.059	281
Russia	847	5.360	10.679	1.261
Ukraine	930	1.080	2.113	227
PMN	**9.572**	**16.898**	**25.390**	**265**
Greece	3.568	4.112	4.641	130
Spain	11.781	23.654	27.566	234
Portugal	3.446	6.093	6.368	185
OLD MED	**18.795**	**33.859**	**38.575**	205

Source: IMF, Direction of Trade Statistics, various issues.

As mentioned earlier, the CEECs have expanded their trade massively since the early 1990s, mainly as a result of the transition process and partly because of free trade arrangements with the EC. Thus their exports to the German market increased by a factor of 3.2 from 1993 to 2002, while those of the 'old Mediterranean' countries to Germany increased by 'only' 56 per cent. But we should note that German exports to these countries also rose spectacularly: by a factor of 2.8 per cent to the CEECs and by two to the 'Old Mediterranean' countries. Anyone worried about Germany's ability to remain competitive in these low-labour cost markets should note that Germany enjoys a comfortable trade surplus with all these countries, with the understandable exception of Russia, whose balance of trade is heavily dependent on the price of oil and where German exports are nevertheless growing spectacularly.

We are now ready for the last piece of the puzzle. If Greece and Cyprus have 'disintegrated' from EC-15 during the 1990s, what have their traders been up to? With which part of the world have they been integrating? Table 1.8 shows that their exports to the new members have risen by a factor of three and ten respectively. Similarly, the CEECs have also been integrating strongly with each other (factor of three).

Greece was of course party to the Europe Agreements with the CEECs during the 1990s, so new trade opportunities developed as the transition progressed. Untangling the two effects is difficult, if not impossible. Was there a free trade arrangement between Cyprus and the Visegrad and Baltic countries during the 1990s? If not, then the spectacular expansion of trade between them is due almost entirely to the transition process, which freed markets for entrepreneurs in a much more fundamental manner than a free trade agreement (which would have been icing on the cake). Was it Greek Cypriot merchants who suddenly spotted an opportunity to import from the Baltics, or Lithuanian entrepreneurs who suddenly discovered a way to export $86 million worth of goods to Cyprus? Or a trader from another country? The trade data cannot tell us. But in any event, many new business opportunities appeared in the 1990s for alert entrepreneurs of whatever nationality or place of residence. Now, membership in the same customs union completes the process.

ENLARGEMENT SEEN FROM THE EC

Generally speaking, enlargement for the EC-15 appears to add little by way of new trade opportunities. The new members take 4.8 per cent of EC-15 exports and supply only 4.4 per cent of EC-15 imports (see Table 1.9). However, this is not the way to look at the issue.

First, the rate of growth noted in the previous section is present again in this one (these trade dependency ratios were 3.4 per cent and 2.5 per cent respectively in 1993). But even if most of the shift in geographic patterns of trade from East to West has already occurred, the importance of these trade flows lies in their dynamics, in their growth and composition. The CEEC's economies are at the threshold of a long period of rapid economic 'catch-up' growth and these trade flows can only grow with them. Through the trade interface, the EC-15 will share in some of the excitement, possibly the only serious growth point on the Continent of Europe in the foreseeable future.

Table 1.8

New members (CEECs + new MED): changing patterns of exports 1993–2002

X to new members	1993 $mn	2002 $mn	change 1993=100
Cyprus	11	104	945
Malta	5	58	1.160
NEW MED	16	162	1.013
Czech Republic	2.667	6.193	232
Hungary	587	2.277	388
Poland	621	4.726	761
Slovakia	1.834	3.957	216
Slovenia	261	843	323
Estonia	116	648	559
Latvia	102	395	387
Lithuania	357	1.060	297
CEECs	6.545	20.099	307
TOTAL NM	6.561	20.261	309
X to EC-15			
Cyprus	626	528	84
Malta	1.038	973	94
NEW MED	1.664	1.501	90
Czech Republic	6.496	26.133	402
Hungary	5.747	25.495	444
Poland	10.019	28.189	281
Slovakia	1.649	8.700	528
Slovenia	3.732	6.143	165
Estonia	356	2.480	697
Latvia	878	1.376	157
Lithuania	854	2.646	310
CEECS	29.731	101.162	340
TOTAL NM	31.395	102.663	327
p.m. exports to Greece	196	546	279
imports from Greece	147	308	210
X to EC-25			
Cyprus	637	632	99
Malta	1.043	1.031	99
NEW MED	1.680	1.663	99
Czech Republic	9.163	32.326	353
Hungary	6.334	27.772	438
Poland	10.640	32.915	309
Slovakia	3.483	12.657	363
Slovenia	3.993	6.986	175
Estonia	472	3.128	663
Latvia	980	1.771	181
Lithuania	1.211	3.706	306
CEECS	36.276	121.261	334
TOTAL NM	37.956	122.924	324

Source: Derived from IMF, International Financial Statistics, various issues.

Table 1.9

Trade patterns with new or potential members and neighbours (PMN), seen from EU-15 (% of EU exports in 1993 and 2002)

EU-15 Exports	to new and potential members			from new and potential members		
			Change			Change
	1993	2002	1993=100	1993	2002	1993=100
	%	%		%	%	
Cyprus	0.14	0.11	81	0.04	0.03	73
Malta	0.14	0.10	73	0.07	0.05	62
NEW MED	**0.28**	**0.22**	**77**	**0.12**	**0.08**	**66**
Czech Republic	0.57	1.13	198	0.47	1.12	240
Hungary	0.52	0.97	185	0.41	1.04	252
Poland	0.90	1.45	161	0.72	1.15	160
Slovakia	0.13	0.34	260	0.12	0.39	329
Slovenia	0.29	0.33	114	0.27	0.28	106
Estonia	0.04	0.14	344	0.03	0.13	517
Latvia	0.03	0.10	298	0.06	0.11	180
Lithuania	0.04	0.16	356	0.06	0.11	185
CEECS	**3.09**	**4.60**	**149**	**2.37**	**4.34**	**183**
total new						
members	**3.38**	**4.82**	**143**	**2.49**	**4.42**	**177**
Turkey	0.99	0.94	94	0.59	0.91	155
Bulgaria	0.12	0.16	136	0.09	0.14	164
Croatia	0.18	0.25	136	0.15	0.10	70
Romania	0.20	0.44	219	0.15	0.42	280
Russia	1.02	1.18	116	1.46	1.90	130
Ukraine	0.13	0.21	168	0.09	0.17	197
PMN	**1.66**	**2.26**	**136**	**1.93**	**2.74**	**142**
total X to EU-15	61.59	61.07	99	59.53	58.62	98
total X to EU-25	64.97	65.89	101	62.02	63.03	102

Source: IMF, Direction of Trade Statistics, various issues.

WELFARE ASSESSMENT OF THE EFFECTS OF ENLARGEMENT

Computable general equilibrium models of the effects of enlargement suggest that the balance of static effects on economic welfare will be positive (Baldwin et al. 1997 and Maliszewska 2004). The reasons are that industrial trade links between the EC-15 and the new members account for 90 per cent of trade and trade diversion risks here are, on the whole, thought to be low and falling. Trade diversion risks are high in the agricultural sector, but this affects only 10 per cent of trade flows. Therefore, in these calculations, trade creation outweighs trade diversion.

However, these models do not capture the distortions that may develop between the farming and non-farming sectors in the new member states. It is to be hoped that CAP prices will continue to fall until they are roughly in line with world market prices, not just because of pressure from the G-20 in the Doha Round, but because the CEECs growth prospects would suffer if they were to remain at current levels. One could imagine a possible scenario wherein a sharp increase in the price of food on joining the EU generates social pressure for a corresponding increase in wages, launching accommodating monetary policies and causing a harmful inflationary spiral ending in a vicious circle of devaluation–inflation–devaluation from which it takes much political courage to disentangle oneself. If high EC food prices remain because of exorbitant levels of EC protection, they will drag down CEEC competitiveness and capacity for growth and causing an unwanted shift of real resources from the dynamic non-farm to the dead-end farming sector. This is one area where the new members risk serious welfare losses.

INVESTMENT PATTERNS IN THE ENLARGED EU

As mentioned above, the dynamic effects of transition to the market economy and membership of the EU should, if all goes reasonably well, overwhelm the negative effects of membership. One of the motors of dynamic change for a growing economy is foreign investment. It is here that membership of the EU may have a measurable impact by reassuring investors. When the Commission confers its seal of approval on a candidate country it is saying to the world 'you can invest in this country without fear of expropriation, inflation, exchange controls, arbitrary tax assessments, theft by unscrupulous business partners left unpunished by a weak judicial system, or too much corruption'. This is definitely worth having and its effect is clear from the statistics on foreign direct investment (FDI).

Generally speaking FDI shrank by 20 per cent in 2002 reflecting recession throughout the developed world. However, it can be seen from Table 1.10 that inward FDI to the CEECs, contrary to this trend, grew in 2002 by 27 per cent and except for Hungary losses were limited. In Cyprus, meanwhile, also a candidate country, FDI fell by over half and in Malta inward flows were actually reversed.

This suggests that the prospect of membership in the EU is not enough, in itself, to attract and keep foreign investment. It is the combination of transition to the market economy, low labour costs and the sure prospect of access to the EU market which attracts investors. In all the 'potential members and neighbours', FDI also fell from 2001 to 2002.

Table 1.10
FDI inflows by host country ($mn)

	1980s av	1993	2000	2001	2002	Growth 1993=100
Cyprus	57	111	804	652	297	268
Malta	25	54	158	294	–375	–694
NEW MED	**82**	**165**	**962**	**946**	**–78**	**–47**
Czech Republic	-	568	4.984	5.639	9.319	1.641
Hungary	-	2.350	1.646	2.440	854	36
Poland	17	1.715	9.341	5.713	4.119	240
Slovakia	-	70	1.925	1.579	4.012	5.731
Slovenia	-	-	136	503	1.865	1.371
Estonia	-	168	387	542	307	183
Latvia	-	20	410	164	396	1.980
Lithuania	-	12	379	446	732	6.100
CEECS	**17**	**4.903**	**19.208**	**17.026**	**21.604**	**441**
TOTAL NM						
Turkey	142	663	982	3.266	1.037	156
Bulgaria	-	55	1.002	813	479	871
Croatia	-	-	1.089	1.561	981	-
Romania	-	94	1.025	1.157	1.106	1.177
Russia	-	700	2.714	2.469	2.421	346
Ukraine	-	200	177	442	77	39
PMN	**142**	**1.712**	**6.989**	**9.708**	**6.101**	**356**

Source: UNCTAD, World Investment Report 2003, Table B1.

If we look at growth rates from 1993 to 2002 (remembering that 2002 was generally a bad year for FDI), we see some truly spectacular leaps – Lithuania, Slovakia (from 2000), Latvia, Czech Republic – probably due more to the sale of previously state-owned enterprises to foreign owners, than to new green-field ventures. These investment flows are in the process of reorganizing economic activity across Europe: firms are re-locating at a great pace from the high-labour-cost West to the lower labour-cost East. This process will continue until labour costs, adjusted for productivity, have converged. Following the same line of reasoning as for trade flows, my (unsubstantiated) guess is that most of the big changes have already occurred and that these spectacular growth rates will soon begin to tail off. Anecdotal evidence supports this hypothesis. According to the

BBC, Renault is having difficulty in recruiting employees to man its brand new plant in the Czech Republic (BBC, World Today, 20 October 2004).

The reason for this may be as follows: (1) wages are never very long out of synchronization with productivity (2) the privatization process is more or less over; from now on new net inward FDI will have to be more creative; (3) as argued above, nominal wages are likely to rise to compensate for loss of real purchasing power due to the adoption of the CAP; (4) the adoption of the acquis communautaire in the sphere of technical norms and safety regulations will raise production costs in the new members and eat away at their initial competitiveness and (5) the CEECs are in competition with a great number of developing countries which are also eager to receive scarce FDI resources.

For these reasons, it is not at all surprising to learn that the CEECs are reviewing their tax codes (UN ECE, 2004) in order to attract high-level FDI and, like Ireland in the 1980s, turn themselves into 'Tigers'. Announced reforms of corporate tax systems include Estonia's zero tax on reinvested corporate profits and Slovakia's 19 per cent flat rate for personal and corporate tax (see Table 1.11 for details).

Table 1.11
Corporate tax rates as % profits

	1999	2004
CEECs	%	%
Estonia	26	0
Latvia	25	15
Slovenia	25	15
Hungary	18	16
Lithuania	29	19
Slovakia	40	19
Poland	34	25
Czech Republic	35	28
PMN		
Russia	-	13
Bulgaria	32.5	19.5
Romania	38	25
Croatia	-	n.a.
Ukraine	-	n.a.
Turkey	-	n.a.
Average EU	32.4	29

Source: UN ECE, Economic Survey of Europe, 2004 No. 1, p.129 T.5.2.2.

Table 1.11 shows that fiscal competition is also in full swing within the EC-15. Other reforms under discussion aim to reduce compulsory state pensions and replace them with voluntary, fully funded systems, increase the private provision of medical insurance and so forth. In short, the new members are fully aware of the need to keep investors interested by maintaining a generally business-friendly environment and offering alternative models of social justice (Curzon Price 2004).

OTHER CAPITAL FLOWS

Besides long-term foreign direct investment (FDI), countries wishing to accelerate the autonomous rate of growth will also attract portfolio investment (equity and bonds), even if this is much more volatile than FDI and could cause a financial melt-down like the Asian crisis of 1997 were investors to lose confidence.

Both types of capital flows represent private investors' assessment of the future growth prospects of the host country. A country in the first stages of catch-up growth, if successful, will typically run a current account deficit (because it is investing (I) more than it saves (S)). The difference (I − S), consisting of a combination of inward FDI and portfolio investment fully finances the necessary deficit on the current account. The credits and debits cancel out, leaving the balance of payments in equilibrium (known as the 'basic balance'). Other big items can be very short-term money flows, but these are volatile by definition and reverse themselves several times a year. They are not included in Table 1.12, which shows the basic balance for various countries for the year 2002.

The column which summarizes the 'basic balance' is entitled CA − FA (current account minus private medium to long-term financial account). We note that from Cyprus through to Portugal all countries enjoy a surplus on the basic balance with only two exceptions (Hungary and Turkey). Hungary's basic balance deficit is equal to 3.9 per cent of GDP and implies that official finance is needed to that degree (private investors are not prepared to supply the difference). It is the only country among the new members which might be considered to be facing 'balance of payments problems'. All of the others are in overall surplus and will either be accumulating reserves or letting their currencies appreciate.

Germany and Switzerland are included for the purpose of comparison. These are mature, slow growing economies which should normally generate a current account surplus and a financial account deficit, as German and Swiss entrepreneurs see better opportunities for profits abroad than at home and export capital. We note that this pattern is indeed borne out by the data. Mature, capital-abundant countries supply capital to rapidly growing youthful economies, while the latter supply goods, services and dividends to pay for their borrowings. The near panic in Germany over firms re-locating to the East is seriously misplaced. It is a perfectly normal phenomenon and will shortly find a new equilibrium (if it has not already done so), as wages begin to rise in the CEECs.

Furthermore, Germany's capital exports to the CEECs are generating a demand for the supply of German capital goods. Finally, Germany will soon be receiving dividends for these investments and higher incomes will generate demand for all sorts of non-traded services, which is where the new unskilled, labour-intensive jobs will appear. This is what Switzerland has done for years without shedding tears (income from Swiss investments abroad supplies 10 per cent of GDP).

It will be noted that Russia, unlike all other countries in Table 1.12, is in surplus on all accounts. This is because it has the typical profile of an oil-exporting country. These surpluses put upward pressure on the exchange rate and/or domestic price levels, both of which discourage FDI (which, as we can indeed see, is correspondingly low and is concentrated in the oil and gas sector) and crowd out all other potential export sectors.

Taking the Czech Republic as an example, it will be noted that the current account deficit is more than offset by the financial account surplus, which puts upward pressure on the exchange rate (the Koruna was indeed revalued in 2003). The same phenomenon occurred in the late 1980s in Spain, giving rise to the so-called 'Spanish paradox' – how could a country with a huge current account deficit see the peseta rise against the mighty German mark? This question for a time puzzled superficial analysts who limited their considerations to the obvious and forgot to push their analysis far enough. But of course, the Spanish current account deficit was due to massive investment in Spain, more than fully financed by inward FDI and portfolio flows, which tailed off thereafter. This is what now awaits the CEECs as they catch up with the rest of Europe. All other CEECs are in equilibrium (see last column, which relates the size of CA – FA balance to GDP).

Table 1.12 also suggests that the moaning and groaning in Germany over loss of competitiveness to the CEECs needs to be tempered. Not only is Germany in substantial over-all trade surplus (as is normal for a capital-abundant country), but we can see from Table 1.6 that its trade with the CEECs is in balance and exports to the East are growing just as fast as imports. The structural changes within these aggregates are, of course, dramatic, but the fact that they are equally dynamic suggests that the necessary entrepreneurial flexibility and adaptability are present in Germany, despite the angst.

Table 1.12
Balance of payments of various countries, 2002, $mn unless otherwise

	Trade Balance	Goods + Services	Current Account (CA)	FDI	Portfolio Investment	Financial Account (FA)	CA – FA	GDP $ bn	CA – FA /GDP
Cyprus (02)	-2.859	-643	-517	614	161	851	334	10	3.34
Malta (02)	-424	-70	-84	-425	-2	217	133	39	0.34
Czechrepublic	-2.240	-1.597	-4.485	9.323	814	11.235	6.750	74	9.18
Hungary (02)	-2.119	-1.506	-2.644	854	1.838	127	-2.517	65	-3.88
Poland (02)	-7.249	-6.400	-5.007	4.131	2.826	6.955	1.948	189	1.03
Slovakia (00)	-895	-459	-694	2.052	1.016	1.472	778	24	3.22
Slovenia (03)	-624	-13	15	180	-31	264	279	22	1.27
Estonia (02)	-1.103	-613	-800	284	345	805	5	6	0.08
Latvia (02)	-1.444	-900	-647	382	-10	699	52	8	0.65
Lithuania (02)	-1.315	-766	-721	712	149	1.048	327	14	2.34
CEECs	-16.989	-12.254	-14.983	17.918	6.947	22.605	7.622	402	1.90
Turkey (02)	-8.337	-457	-1.521	1.038	1.503	1.328	-193	183	-0.11
Bulgaria (02)	-1.594	-1.000	-682	874	-302	1.692	1.010	15	6.73
Croatia (02)	-5.640	-2.485	-1.908	1.124	410	3.145	1.237	22	5.62
Romania (02)	-2.611	-2.602	-1.525	1.144	382	4.079	2.554	46	5.58
Russia (02)	46.335	36.449	29.520	3.442	3.295	907	30.427	346	8.80
Ukraine (02)	710	1.857	3.174	693	-1.718	-1.065	2.109	41	5.09
Greece (02)	-21.452	-11.906	-10.405	53	12.315	11.574	1.169	183	0.64
Spain (02)	-33.098	-8.228	-15.942	21.284	35.137	18.842	2.900	902	0.32
Portugal (02)	-12.115	-8.994	-8.813	4.235	10.173	9.177	364	168	0.22
Germany	122.180	77.690	46.590	-25.300	-63.320	-25.300	21.290	2.243	0.95
Switzerland	6.432	18.705	26.011	-10.069	-29.914	-33.692	-7.681	268	-2.87

Source: IMF, International Financial Statistics, April 2004.

Table 1.12 also suggests that it might be difficult for the CEECs to try to stabilize their exchange rates too soon. The Czech Republic could have discouraged capital imports in 2002 (by taxing them, withdrawing red-carpet treatment, etc.) and thus avoided the appreciation of the Koruna in 2003. But would this have been the right choice? Is it worth slowing down the rate of catch-up growth in the name of currency stability? And all this without even mentioning a possible Balassa-Samuelson effect.

It is frequently assumed that after enlargement capital will move East and labour will move West. I would like to suggest a different hypothesis, based on the fact that capital and labour are more complementary than competitive factors of production. Capital will move to where after-tax returns are highest and not necessarily to where labour costs, or even tax rates, are lowest. The whole calculation is much more complex and takes into account total factor productivity, as well as social and political considerations. In years to come, members of the EC-25 will compete fiercely with each other to attract these mobile capital and labour resources (Table 1.10 shows how corporate tax rates have already shrunk and not just in the CEECs, but this is only one dimension of public policy competition). If successful, they will attract both types of factors. The EC is still all about the undistorted allocation of resources in a reasonably competitive environment and this will – or at least should – determine the location of economic activity across the continent. The EC Commission and Court of Justice watch over forbidden (discriminatory) taxes and subsidies, which artificially alter the rules of the competitive game between people and sectors. Differences in non-discriminatory rules between different member states do not distort competition and are, indeed, the basis upon which all federal states stand (otherwise they would be unitary states). In a few years time we should be able to take an economic satellite picture of Europe, showing where the high-growth areas are located: they will be on both sides of the current East–West divide. It is up to governments to provide the right mix of supportive policies consistent with their EC obligations.

CONCLUSION

The process of economic integration through trade and investment flows began over 10 years ago. The initial tidal wave of change is probably mostly behind us. The reason is that while the 1990s were years of transition for the CEECs from planned to market economies, the early decades of this century will be a time of consolidation. The change was vast and non-marginal (see Table 1.3).

Trade and investment flows are now in the process of re-shaping economic activity across the European Continent. Some mis-allocation of resources is bound to occur, especially on the interface between agricultural and non-agricultural activities. However, hoping for the best, these losses should be contained, especially if the Doha Development Round is brought to a successful conclusion with regard to agriculture. Under this assumption, enlargement will contribute to rapid economic growth in the CEECs. Access to markets, capital and technology will put them, inter alia, in an ideal position to supply the huge (and growing) Russian market. It is true that Greece, Spain and Portugal will find new competitors on their path, but they will also find new markets and new suppliers. Trade is a two-way street.

Competition for mobile factors of production will be fierce, but conducive to economic growth, on both sides of the former East–West divide. Competition is a beneficial force in ordinary markets for goods and it is not to be disdained in the 'market' for good public policies. It weeds out ineffective private and public strategies.

Rapid economic growth in the CEECs will of course benefit their own citizens, providing necessary resources to finance both private consumption and independently determined social policies, but it will also benefit the old EC-15 for reasons which were first put forward by David Hume 250 years ago and who provides, I believe, a fitting conclusion to this chapter:

> I will venture to assert, that the increase of riches and commerce in any one nation, instead of hurting, commonly promotes the riches and commerce of all its neighbours; and that a state can scarcely carry its trade and industry very far, where all the surrounding states are buried in ignorance, sloth and barbarism . . .I shall therefore venture to acknowledge, that, not only as a man, but as a British subject, I pray for the flourishing commerce of Germany, Spain, Italy and even France itself . . .

REFERENCES

Baldwin, R., Francois, J. and Portes, R. (1997), 'The costs and benefits of eastern enlargement: the impact on the EU and eastern Europe', *Economic Policy*, April 1997, pp. 125–70.

Curzon Price, V. (1999), 'Reintegrating Europe: economic aspects', in V. Curzon Price, A. Landau and R.G. Whitman, *The Enlargement of the European Union, Issues and Strategies*, London and New York, Routledge, pp. 25–55.

Curzon Price, V. (2004), 'Costs and benefits of membership: making the most of the principle of subsidiarity within the EC', paper presented to the Institute of Economics and the Faculty of Law, University of Wroclaw, 20–21 May 2004.

GATT/ WTO (2002), *International Trade* (various years), Geneva.

Hume, D. (1752), *Of the Jealousy of Trade*, Political Discourses.

International Monetary Fund, Direction of Trade Statistics 2002, Washington.

International Monetary Fund (2004), *International Financial Statistics*, Washington, April 2004.

Maliszewska, M. (2004), *EU Enlargement: Benefits of the Single Market Expansion for Current and New Member States*, Series: Studies and Analyses No. 273, Warsaw 2004. See http://www.case.com.pl/upload/publikacja_plik/1861894_273.pdf
UNCTAD (2003), World Investment Report 2003, New York and Geneva.
UN ECE (2004), 'Tax reforms in the EU acceding countries', *Economic Survey of Europe* 2004, No. 1, pp. 119–44.
UN ECE, *Economic Survey of Europe*, various issues.

2. Economic Integration and Spatial Location of Production

Miroslav N. Jovanović*

INTRODUCTION

One of the most important and challenging questions in economics is: where will economic activity locate in the future?

Progress in technology, changes in demand and moves towards a liberal economic policy and international economic integration create new challenges for theorists, policymakers and business executives. As a number of economic activities became 'footloose' and highly mobile, one of the most demanding and intricate questions in such a situation is where firms and industries would locate, re-locate or stay.

This chapter is structured as follows. The next section outlines the basic theoretical strands, while the gains of economic integration are presented in the third section. The fourth and fifth sections, respectively, discuss production geography with trade barriers and the situation when these barriers are reduced. Experiences and possible gains for the new European Union (EU) member countries are the subject matter of the sixth section. At the end, there are conclusions and policy implications.

THEORETICAL BACKGROUND

The spatial location of a firm is an issue only in the situation with market imperfections. Without market imperfections such as transport cost (affected by

* Un ringraziamento va a Silvia Bonato che mi ha aiutato senza saperlo. I have benefited from discussions with and intellectual capital of many friends and colleagues, but I owe special gratitude to Lisa Borgatti. This paper is based on the chapter 'Spatial location of production and regional policy' from my book *The Economics of European Integration* (2005). The views expressed are my own and do not reflect the position of the organisation for which I work.

location), the production location decision becomes irrelevant. This is to say that without market failures firms may split into units of any size and operate in all locations without any cost disadvantage. However, in a situation with market imperfections, recent empirical research found 'that the degree of production indeterminacy is greatest when trade barriers and trade costs are relatively low' (Bernstein and Weinstein, 2002, p. 73).

To a large extent, in the distant past wealth creation used to depend on the availability of local natural resources.[1] As the economy evolved, wealth creation started to depend more on physical assets (mainly equipment and finance). In modern economies, prosperity and competitiveness of output depend not only on the physical, but also and increasingly on intangible assets such as knowledge, information processing, as well as on organisational and control potentials and capabilities. In the new situation, in which most determinants for the spatial location of firms and industries are mobile and man-made, the location determinants for (footloose) industries include considerations of:

- **Costs and prices:** availability, substitutability, quality and prices of inputs (raw materials, energy, labour); cost of market access (trade costs); economies of scale; utility costs; infrastructure; transport cost of inputs and output; earlier sunk costs in other locations (not yet depreciated); availability of investment funds; and cost of the project.
- **Demand:** its real and potential size, its growth and consumer preferences.
- **Organisation and technology:** input–output production links; externalities; competition and market structure; location decisions of other competing or supplying firms; technology and the speed of its change; and local R&D resources and capabilities.
- **Policy related factors:** incentives; taxes; subsidies; public procurement; permissions; and mandatory or voluntary unionisation of labour.
- **Social factors:** system of education of management and training of labour; brain drain; general quality of life; distribution of income;[2] and retirement patterns.

---

[1] Abundant natural resources may often be a problem for a country, not a benefit. This is particularly relevant for certain developing countries. A discovery of resources attracts gamblers, opportunists and crooks such as Francisco Pizzaro (Latin America), Robert Clive (East India Company) or Cecil Rhodes (South Africa). These resources provoke or contribute to civil wars: Angola, Congo or Nigeria. Elsewhere, abundant oil reserves and exports as is the case in Saudi Arabia, Bahrain or Kuwait keep local wages too high to permit the local development of the manufacturing industry. Foreigners from less well-off countries fill jobs in services in these countries. However, developed countries such as Norway and Iceland manage relatively well the discovery of natural resources. In addition, certain countries that are exceptionally poor in natural resources such as Switzerland, Austria or Japan are highly developed and amongst the wealthiest in the world. They base their prosperity on the most important resource: human capital.

[2] Income distribution also affects the location of production. If, for example, income is distributed to a small segment of the population (landowners or owners of capital) who spend it on imports of luxury goods and services, there may not be a spread of development of industries in their area or country. If,

Hence, the decision about the location of a firm or an industry is a complex, uncertain and risky task. It comes as no surprise that national or regional production geography does not always change very fast.

Multiple equilibria create a situation for welfare ranking and set up many temptations for policymakers to try to 'pick winners'. The selection problem, however, remains unresolved. Hence a small historical accident (chance, arbitrariness)[3] remains the unique deciding factor that counts heavily in deciding the location (Arthur, 2002, p. 6). If governments want to tip markets towards a preferred solution, then it is timing and, to an extent, instruments that are crucial. There is only a narrow window of opportunity during which the policy may be effective. Otherwise, governments with their limited knowledge, instruments and resources try to stabilise artificially a 'naturally' unstable and evolving process.

Arthur (1989, 1990, 1994a, and 1994b) argued that certain models of production geography give weight to differences in factor endowment, transport costs, rents and competition. In such cases, the pattern of production locations may be in equilibrium. Hence, in these models history does not matter. The location system is determinate and predictable (Arthur, 1994a, pp. 49–50). However, if one takes increasing returns and multiple equilibria into consideration, the new model has four properties that cause serious difficulties in analysis and policymaking. These features are (Arthur, 1989, pp. 116–17):

- **Multiple equilibria (non-predictability):** ex ante knowledge of firms' preferences and potentials of technologies may not be sufficient to predict the 'market outcome'. The outcome is indeterminate.[4]
- **Potential inefficiency:** increasing returns (*i*-activities) may uplift the development of technology with inferior long-run aptitude as firms make irreversible investments under uncertainty.[5] Basically, a superior technology may have bad luck in gaining early adherents. For example, the American nuclear industry is dominated by light-water reactors as a consequence of the adoption of such reactor to propel the first nuclear submarine in 1954. Engineering literature asserts, however, that gas-cooled reactor would have

---

however, income is distributed in favour of a large number of families that demand domestically produced goods and services, this may have a positive impact on the location of firms and industries closer to the domestic market.

[3] Marriages (chances or historical accidents) of the Habsburgs created the Austro-Hungarian Empire that altered economic space in central and eastern Europe.

[4] Murphy *et al.* (1989) discuss multiple equilibria with respect to the process of industrialisation, postulating that a certain critical mass of industries may have to be involved in order for industrialisation to be successful. A parallel could be drawn with location theory, and a role for government policy to aid the 'take-off' of a particular location, and encourage firms to move to that location.

[5] Positive feedback economics may also find parallels in non-linear physics. For example, ferromagnetic materials consist of mutually reinforcing elements. Small perturbations, at critical times, influence which outcome is selected (bifurcation point), and the chosen outcome may have higher energy (that is, be less favourable) than other possible end states (Arthur, 1990a, p. 99).

been a superior choice (Arthur, 1989, p. 126). If engineers claim that Betamax is a technically superior system for video recorders, then the market choice (around 1980) of VHS did not represent the best outcome. Similar arguments could be used for the triumph of DOS over Macintosh during the mid-1980s. In addition, the 'qwerty' arrangement for typewriter keyboards was designed in the 19th century; its name refers to the first six top line letters. Even though it has repeatedly been shown that this distribution of letters was sub-optimal, the 'qwerty' system continues to be the standard for keyboards.

- **Inflexibility:** once an outcome such as a dominant technology begins to surface it turns out to be more 'locked in' and persist for a long period of time. In order to replace an entrenched product or technology, the new one must be several times superior to the existing one. It must significantly increase convenience of use for consumers and it has to be available at a price that takes into account three factors: culture (openness to change); investment of capital and time (learning) into the new good or service (once people learn to use something, they do not want to switch easily); and convenience of use. VCRs were introduced during the 1970s. It took three decades to replace them by DVDs and full replacement is not yet finished.
- **Path dependence (non-ergodicity):**[6] small, unpredictable, random and arbitrary events (chances and accidents), path dependence and economies of scale in a non-ergodic system may set in motion mutations in economic structures and irreversibly decide the final outcome. These events are neither normalised, nor averaged away, nor forgotten by the dynamics of the system. There is no homeostasis (habitual return to the initial equilibrium).

In this model history matters, but the system's dynamics, increasing returns, multiple equilibria, lock-in effect and path dependence generate theoretical and practical limits to predicting the future spatial location of an industry with a high degree of certitude

The probability of the location of an industry resulting from a historical accident is shown in highly stylised, graphical form in Figure 2.1. If the distribution of potential locations of an industry is concave (see Figure 2.1a), with a single minimum and a corresponding single outcome, the location is not influenced by a historical chance. This type of distribution is exemplified by the mining and steel-making industries, which are normally located close to their source of raw materials. If, however, the distribution is convex (see Figure 2.1b), with two minima, then there are two potential outcomes, each resulting in a different location which may depend on the historical chance. The third case represents a sphere in which there are *n* solutions for the location of footloose industries (see Figure 2.1c). Hence, multiple equilibria make policy analysis

---

[6] An ergodic system (a pendulum, water in a glass) returns at the end to its original state, no matter the disturbances between the starting and ending points in time.

conceptually difficult. Corner shops, bakeries and petrol stations exemplify this type of distribution. However, firms in most industries need to be close to each other (i.e. they tend to agglomerate and create towns and cities), not only to be close to common suppliers of inputs, but also to foster competition and to facilitate exchange of information, which can be hampered if firms are spatially dispersed.

Figure 2.1
Concave (a), convex (b) and spherical (c) distributions of potential industry locations

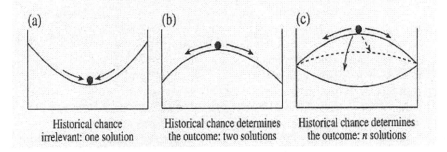

Historical chance irrelevant: one solution	Historical chance determines the outcome: two solutions	Historical chance determines the outcome: n solutions

The **convergence or neo-classical school** of thought regarding regional matters did not consider either market imperfections such as economies of scale, sunk costs and externalities or institutions that set organisational environment. This school argued that the 'regional problem' and the spatial location of economic activity are no problems at all. Free trade and unimpeded factor mobility would produce a smooth spatial dispersion of people, skills, technology and economic activity. This would equalise factor earnings and living standards in all regions and countries. Apart from transport costs, it should not matter where a tradable good or service is produced. Hence, the spatial location of output is not more than an operational detail. This is because transport, communication and other trade costs have been declining over time because of innovation and increases in productivity. The peripheral regions and countries are expected to gain from trade liberalisation and integration in terms of an increased relocation of industries and trade. At the limit, there would be a full equalisation in factor prices.

The neo-classical one-sector growth models based on exogenous technological progress anticipate economic convergence among regions. This expectation, based on comparative advantages, depends on the starting conditions (including the endowment of factors). However, different regions may have different long-run growth rates because of different starting situations. As technological progress in this model is exogenous, developing counties should grow faster than the developed ones. If, however, technological progress is endogenous, the convergence school does not give a clear prediction about growth rates and patterns.

This liberal (non-interventionist) attitude in the field of regional policy in the market economies had certain validity until the economic crisis of the 1930s. With free trade, perfect allocation and use of resources, intervention in regional policy is not necessary because markets clear and bring the economy to equilibrium. Such a convergence approach was not validated by time and experience. In spite of expectations about convergence, even the **laissez-faire** governments may consider it necessary and beneficial to intervene, as the adjustment process may take too long to be politically acceptable.

The new spatial economics emphasises potentially growing disparities, rather than convergence among regions and countries. This **divergence school** of thought offered theories that refer to the growing discrepancy among regions. Explanations are based principally on economies of scale. Sources of economies of scale include very high set-up or sunk costs (in fixed capital and R&D); learning effects (the more people learn how to use one Microsoft program, the easier is for them to learn and adjust to other programs); and network and coordination effects (the more people use mobile phones or electronic banking, the greater is the utility of that to all network users). Together with the new geography of production (spatial economics), divergence theories consider market imperfections and institutions that set rules which streamline liberties and behaviour. Institutional organisation, social regulation and political intervention may have a significant influence on the location of production. This moves theoretical concepts closer to reality. The list of new assumptions includes economies of scale, high fixed costs, trade and adjustment costs, entry and exit barriers, constrained mobility of factors, transport costs, externalities, multiple equilibria, path dependence, multiplier effect, cumulative causation, non-ergodicity and inflexibility. Cumulative causation mixes causes and effects of an event. They are combined in a chain reaction that is increasingly circular, snowballing, herding or perpetually accumulative. This type of self-reinforcement has different labels in economics which includes economies of scale, path dependency, virtuous and vicious circles, as well as threshold effects. The sources of this process are large sunk costs, learning, network and coordination effects. If applied to intermediate production, these forces can combine and influence each other in such a complex way that their behaviour becomes fickle. They can produce highly unpredictable outcomes regarding locations of firms and industries. In many cases history, chance and expectations set the final outcome.

The Heckscher-Ohlin theory is inadequate for providing the reason for the location of an industry in regions with high mobility of factors (US) or in the countries with broadly similar endowment of factors (France and Germany).

Patterns of regional specialisation and location of firms and industries are often created by historical accident. Ohlin noted that 'Chance plays a significant part in determining the localisation of industry'... A different distribution of inventions would have caused a different localisation (Ohlin, 1933, p. 137). More recently Krugman wrote: 'I at least am convinced that there is a strong arbitrary, accidental component to international specialization; but not everyone agrees, and the limitations of the data make a decisive test difficult' (Krugman, 1992, p. 9).

Production and trade in goods are increasingly becoming elaborate and difficult. They heavily depend on sophisticated information and services that are included in the final good and its price. Internal trade within each Transnational Corporation (TNC) may take a big part of total trade. Hence, national and international markets become more incomplete and harder to manage. In addition, the new elements listed that are considered by the divergence theory, exert a strong influence on the location of production, trade and **absolute** advantages (which widen regional gaps), while **local comparative** advantages may play a less important role. In this case, competition, liberalisation and economic integration generate concentration (or increase the attractiveness of the already developed areas), they generate economic divergence and widening of regional gaps, not economic convergence among regions and countries.

Given that spatial concentration is the most striking feature of the geography of production, there exists clear evidence of some kind of increasing returns to scale (Krugman, 1992, p. 5). New technologies in select industries may overcome some of the obstacles to the spread of production, but not many. Hence, the pattern of regional specialisation and trade can be arbitrary and potential gains from specialisation and trade are likely to be ambiguous.[7]

ECONOMIC INTEGRATION: GAINS

Economic integration may increase the average welfare of consumers directly and indirectly. The problem is that the benefits accrue to everyone in relatively small instalments and only in the medium and long term. Some of those gains include:

- secure access to markets in partner countries,
- increased investment opportunities as expectations may be established with an increase in security,
- improved efficiency in the use of resources,
- elimination of trade barriers reducing trade costs,

---

[7] The interested reader is invited to consult Brülhart (1998a) for a brief survey of theoretical strands.

- increased competition on internal market pushing down prices,
- facilitation of exchange of technical information,
- competition forcing firms to implement new ideas and technologies,
- the enlarged market encouraging producers to exploit and benefit from economies of scale,
- potential for coordination of specific economic policies,
- improved bargaining position with external partners,
- research and innovation being stimulated by tougher competition in a larger market and the possibility to share fixed costs in this market,
- more opportunities in an integrated market for a wider range of goods and services for consumers, hence an improvement in individuals' utility function and a reduction in X-inefficiency which moves the production activities of firms closer to best practice business organisation.

However, one must always keep in mind that international economic integration is never more than a useful **supporting** tool to the sound domestic macro and micro economic policies and that it can not act as their replacement. If these domestic policies are not healthy, integration cannot be their substitute.

PRODUCTION GEOGRAPHY: WITH TRADE BARRIERS

International economic integration may influence the geography of production in several ways. Three are most obvious. They were neglected in earlier analysis because of non-linear analytical complications that arrive from externalities and they deal with trade costs (Fujita *et al.*, 1999, p. 251):

- With transport costs and high trade barriers (or autarky), each country is likely to have manufacturing to supply its local consumers.
- With low or no transport and trade costs (free trade), the world gets 'smaller' and markets larger, forward and backward linkages (presence of tradable intermediate goods) dominate and there are possibilities for footloose manufacturing to agglomerate in a single country or a single location (American outcome). There is no need for producers and consumers to be in vicinity as trade is costless. Firms move to the lowest cost locations.
- At intermediate transport costs concentration becomes possible and necessary. Costs of production may differ between countries depending on country size (market) and economies of scale. In a smaller or peripheral country, firms producing tradable goods depend, on average, more on foreign trade than firms in larger countries. Therefore, if trade is liberalised, firms from the small country may gain more than firms from the large countries. However, firms from the large country may exploit economies of scale and have lower costs of

production and prices of output than the firms in a small country. Once trade is liberalised and trade costs fall, firms from the large country may capture a large part of the small country's market. Then comes a period of adjustment. Some firms may relocate, searching for low cost immobile factors (land, labour) and larger markets. In small countries such as Austria, Switzerland or Luxembourg, firms may successfully adjust and penetrate niche markets in a large country.[8] Although the national production geography (distribution of industries) is altered, this does not mean that there is going to be a divergence in national per capita income. Each country may have a cluster of industries that supply the entire integrated market. However, this case brings with it a range of stable and unstable equilibria (European outcome).

Suppose that transport costs in the real world have a declining path over time. This is a relatively reasonable assumption from the time of Ricardo. One may observe a trend in the narrowing of the income gap between the advanced countries (North) and certain developing countries (South). 'Declining trade costs first produce, then dissolve, the global inequality of nations' (Fujita *et al.*, 1999, p. 260). The problem is that industrialisation and economic development is not a uniform process. It takes place in a series of waves. Labour intensive industries are the first to leave the industrialised country because of high wages. The less labour intensive industries that move at a later stage, do so possibly faster than the earlier movers. Usually upstream industries move first and create the potential for forward and backward production links in the target country which facilitates the entry of firms from other downstream industries.

PRODUCTION GEOGRAPHY: REDUCTION IN TRADE BARRIERS

There is, however, a drive that may help regions which fall behind in an integrated area. Suppose that the initial elimination of barriers to the movement of goods, services and factors in a common market spurs an inflow of factors to already industrialised areas where they benefit from economies of scale and various externalities. If all barriers to internal trade and factor movements are eliminated or become insignificant, firms may benefit from economies of scale and externalities in other (less advanced or peripheral) regions where the variable costs of production are potentially lower than in the centre of the manufacturing or service activity (Krugman and Venables, 1990, p. 74;

---

[8] Casella (1996) discusses the case of reallocation of resources and gains from an enlargement of a trade block in small and large countries that already belong to that bloc. She showed that smaller EU countries gained more from the entry of Spain and Portugal of the EU than the large EU countries.

Venables, 1998, p. 3). In this case, the less developed region or a country that takes part in a common market is likely to benefit on two accounts:

• it gets firms that benefit from economies of scale and
• the former regional production structure that was typified by a lack of open competition is altered.

Kim confirmed this type of reasoning for the manufacturing industry in the US during the period 1860–1987. Industry specialisation rose substantially prior to the turn of the 20th century. At about the same time, the US was developing its transport and communication network in order to become a fully integrated economy. During the inter-war years, the level of regional specialisation 'flattened out', but then fell substantially and continually between 1930s and 1987. Economic integration made the US regions less specialised today than they were in 1860 (Kim, 1995, pp. 882–6). This trend of dispersion of industries and increasing similarity in the US continued throughout the 1990s (Midelfart-Knarvik *et al.*, 2000, p. 44).

In theory, economic integration may, but not necessarily will, bring greater benefits to the regions/countries whose development lags behind the centre of economic activity. However, if production linkages (forward and backward) are strong (meaning that production is indivisible) and **internal** to an industry such as in chemicals or financial services and imperfect competition prevails, economic integration would trigger agglomeration (clustering) tendencies. If those linkages are not limited to a relatively narrow industry group, but are strong **across** industries and sectors, integration would produce agglomeration tendencies in specific areas. If labour is not mobile, the whole process would tend to open new as well as widen existing regional wage differentials (Venables, 1996). Although this may produce deindustrialisation tendencies in the peripheral regions, it does not mean that integration is not desirable. For instance, education and regional policies increased the attractiveness of Spain as a location for various manufacturing industries, discovered by the EU and other foreign investors. This was particularly obvious following the Spanish entry into the EU in 1986. Integration of Mexico with the US shifted a lot of manufacturing industries from the area of Mexico City northwards, along the border with the US. This took place not only because there was a growing demand in the US, but also because of the general trade liberalisation policy in Mexico. Once the economy turns outwards, internal production linkages weaken and firms have fewer incentives to stay in the congested hub.

If costs of trade are high, industries tend to disperse. When this cost is reduced, agglomeration can take place as demand in distant places can be met by exports. When these trade costs approach zero (as is the case in writing computer software in Bangalore or data entry in Manila and the use of the Internet), footloose production may be dispersed and located according to the availability of the specific resource inputs.[9] Globalisation of certain industries (integrated international production) reduces the weight of physical proximity between various production units, as well as between producers and consumers. However, in industries that have strong internal links such as the ones based on new knowledge (innovation activities are still highly clustered in the world), financial services or chemicals, there is a strong propensity to cluster in spite of 'globalisation' of other businesses.

Deepening economic integration in the EU through the elimination of non-tariff barriers (NTBs) during the introduction and after the establishment of the Single European Market, reduction of transportation costs and the Eurozone may diminish motives for regional and national self-sufficiency. However, integration may also stimulate agglomeration tendencies and reinforce the core–periphery problem. Production in the EU may resemble the US where industrial output (both in manufacturing and in services) is concentrated in distinct geographical locations. Hence, if this does take place in the future, internal EU trade between Member States will no longer be intra-industry, but rather inter-industry in nature. Further reduction of trade costs in the EU may lead to further concentration of production, which is subject to the economies of scale in the already existing core locations, while the periphery may specialise in the manufacturing production that does not depend on economies of scale. This provides support to the arguments of the new economic geography and trade theories (Brülhart and Torstensson, 1996; Amiti, 1999).

Industry characteristics set the locational response to lower trade costs. Industries that have significant economies of scale and important intra-industry links have a hump (∩) shaped relation between integration and concentration. When there are high trade costs trade production is dispersed so industrial concentration is low; as these costs are lowered and reach intermediate level, there is an increase in industrial concentration; as trade costs fall to low levels, there is a decrease in concentration (spread) as industries start to respond to factor markets.[10] These industries are metals, chemicals, machinery and transport equipment. Industries that are not strongly based on economies of scale (textiles, leather and food products) have a monotonously increasing path towards concentration as trade cost decrease because of integration (Forslid *et al.*, 2002, p. 293). This kind of reasoning and regional compensation funds of the group may be used in convincing the adversely affected peripheral regions to put up with hard transition times that may follow trade liberalisation and economic

---

[9] There are, however, certain limits to such type of 'off-shoring' and migration of such services jobs towards the developing countries. Tastes and needs change, markets are fickle, hence there will always be necessary certain local presence, close to consumers. It may be tough to service such consumers and markets in the EU from Bombay.

[10] Spain as a peripheral country attracted a relatively large number of foreign investors.

integration (Puga and Venables, 1997, p. 364). Similar arguments may be used in the case of the CEE countries.

If local entrepreneurs are flexible, then the regional geography of production can be altered within a large integrated area without a substantial external assistance or even without a separate regional currency. A clear example is the conversion of New England's production geography from the production of shoes and textiles in the 1960s (coupled with relatively high unemployment) to an economy based on 'high technology' and low unemployment in the 1980s.

Centripetal forces may explain relatively low indices of intra-industry trade (agglomeration, clustering) in industries subject to high economies of scale. Conversely, relatively high indices of intra-industry trade (in 'labour-intensive' industries) may suggest the spread of industries. In the case of the EU, Brülhart (1998b, pp. 340-1) suggested that in the period 1980–90:

- there was no further concentration of already clustered industries that are subject to increasing returns in the central regions,
- there was further concentration of textile-related industries at the periphery, and
- there were certain indicators of spread of 'high-technology' industries towards the periphery.

Others may, however, argue that the outcome may be reversed from the one just described and that an active regional policy is necessary particularly in an economic and monetary union (EMU). Emigration of people would discourage an entry of new businesses into such a region. That trend would further weaken the economic position of the region in question. None the less, such a vicious circle has not taken place in the EU. Even though there are severe problems regarding data, particularly regarding the 1950s and 1960s, one may uncover certain leanings. What seems likely to be the case in the EU is that the regional disparities were slowly narrowing until the early 1970s. This was followed by a decade-long period of widening of regional gaps and a mixture of stabilisation and widening of regional gaps between member countries ever since. It is not yet clear what prompted the halt in the convergence process after the 1970s. This does not mean that specific regions are irrevocably affixed to a specific position in the regional rank order. Evidence is available that there is quite a lot of switching over from one position on the regional rank to another (Armstrong and de Kervenoael, 1997, p. 41; Midelfart-Knarvik *et al.*, 2000).

Economic history of integrated states such as the US points to the fact that integration is associated with regional convergence which predominates over economic divergence in the long run. This process is rather slow, around 2 per cent a year, but it is sustained over a long period of time (Barro and Sala-i-Martin, 1991, p. 154). General, but very slow regional convergence has been confirmed by the literature, however, a poor region can expect the gap between its initial level of income and the aggregate to be reduced by only 30–40 per cent in the limit (Canova and Marcet, 1995, pp. 1 and 24). Armstrong (1995, p. 149) found that the convergence rate between 1970 and 1990 was only 1 per cent a year, which is half the rate estimated by Barro and Sala-i-Martin.

In a critical survey of new geographical turn in economics, Martin found that regional convergence is remarkably similar across the US, EU, Canada, Japan China and Australia and stated that 'the observed rate of regional convergence is very slow, about 1–2 per cent per annum, and considerably lower than predicted by the simple neoclassical growth model' (Martin, 1999, p. 72). In any case, there are endogenous growth factors (increasing returns) at work and regional policies based on pure transfers of funds are not working unless linked with structural changes and factor mobility.

The change in the production structure data in the EU found certain support in the change in the structure of EU trade. Trade data support the finding that there was a decrease in specialisation during the 1970s. The picture is, however, mixed from the beginning of the 1980s. The growing specialisation revealed in the production data is not reflected in the change in the structure of trade. The main reason for the faulty display of changing specialisation in production is the growing volume of intra-industry trade (Midelfart-Knarvik *et al.*, 2000, p. 12). In addition, trade data may not be a suitable substitute for the production records. The structure of trade may change as a response to changing demand without any change in production. If there is a change in domestic tastes, then the domestic producers may sell goods on the home market rather than make extra efforts to sell abroad. The structure and volume of trade are altered in this case, while there may be no change in the composition of the domestic output.

Compared with the pre-Single Market Programme, the EU 'problem regions' saw improved economic performance in the period following the completion of the Single European Market. This improvement was obvious in terms of both growth in employment rates and growth in gross value added (European Commission, 1997, p. 5). Concerns that the Single Market Programme would lead into a concentration of economic activity into the 'core' EU countries were not fulfilled. There has been only a limited spread of economic activity to the 'peripheral' EU countries which enjoy certain cost advantages (European Commission, 1998, p. 145). This is consistent with the view that as costs of trade fall for products of certain industries, the periphery may become more attractive for investment as the returns on the capital are greater. However, this development in the EU may also be the consequence of the impact of regional aid (European Commission, 1997, p. 34).

One of the outcomes of the Single European Market was that certain clusters of firms and industries in the EU became more visible. Relatively high geographical concentration of similar firms in relatively small areas eased exchange of information. Following these changes, Frankfurt, London and Paris are the areas that create jobs faster than the rest of the national economy. However, the problem is in the regions outside a large metropolitan area which still seem to remain 'poor'. Success, like many other things, also appears to cluster.

The impact of the Single European Market on regional disequilibria in the EU is ambiguous. There is an identification problem. First and foremost, one needs to answer difficult questions: what are the short- and long-term effects of the Single European Market Programme (1985–92) on the regions and, what is the impact of the changes on the regional disequilibria that would have happened on their own? If the longer-term effects of the Single European Market include the liberalisation of EU trade, then output may continue to be concentrated in the already advanced regions in order to benefit from positive externalities (this implies a fall in output and wages in the less advanced regions). However, internal trade liberalisation may reallocate some EU production activities towards the periphery in order to take advantage of lower wages and other production costs there. As the outcome is uncertain in a situation with market imperfections and multiple equilibria, the effects of the Single European Market on the regions will continue to be debated for quite some time in the future.

In spite of substantial regional expenditure by the EU, Boldrin and Canova (2001) showed that neither convergence, nor divergence was taking place among the EU(15) regions during the period 1980–95. The adopted and implemented regional policies, as well as substantial public resources channelled to less developed regions do not appear to enhance the capacity of these regions. These funds only redistributed income among regions. With no prospects for change and if income distribution is the principal concern, such transfers will be necessary on a continuous basis. Therefore, there was no evidence that the adopted policies of redistribution of income were the most appropriate. As most regions were growing at a fairly uniform rate, these policies reflected internal political compromises which have little effect on fostering economic growth and convergence in the EU (Boldrin and Canova, 2001, pp. 211 and 242).

In spite of substantial expenditure on regional matters by the EU during 1980s and 1990s, regional inequalities have not narrowed during this period, and by some measures have even widened. 'Income differences across states have fallen, but inequalities between regions within each state have risen. European states have developed increasingly different production structures' (Puga, 2002, p. 400). A similar observation came from Midelfart-Knarvik and Overman (2002, p. 333) who noted that despite the fact that the EU(15) spent around a third of its overall annual budget on regional matters, there was an increasing regional inequality. If the EU regional policy and instruments were successful on the country level, they were less so on the sub-national plane.

EUROPEAN UNION'S PERIPHERY AND NEW MEMBER STATES

International economic integration brings multiple equilibria and may, in some cases, aggravate the situation of already weak and peripheral regions in comparison with previous circumstances. This is recognised in part by the existence of national and EU regional policies. Nonetheless, having a peripheral location does not mean that a country is destined to have poor economic performance. The accumulation and efficient employment of human (and physical) capital is the most important factor in a country's economic performance. Although countries such as Finland, Sweden, New Zealand, Australia and even Japan and South Korea have relatively unfavourable geographical locations regarding major transport routes, the irreversibility of their 'peripheral' geographical position is mitigated and more than compensated for by the accumulation and efficient employment of their national human and physical capital, as well as adjustments in their domestic investment-friendly economic policies. The most striking feature of this process was a change in the industrial structure of Ireland and Finland. New high–technology industries and the ones subject to increasing returns to scale were located in these two peripheral countries. In addition, the expansion of infrastructure and further development of human and physical capital alleviated Spain's location at the fringe of the EU. It is expected that the CEE countries will do likewise in the future.

One of the reasons why Peugeot-Citroën announced in 2003 that it intends to invest and to locate a large (700 million) car assembly factory in Trnava, Slovakia (over alternative locations in Poland, the Czech Republic and Hungary) is that this country has good access to transport links and that it is 'in the centre of Europe'.[11] The factory would start production of about 300,000 small cars from 2006. The management intends to be closer to fast-growing markets in the EU accession countries and to profit from wage rates that are a fifth of the rates paid in the EU(15) for similar industrial operations.

In 2004, Hyundai selected Slovakia over Poland (known for the aggressive reputation of its labour unions) to build a 700 million car assembly plant in Zilina. This is Hyundai's first car assembly plant in Europe. It would assemble 200,000 cars a year (potentially 300,000 from 2008). The reasons for the decision to locate in Slovakia include wage costs (a quarter of the prevailing rates in western Europe); half the car ownership levels of western Europe; laws that made labour market flexible; reduced corporate and income taxes; existing network of suppliers (expected to expand further); and membership of the EU. As Volkswagen already produces cars in Slovakia (Bratislava), this 'tiny' (5.4

---

[11] R. Anderson, M. Arnold and J. Reed, 'Peugeot to build new plant in Slovakia', *Financial Times*, 15 January 2003.

million people) central-European country becomes one of the European motor giants. The three Slovak car plants could produce over 800,000 cars a year from 2006. That would make the highest per capita car production in the world.[12]

Slovakia may produce about 900,000 cars a year from 2008. The automotive industry contributes a quarter to the manufacturing output and a third to exports (this will increase to a half once the two plants are completed). The problem may be in the increasing unbalance in the Slovak industrial structure. Although Slovakia may be the victim of its own success, some of the neighbouring countries that lost out to Slovakia (Poland, for example) may like to have such 'troubles'.

CONCLUSIONS AND POLICY IMPLICATIONS

A century ago, even a half of a century ago, economic theory looked at the location of firms and industries in a rather technical and deterministic way. Subjects and causes were separated from objects and effects, and everything ended up in equilibrium. Parts of modern spatial economics and the new geography of production consider the location of firms in an evolutionary way where the state of equilibrium is only a temporary special case as everything is in an unstable organic process.

Where a firm or an industry should locate is not a question with a straightforward answer. Rich nations fear the relocation of firms and industries to low-wage nations; poor nations worry that the production of goods and services will migrate to developed countries; while small countries are concerned that businesses will move to large countries. At the time and age of 'globalisation' of business, one might expect the importance of firm location to be diminishing. Some argue that distance is dead in terms of production and business because of astonishing changes in communications and computers. 'Time zones and language groups, rather than mileage, will come to define distance' (Cairncross, 2001, p. 5). But this may be relevant only for certain manufacturing and services activities that are simple, routine and with codified knowledge.

Local proximity (clusters) of firms that produce similar, competing and/or related products together with supporting institutions still matters for complex activities, with no or lightly codified knowledge and where market changes and uncertainty require a rapid reaction. Economies of scale, activity-specific backward and forward linkages (indivisible production), accumulated knowledge, innovation, lock-in effects, existence of sophisticated customers and a fall in transportation costs play relevant roles in the protection of clusters and

---

[12] R. Anderson and J. Cienski, 'Hyundai picks Slovakia for new 700m car assembly plant', *Financial Times*, 3 March 2004.

the absolute advantage of certain locations. 'Global' competitiveness often depends on highly concentrated 'local' knowledge, capabilities and a common tacit code of behaviour which can be found in a spatial concentration (a cluster) of firms. Hence, successful managers must often think in regional and act in local terms.

The new economic geography differs from the traditional model in several important dimensions. The new model makes a case that production specialisation in a given locality is not only based on certain comparative advantages, but rather on a self-reinforcing lock-in effect, path dependence, accumulated knowledge, agglomeration, clustering and linkages (indivisible production). In addition, while the traditional models reason that a reduction in trade costs among locations favours local specialisation, the new economic geography claims that the effect on local specialisation is ambiguous. The final outcome is industry specific and depends on the functional intra-industry production linkages, market structure, consumer preferences (homogeneity of tastes) and factor market (availability and mobility of factors and flexibility in prices). In general, the choice of location for a new investment or a new firm that produces tradable goods and services depends on a complicated interplay of at least three elements: factor intensity; transport intensity; and each in relation to the already established firms and their activities and (re)actions. Remote places do not necessarily need to be poor locations for firms as their remoteness is already reflected in their factor prices (Venables and Limão, 2002, pp. 260-1).

As a reaction to trade liberalisation and economic integration various industries follow different paths. Depending on the functional intra-industry production links, some industries concentrate (reinforcing absolute advantages of certain locations), while others spread. This is contrary to the expectations of neo-classical theory, which predicts that all industries will be affected in the same way. Different forces, therefore, propel such changes in the spatial structure of production. Strong functional intra-industry linkages (high share of intermediate goods from the same industry and/or the need for a large pool of highly skilled labour and researchers) stimulate agglomeration. Where these functional linkages are weak, this acts as an incentive to spread production.

In the end, one may reason that there is an important lacuna in our understanding of spatial economics. It comes as no surprise that there are many disagreements and perhaps only four theoretical agreements:

- First, if one wants to start a new activity in a specific location, one has to build on already existing expertise and specialisation of that location.
- Second, if one wants to use policy intervention to influence the location of firms, this is most effective only very early in the process.[13]

---

[13] A century ago a man went to a Belfast bank and asked for a loan to start a company. He explained to the bank managers that his invention was a mechanical horseless device that would replace horses in

- Third, economies of scale and functional linkages in production have a certain impact on the location of firms and industries.
- Success or failure of a region or a policy sometimes depends on uncontrollable factors and events that are located outside regions themselves.[14]

Enterprise policy and the policy of macroeconomic stability are gradually being used instead of regional policy to tackle the regional (spatial) problems of a country. The new regional (development) policy ought to change the traditional intra- and inter-regional relations of dependence and hierarchy. This type of rigid structural organisation of firms, industries and institutions (state commands, taxes and shelters; big firms are protected; small and new firms are tolerated, but not highly encouraged; while the family ties and 'old boys' connect everything) ought to be replaced by structures that are open for contacts based on affinity, support and perception of common growth and positive sum game. This new policy ought to include the following features:

- assistance to innovation and permanent learning;
- aid to increase flexibility to face and adapt to challenges;
- reduction in the traditional financial regional support;
- emphasis on small and medium-sized enterprises, business 'incubators' and start-ups of new firms;
- backing of the producers' services; and
- coordination with other policies.

The critics of this policy stance believe that lacks the firmness needed to have a direct influence on a given spatial problem.

As the CEE countries brought in serious regional disequilibria into the EU, cohesion will remain one of the major long-term issues in the EU(25). Hence, there are at least three major arguments in favour of certain EU regional policy in order to preserve unity with diversity in the EU(25):

- In the absence of policy instruments such as tariffs, NTBs, devaluation or changes in rates of interest, regions that are not able to adjust as fast as the rest of the EU face increases in unemployment and decreases in living standards. In this situation, there is some case for the demand for short-term fiscal

---

ploughing. This was too risky for the bank, as it could not foresee that happening at all with a commercial success. Hence, this man by the name of Ferguson went to Canada. He met another men by the name of Massey, they teamed up, and the rest of the story is generally known. Massey Ferguson became one of the major world producers of tractors and agriculture-related machinery. The moral of this story is that one needs to recognise and seize the opportunity. Carpe diem!

[14] Coalmining regions weakened and declined when liquid fuels started to be used as principal sources of energy.

transfers at the EU level to ease the adjustment process. The possibility of such transfers in unforeseen cases ought to be permanent in an EMU (Eurozone). Otherwise, when in need, the regions that are in trouble may not be sure that other partner countries will provide resources on a case-by-case basis. The Eurozone may not be able to operate efficiently in the long term without an effective regional policy. However, there is high uncertainty regarding the size of the EU(25) structural funds during the period 2007–13. There are serious political pressures to limit and to scale down the overall EU budgetary expenditure.

- Coordination of national regional policies, as well as other principal economic policies at the EU level can avoid self-defeating divergent regional programmes that are taken in isolation.
- Footloose industries, multiple equilibria, economies of scale and externalities do not guarantee that integration will bring an equitable dispersion of economic activities. Some direction for economic adjustment and allocation of resources in the form of regional policy may be necessary.

BIBLIOGRAPHY

Amiti, M. (1999), 'Specialization patterns in Europe', *Weltwirtscahftliches Archiv*, pp. 573–93.

Armstrong, H. (1995), 'Convergence among regions of the European Union, 1950–1990', *Papers in Regional Science*, pp. 143–52.

Armstrong, H. and Kervenoael, R. de (1997), 'Regional economic change in the European Union', in J. Bachtler and I. Turok (eds), *The Coherence of EU Regional Policy*, London: Jessica Kingsley, pp. 29–47.

Arthur, B. (1989), 'Competing technologies, increasing returns, and lock-in by historical events', *Economic Journal*, pp. 116–31.

Arthur, B. (1990a), 'Positive feedbacks in the economy', *Scientific American*, (February), pp. 92–9.

Arthur, B. (1990b), 'Silicon Valley locational clusters: when do increasing returns imply monopoly', *Mathematical Social Sciences*, pp. 235–51.

Arthur, B. (1994a), 'Industrial location patterns and the importance of history', in Arthur B. (ed.), *Increasing Returns and Path Dependence in the Economy,* Michigan: University of Michigan Press, pp. 49–67.

Arthur, B. (1994b), 'Urban systems and historical path dependence', in Arthur B. (ed.), *Increasing Returns and Path Dependence in the Economy,* Michigan: Michigan University Press, pp. 99–110.

Arthur, W.B. (2002), 'How growth builds upon growth in high-technology', *Annual Sir Charles Carter Lecture*, Belfast: Northern Ireland Economic Council.

Barro, R. and Sala-i-Martin, X. (1991), 'Convergence across states and regions', *Brookings Papers on Economic Activity*, pp. 107–82.

Bernstein, J. and Weinstein, D. (2002), 'Do endowments predict the location of production? Evidence from national and international data', *Journal of International Economics*, pp. 55–76.

Boldrin, M. and Canova, F. (2001), 'Inequality and convergence in Europe's regions:

reconsidering European regional policies', *Economic Policy,* pp. 207–53.

Brülhart, M. (1998a), 'Economic geography, industry location and trade: the evidence', *World Economy,* pp. 775–801.

Brülhart, M. (1998b), 'Trading places: industrial specialization in the European Union', *Journal of Common Market Studies,* pp. 319–46.

Brülhart, M. and Torstensson, J. (1996), 'Regional integration, scale economies and industry location in the European Union', *CEPR Discussion Paper* No. 1435.

Cairncross, F. (2001), *The Death of Distance* 2.0. London: Texere.

Canova, F. and Marcet, A. (1995), 'The poor stay poor: non-convergence across countries and regions', *CEPR Discussion Paper* No. 1265.

Casella, A. (1996), 'Large countries, small countries and the enlargement of trade blocs', *European Economic Review,* pp. 389–415.

European Commission (1997), *Regional Growth and Convergence,* London: Kogan Page.

European Commission (1998), *Foreign Direct Investment.* London: Kogan Page.

Forslid, R., Haaland, J. and Midelfart-Knarvik, H. (2002), 'A U-shaped Europe? A simulation study of industrial location', *Journal of International Economics,* pp. 273–97.

Fujita, M., Krugman, P. and Venables, A. (1999), *The Spatial Economy,* Cambridge, MA: MIT Press.

Jovanović, M. (1998), *International Economic Integration: Limits and Prospects,* London: Routledge.

Jovanović, M. (2001), *Geography of Production and Economic Integration,* London: Routledge.

Jovanović, M. (2003a), 'Spatial location of firms and industries: an overview of theory', *Economia Internazionale,* pp. 23–81.
http://papers.ssrn.com/sol3/papers.cfm?abstract_id=451800

Jovanović, M. (2003b), 'Local vs. global location of firms and industries', *Journal of Economic Integration,* pp. 60–104.
http://papers.ssrn.com/sol3/papers.cfm?abstract_id=394760#Paper%20Download

Jovanović, M. (2005), *The Economics of European Integration,* Cheltenham:, UK and Northampton, MA, USA: Edward Elgar.

Kim, S. (1995), 'Expansion of markets and the geographic distribution of economic activities: the trends in U.S. regional manufacturing structure, 1860–1987', *Quarterly Journal of Economics,* pp. 881–908.

Krugman, P. (1992), *Geography and Trade,* Cambridge, MA: The MIT Press.

Krugman, P. (1998), 'What's new about the new economic geography', *Oxford Review of Economic Policy,* pp. 7–17.

Krugman, P. and Venables, A. (1990), 'Integration and the competitiveness of peripheral industry', in C. Bliss and J. Braga de Macedo (eds), *Unity with Diversity in the European Economy: The Community's Southern Frontier,* Cambridge: Cambridge University Press, pp. 56–75.

Lucas, R. (1988), 'On the mechanics of economic development', *Journal of Monetary Economics,* pp. 3–42.

Martin, R. (1999), 'The new geographical turn in economics: some critical reflections', *Cambridge Journal of Economics,* pp. 65–91.

Midelfart-Knarvik, K., Overman, H., Redding, S. and Venables, A. (2000), 'The location of European industry', *Economic Papers,* No. 142, European Commission.

Midelfart-Knarvik, K. and Overman, H. (2002), 'Delocation and European integration', *Economic Policy,* pp. 323–59.

Murphy, K., Shleifer, A. and Vishny, R. (1989), 'Industrialization and the Big Push',

Journal of Political Economy, pp.1003–26.
Ohlin, B. (1933), *Interregional and International Trade*, Cambridge, MA: Harvard University Press.
Porter, M. (1990), *The Competitive Advantage of Nations*, New York: The Free Press.
Porter, M. (2000), 'Locations, clusters and company strategy', in G. Clark *et al.* (eds), *The Oxford Handbook of Economic Geography*, Oxford: Oxford University Press, pp. 253–74.
Puga, D. (2002), 'European regional policies in light of recent location theories', *Journal of Economic Geography*, pp. 373–406.
Puga, D. and Venables, A. (1997), 'Preferential trading arrangements and industrial location', *Journal of International Economics*, pp. 347–68.
Rugman, A. (2002), 'Multinational enterprises and the end of global strategy', in J. Dunning and J. Mucchielli (eds), *Multinational Firms*, London: Routledge, pp. 3–17.
Rugman, A. and Hodgetts, R. (2001), 'The end of global strategy', *European Management Journal*, pp. 333–43.
Venables, A. (1996), 'Localization of industry and trade performance', *Oxford Review of Economic Policy*, pp. 52–60.
Venables, A. (1998), 'The assessment: trade and location', *Oxford Review of Economic Policy*, pp. 1–6.
Venables, A. and Limão, N. (2002), 'Geographical disadvantage: a Heckscher-Ohlin-von Thünen model of international specialisation', *Journal of International Economics*, pp. 239–63.
Yamawaki, H. (1993), 'Location decisions of Japanese multinational firms in European manufacturing industries', in K. Hughes (ed.), *European Competitiveness*, Cambridge: Cambridge University Press, pp. 11–28

3. The Impact of Enlargement on EU Agriculture

Nicholas C. Baltas

INTRODUCTION

Ten countries of Central and Eastern Europe (Bulgaria, the Czech Republic, Estonia, Hungary, Latvia, Lithuania, Poland, Romania, Slovakia and Slovenia) and two small insular countries (Cyprus and Malta) have negotiated full membership with the EU. At the Copenhagen European Council in December 2002, it was resolved that ten countries would join the EU in May 2004. Bulgaria and Romania's tentative date of accession was set as 2007. Turkey became a candidate country at the Helsinki European Council Summit in 1999, with membership negotiations likely to start in October 2005.

The purpose of this chapter is to consider the economic impact of the enlargement for EU agriculture, especially on the characteristics of the new member states and on the economic implications of the enlargement for Greek agriculture. Emphasis will also be given on the effects of Common Agriculture Policy (CAP) reform on EU agriculture.

The chapter consists of six sections. In the second section the economic structure in the acceding countries is examined. In the next section the implications of the enlargement with regard to EU agriculture is presented. In the fourth section the effects of the reform of the CAP is evaluated. In the fifth section, the impact of the enlargement on Greek agriculture is presented. Finally, the sixth section contains some concluding remarks drawn from the previous analysis.

THE ECONOMIC STRUCTURE OF THE NEW MEMBER STATES

The accession of 10+2 states will increase the EU's population by 28 per cent but its GDP only by 7 per cent at 2001 prices and by 15 per cent in terms of purchasing power standard (PPS) (Eurostat, 2002). Measured by GDP per capita in PPS, the 10+2 countries are at a significantly lower level of development than the EU-15 average (see Table 3.1). All of them are eligible candidates for the Cohesion Fund. With the exception of Cyprus and Slovenia, in all the other new member states GDP per capita is less than 60 per cent of that the EU-15 average. Classified in descending order, the other groups consist of the Czech Republic, Malta, Hungary and Slovakia (with GDP of around of half of EU average); then come Estonia, Poland, Lithuania and Latvia (with GDP of around one - third of EU average); Bulgaria and Romania (with GDP of around one - fourth of EU average) are in the bottom group (Baltas, 2004).

Table 3.1
GDP per capita, measured at purchasing power standard and population in the 10+2 states and EU-15 (2001)

Country	GDP per capita (in EUROs)	Population (in million)
EU-15	23.160	380.5
Cyprus	18.460	0.7
Slovenia	15.970	2.0
Czech Republic	13.280	10.3
Malta (2000)	11.900	0.4
Hungary	11.880	10.2
Slovakia	10.780	5.4
Estonia	9.820	1.4
Poland	9.210	38.6
Lithuania	8.730	3.5
Latvia	7.710	2.4
Bulgaria	6.510	7.9
Romania	5.860	22.4

Source: Eurostat (2002).

The economic structure of the 10+2 states shows that, as in the EU-15, services constitute the predominant economic sector (see Table 3.2). As GDP has grown, demand for services has increased due to higher income elasticities. However, despite the substantial fall in output in the early 1990s, industrial production still accounts for between 20 and 30 per cent of GDP in most Central and Eastern European Countries (CEECs), which is significantly higher than most EU-15 countries. This implies the important role of the manufacturing sector in the economies of the CEECs. Their long-standing tradition in manufacturing along with low costs for labour and raw materials helps to explain why there has been a rapid inflow of foreign direct investment (FDI) in the CEECs (Baltas, 2001a).

There are considerable concerns regarding agriculture, the contribution of which to the GDP in many of the new member states is much higher than in the EU-15. The share of agriculture in GDP ranges from 2.4 to 14.6 per cent compared to 2.1 per cent for the EU (see Table 3.2). Bulgaria and Romania in particular are large producers of farm products. These percentages are almost double those of Greece, whose agricultural sector has the highest share in GDP among the existing member states.

Table 3.2

Structure of GDP in the 10+2 states and the EU-15 in 2001 (per cent)

Country	Agriculture, hunting, forestry and fishing	Manufacturing excluding construction	Services
EU-15	2.1	22.3	75.6
Bulgaria (2000)	13.8	23.0	63.2
Cyprus (1999)	4.2	13.3	82.5
Czech Republic	4.2	32.8	63.0
Estonia	5.8	22.7	71.5
Hungary (2000)	4.2	28.3	67.5
Latvia	4.7	18.7	76.6
Lithuania	7.0	28.3	64.7
Malta	2.4	24.5	73.1
Poland	3.4	25.4	71.2
Romania	14.6	28.5	56.9
Slovakia	4.6	27.5	67.9
Slovenia	3.1	31.0	65.9

Source: Eurostat (2002).

Differences in agricultural employment patterns are particularly pronounced. Romania heads the list, with 44 per cent of the labour force employed in agriculture, which is more than ten times the EU-15 average (see Table 3.3). In Bulgaria, around one-quarter of the labour force is employed in agriculture and in Poland just under one-fifth. An indication of the challenge this poses not only for new member states but also for the enlarged EU is seen in the fact that the nearly 20 per cent of the Polish population engaged in agriculture contribute little more than 3 per cent to Poland's GDP. This compares with figures of 4.2 and 2.1 per cent, respectively, for the EU-15. Labour migration to the cities should increase agricultural productivity in Poland and other CEECs, but if there are not enough new jobs in the manufacturing and services sectors to absorb such an inflow there may be a significant rise in social tensions (Jovanovic, 2002).

Table 3.3
Share of agriculture in total employment in the 10+2 states and in the EU-15 in 2001 (per cent)

Country	Agriculture in total employment
EU-15	4.2
Bulgaria	26.7
Cyprus	4.9
Czech Republic	4.6
Estonia	7.1
Hungary	6.1
Latvia	15.1
Lithuania	16.5
Malta	2.2
Poland	19.2
Romania	44.4
Slovakia	6.3
Slovenia	9.9

Source: Economic Commission for Europe (2002); Eurostat (2002).

THE IMPLICATIONS OF ENLARGEMENT FOR EU AGRICULTURE

Labour employed in agriculture was discussed in the previous section, but it merits being noted here that all of the 10+2 states apart from Malta have a higher proportion than the EU-15 average of 4.2 per cent. Enlargement doubles the EU-15's agricultural labour force. The Union's agricultural area increases by 60 million hectares (ha) to close to 200 million ha. Of these 60 million ha, two - thirds is arable land, adding 55 per cent to the EU's existing arable area of 77 million ha. The share of agriculture in GDP of the new member states ranges from 2.4 (Malta) to 14.6 per cent (Romania) compared to 2.1 per cent for the EU-15 (see Table 3.2). The share of the agro-food sector in total trade is also important in many of the CEECs. Hungary had the highest export share (20 per cent) and, at the same time, the lowest import share (6 per cent) of agro-food trade in its total 1996 trade; a similar pattern can be observed for Bulgaria. In Estonia, too, agro-food accounted for a relatively large proportion of total exports (15 per cent) and, in contrast to Hungary and Bulgaria, an even larger share in total imports (23 per cent). In the Czech and Slovak Republics, agricultural and food products, with 5 to 8 per cent shares, were of minor importance in their total trade in 1996, both on the export and import sides (Eiteljorge and Hartmann, 1999, p. 189). The fact is that there is a pressing need for structural improvement in the agricultural sectors of most of the 10+2 states – most obviously on the farms themselves, but also in the up and downstream sectors (Mergos, 1998). Restructuring can be expected to reduce agriculture's labour absorption capacity, implying a need for diversification of these countries' rural economies.

Concerning the budgetary implications of the enlargement, various early estimates have been made, ranging from 5 to 50 billion ECU, depending on the assumptions used to develop alternative scenarios. According to EU estimates (European Commission, 1997), the cost of enlargement would require a 25 per cent increase of the CAP budget, which stands at 36 billion ECU. Despite these initial high estimates, the Berlin Summit (European Council, 1999) agreed to set aside a budget for the enlargement rising from Euro 6.45 billion in 2002 to Euro 16.78 billion in 2006 (see Table 3.4). This assumed (very optimistically) that enlargement would begin from 2002. Agricultural spending would play a limited role, rising from Euro 1.6 billion in 2002 to Euro 3.4 billion in 2006, despite the addition of ten less-developed countries, some of which have relatively large agricultural sectors.

Table 3.4
EU budget resources available for accession (appropriations for payments) (in million Euros, 1999 prices)

	2002	2003	2004	2005	2006
Payment appropriations	6.450	9.030	11.610	14.200	16.780
Agriculture	1.600	2.030	2.450	2.930	3.400
Other expenditure	4.850	7.000	9.160	11.270	13.380

Source: European Commission (1999).

The enlargement of the EU would require extending CAP price support to new members. It is generally assumed that this would involve a significant increase in producer prices in the new member states, taking into consideration that farmgate prices in the CEECs stood at 40 to 80 per cent of the EU level in 1999. These gaps[1] were considerably reduced but not

---

[1] For example, for cereals, oilseeds and protein crops they are around 10 per cent, for sugar beet somewhere between 40–50 per cent, for dairy products in the order of 15–25 per cent, for beef in the region of 15–25 per cent, while for certain fruit and vegetables price differences can be as high as 80 per cent (which is the case for tomatoes) (Baltas, 2001b).

eliminated after the Berlin Agreement. In any case, it is not possible for the new member states to be immediately integrated in the CAP for the following reasons. First, it would trigger large supply responses in the new EU member states, in particular for cereals, oilseeds, sugar, milk and meat; second, it would reduce competitiveness in the food industries of the new member states; third, it would occasion sudden and undesirable changes to consumer prices resulting in a substantial reduction of consumers' real incomes, taking into consideration that households in the CEECs spend on average a relatively high proportion – 30 to 60 per cent – of their disposable income on farm products; and fourth, the funds available from the EU budget are insufficient to finance the full application of the CAP in the CEECs. Within the Commission, the debate over the feasibility of compensating CEEC farmers was very much alive, since no losses were foreseeable for them as a result of the application of the CAP. Indeed, upon entering the EU, the CEECs would enjoy a higher level of agricultural prices and overall support to agriculture than at present. This would increase the EU's surplus of principal agricultural products in the majority of the new member countries and place great pressure on the finely balanced arrangements of the GATT Agreement. Moreover, future exports from the CEECs would rise, as would the degree of protectionism toward their imports. These factors would create no small problems for the position from which Europe has been negotiating in the WTO negotiations.

Hence, it would be difficult to convince the accession countries not to increase farm production, unless they could see clear signs that the CAP is changing prior to their entry. One thing is clear: enlargement of the EU-15 cannot easily proceed without a prior change in the CAP, taking into consideration that there is reluctance to increase the European budget from the existing level of 1.27 per cent of EU GDP. The European Council in Brussels 24–25 October 2002 reconfirmed its Berlin decision that the ceiling for enlargement-related expenditure set out for the years 2004–2006 must be respected. Moreover, the European Council decided on the 'adjustment' of future CAP payments. From 2006, total CAP subsidies would have a ceiling. This would keep payments fixed at current levels during the 2007–2013 period with an allowance of 1 per cent per year for inflation. In real terms, these payments would almost certainly represent a steady decrease. Regarding subsidies to farmers in the new member states, the European Council in Brussels (October 2002) decided on a gradual introduction of direct subsidies over a ten year transitional period. In years 2004, 2005, 2006 and 2007 direct subsidies will be equal to 25, 30, 35 and 40 per cent respectively of the amount provided by the existing system. In the second stage, direct subsidies will be granted gradually, reaching 100 per cent in 2013.

THE REFORM OF THE COMMON AGRICULTURAL POLICY[2]

Undoubtedly, reform of the CAP represents one of the most serious challenges for the EU. The reform of the CAP is necessary on two grounds. First, CAP payments during the 2007–2013 period will be capped at their 2006 level, also taking into consideration EU enlargement. Second, support for EU agriculture will have to reflect clearly the international constraints imposed on the EU following the WTO negotiations.[3] The reform will also strengthen the EU's negotiating hand in the ongoing WTO trade talks. To this end, a set of proposals for the adjustment of the CAP was put forward by the European Commission and was adopted by the Council of Ministers of Agriculture on 26 June 2003 (Council of the European Union, 2003, June).

The main elements of the CAP reform are the decoupling of direct support to farmers from production (single farm payment); to make direct payments conditional on compliance with environmental, food safety, animal welfare and occupational safety standards (cross-compliance); to increase support for rural development by modulating direct payments for all except small farmers (modulation); to introduce a new farm audit system for financial discipline and new rural development measures; and to improve production quality. The reform will alter the CAP system significantly, most especially because the majority of subsidies will not be tied to the volume of production. Finally, the reform includes modifications to the market arrangements for a number of products (cereals, durum wheat, rye, drying aid, rice, starch potatoes, nuts, meat and dairy products).

To evaluate the medium term economic consequences of the reform, the findings of a series of studies analysing the impact of the Mid-Term Review proposals on the agricultural markets and incomes in the EU are used. The final decisions reached by the Council of Ministers of Agriculture regarding CAP reform are also taken into account. Four of these studies were carried

---

[2] For more details regarding the effects of the CAP reform, refer to Baltas (2004).

[3] The GATT Uruguay Round agreement on agriculture imposes disciplines on member countries in three separate areas: reduction of domestic subsidies by 20 per cent over six years; market access, i.e. all import restrictions were converted to customs tariffs which were reduced by 36 per cent over a period of six years; and reduction of export subsidies by 21 per cent in volume and by 36 per cent in value over six years. Regarding domestic support the agricultural policy measures are classified into three boxes according to the degree of production and trade distortion. The 'green' box includes measures which do not distort production and international trade and characterized as 'neutral', such as structural policy measures, i.e. incentives to young farmers, compensations for natural disasters, etc. The 'blue' box includes aid per hectare or per animal, which concerns arable crops, rice, beef and sheep or good meat. These aid measures were decided in the framework of the 1992 CAP reform. Finally, the 'yellow' box includes production measures and direct subsidies granted according to the volume of output. These measures are not compatible with GATT/WTO (Baltas, 2001b, pp. 105–7).

out by external organizations at the request of the EU Commission and two others by Commission services[4] (Directorate General for Agriculture) on the basis of two in-house models (European Commission, 2003, February and March).

In all models, the impact of the MTR proposals is analysed for the year 2009 with reference to a status quo policy situation, which corresponds to the continuation of the Agenda 2000 agricultural policy over the medium term. However, these status quo scenarios vary substantially across studies with regard not only to key underlying assumptions concerning the trade policy framework, the macro-economic environment (notably GDP growth, inflation and the EUR/$ exchange rate) and medium-term developments on world agricultural markets, but also to the overall market developments

---

[4] The first DG AGRI analysis has been undertaken on the basis of a set of partial equilibrium, dynamic models covering the most important arable crops, animal and dairy products in the EU. These models are used annually to develop the outlook for agricultural markets and to form the baseline for policy simulation.

The second DG AGRI study has been conducted with the European Simulation Model (ESIM), which is a price driven, world, multi-country non-linear, agricultural sector model, with an extended policy representation. Although originally designed to analyse the impact of EU enlargement to Eastern Europe, it has been further developed and updated to assess the impact of the MTR proposals.

The first external impact assessment study has been conducted by a unit in the Food and Agricultural Policy Research Institute (FAPRI) at the University of Missouri (USA). The FAPRI models used in this exercise consist of a set of non-spatial partial equilibrium models for major agricultural markets used every year to develop projections of world agricultural markets which form the baseline for policy analysis on behalf of the US Congress. These models estimate production, consumption, stocks, trade and prices of major trading countries and agricultural commodities. This specific FAPRI-Missouri study used a detailed EU module which is of a similar general structure to the standard FAPRI models and covers the most important EU policy instruments.

The second external study, carried out by the University of Bonn, has been undertaken at regional level based on the CAPRI modelling system. It is designed as a projection and simulation tool for the agricultural sector based on a physical consistency framework, economic account principles and a detailed policy representation. The model consists of separate supply and market modules which are interactively coupled and operates at NUTS II level. It allows the impact of policy changes on agricultural markets, producers' income, the EAGGF budget, consumer welfare and some environmental indicators to be evaluated.

The Centre for World Food Studies of the University of Amsterdam (CWFS) and the Netherlands Bureau for Economic Policy Analysis (CPB) in the Hague jointly realized the third analysis using the CAP Modelling and Accounting Tool (CAPMAT) of the EU agricultural sector. It performs dynamic policy simulations on the basis of an analytical model of the applied general equilibrium type that generates developments in supply, demand and cross-commodity substitution. It incorporates the CAP instruments and farmers' behavioural responses to policy changes through agricultural supply models at national and EU level.

Finally, a further impact assessment has been provided by the University of Bonn based on the CAPSIM model for Eurostat (The Statistical Office of the European Communities). This partial equilibrium model allows forecasting and simulating policy changes on area allocation, production, consumption and income variables of the agricultural sector at national level. It consists of a supply component and a demand component dynamically linked in an overall system that determines price formation.

projected for some specific sectors. Therefore, for comparative purposes, the simulation results are presented in the form of deviations from the status quo scenario. Furthermore, results should not be interpreted as changes relative to the current situation in 2003.

The impact studies on the agricultural sector focus on the sectors most concerned by the MTR proposals, namely arable crops, meat production and the dairy sectors, with specific reference to area allocation, the main market variables (production, consumption, external trade, stocks and prices) and income changes.

It is difficult to model the impact of decoupling directly. The decoupling impact is extremely complex and at the level of the individual farm will depend on the extent to which farms are willing and able to shift production to more profitable sectors and to bring about further efficiency gains through further restructuring. Decoupled payments to be modelled is a major subject in its own right, and thus could not be treated in a chapter that is concerned with policy results not policy analysis per se.

The studies show that decoupling will favour extensification of production and improve producer incomes as producers no longer have to produce at a loss to receive a subsidy. The impact of the CAP reform on total cereal and oilseed production will tend to leave the situation unchanged. The effects will be significant on rye, durum wheat and rice given the considerable reduction of their support. EU-15 beef and butter production will fall over the medium term, triggering a higher rise in domestic producer prices and reducing exports considerably. The impact of the reform on agricultural income in the EU-15 will be marginally smaller than would have been the case under Agenda 2000 until 2009. The Commission's expenditure forecast for Pillar 1 will rise from 41.4 billion Euro in 2004 to nearly 43.7 billion Euro in 2009, which is in line with estimates by Defra (Agricultural Policy and Food Chain Economics, 2003, p. 4). Overall, the effects on the environment are expected to be positive. There will be potential benefits from decoupling and cross-compliance but there may be adverse effects in certain localized areas which will need special consideration.

Decoupling in the enlarged EU should produce similar trends to those in the EU-15, as producers' decisions will be driven by market considerations rather than by the maximization of direct payments. The CAP reform will generally reduce most of the downside risks of agricultural markets in the EU-25, notably in the area of structural surpluses. In the new member states, market income should increase in real terms not as a result of the CAP reform but as compared to the pre-enlargement situation in 2002. According to estimates made by the Commission for the new member states, expenditure will reach 6.3 billion Euro by 2013, a figure higher than the forecast by Defra for that year which is 5.3 billion Euro.

Decisions on the reformed CAP regime for olive oil, cotton and tobacco were reached by the Council of the EU in April 2004. These products are known collectively as the Mediterranean products since they are of key importance to Spain, Italy and Greece, which dominate EU production. The main element of the reforms is the shift from the current production-linked payments to the decoupled single farm payment. The reform will start in 2006 and have a neutral effect on the CAP budget, which amounts to nearly half of the EU's annual budget of some 100 billion Euros. Subsidies for the three regimes cost over four billion Euros a year, less than 10 per cent of CAP spending.

CASE STUDY: THE IMPACT OF EU ENLARGEMENT ON GREEK AGRICULTURE

Regarding the expected impact of EU enlargement on Greek agriculture, the main problem relates to the fiscal sector. On the one hand, the sources of the EU budget cannot increase further and on the other hand most of the CEECs have serious structural weaknesses. As a result, it is to be expected that a redistribution of resources will decrease EU budget flows to Greece. However, it should be pointed out that agricultural production in the new member states is not directly competitive with Greece, with the exception of sheep or goat meat. But this case is postponed until 2007 when Bulgaria and Romania are expected to accede to the EU. Moreover, the CEECs' internal markets will be a potential outlet for exports of Greek agricultural products given that with accession to the EU-15 some of the existing barriers will be abolished. In fact, there is already some penetration of Greek agricultural products which is expected to deepen after enlargement. The present position and future prospects of Greek farm exports to the new entrants can be summarized as follows:

- **Fish products**. Due to the low level of per capita incomes in these countries, these products are relatively expensive for local consumers, so that no significant penetration of Greek products is expected.
- **Olive oil**. It too is a rather expensive product for CEEC consumers and it will be hard to penetrate the new markets. Moreover, most exports of Greek olive oil go through Italy for blending, standardization, etc.
- **Durum wheat**. Similar to olive oil. Greece exports small quantities of soft wheat flour-mill products.
- **Drinks**. Greek exports make up a substantial percentage of the Bulgarian and Romanian markets. Keen competition is expected from other exporting countries in the markets of the other acceding countries.

- **Cotton**. Since the early 1990s, Greek cotton has made up a significant percentage of the CEECs' markets, where the textile industry occupies an important place even in the absence of locally produced raw materials. Moreover, there is no direct competition from other EU-15 member states. About 30 percent of Bulgaria's cotton is imported from Greece.
- **Tobacco.** Significant quantities of Greek tobacco are exported to the CEECs. It is worth mentioning that until 1988, Bulgaria, like Greece, was one of the most important tobacco producers and exporters.
- **Fruit and vegetables**. Greece accounts for a satisfactory share of the CEECs' markets and a particularly significant one in two Balkan candidates. However, keen competition is expected from Italy and Spain. Nevertheless, given the dilemma between better quality and higher price or moderate quality and lower price, in the medium term CEEC consumers are expected to opt for the latter, which will favour Greek exports.

In any case, the main goal of Greek agricultural policy must be oriented towards quality products. The Greek agricultural sector is characterized by a multitude of smallholdings, which are unable to compete successfully with countries with extensive agricultural lands in which the use of large scale production technology is favoured. Therefore, emphasis should be given to traditional and biological products in which the country can claim a competitive advantage. Also, Greece should strive to make the most of the new rural development policy.

The single farm payment which will replace most of the premia under the various Common Market organizations will no longer be linked to production. However, there is always the danger of abandonment of production from marginal farmers, since they will be receiving subsidies without even producing. Obviously, such developments will have a negative impact on the productive structure of Greek rural areas, particularly on employment and farmland utilization.

CONCLUSION

The main problems that arise for EU agriculture from the expansion of the EU to include the CEECs can be summarized as follows. Given that the current level of own resources in the European budget (1.27 per cent of GDP which will be maintained not only from 2004 to 2006 but also during the period 2007–2013) is insufficient for financing the accession of so many CEECs, it was necessary for the EU to reform its agricultural policy before extending the CAP to the CEECs. Moreover, CAP reform was also a consequence of international pressures. From 2006, total CAP subsidies will have a ceiling. This will keep payments fixed at current levels during the 2007–2013 period with a light inflation proof of 1 per cent/year. Subsidies to farmers in new member states will be gradually introduced over a ten year transitional period. According to European Commission estimates, these adjustments will cause a reduction of the total subsidies to the existing EU member states by 5 per cent by 2013.

The impact of the reform on total cereal and oilseed production will be negligent and will leave the situation more-or-less unchanged. The effects will be significant on rye, durum wheat and rice given the considerable reduction of their support. EU-15 beef and butter production will fall over the medium term, triggering a rise in domestic producer prices and considerably reducing exports. Until 2009, the impact of the reform on agricultural incomes in the EU-15 will be marginally smaller than would have been the case under Agenda 2000.

Decoupling in the enlarged EU should produce similar trends to those in the EU-15 as producers' decisions will be driven by market considerations rather than by the maximization of direct payments. The CAP reform will generally reduce most of the downside risks of agricultural markets in the EU-25, notably in the area of structural surpluses. In the new member states, market income should increase in real terms compared to the pre-enlargement situation in 2002.

Regarding the expected impact of EU enlargement on Greek agriculture, the main problem is related to the danger of a decrease of EU budget flows to Greece. However, it should be pointed out that the structure of agriculture production in the CEECs is not directly competitive with that in Greece. Moreover, the CEECs' markets will be a potential outlet for exports of Greek agricultural products.

REFERENCES

Agricultural Policy and Food Chain Economics (APFCE-Defra) (2003), *Assessment of the Economic Impact of the Commission's Long Term Perspective for Sustainable Agriculture*, March, London.
Baltas, N.C. (2001a), 'European Union Enlargement: An Historic Milestone in the Process of European Integration', *Atlantic Economic Journal*, 29 (3): 254–65.
Baltas, N.C. (2001b), 'Common Agricultural Policy, Past, Present and Future' in F. Colombus, (ed.), *European Economic and Political Issues III*, New York: Nova Science Publishers, Inc, pp. 97–116.
Baltas, N.C. (2004), 'The Economy of the European Union' in N. Nugent (ed.), *European Union Enlargement*, Hampshire: Palgrave Macmillan, pp. 146–57.
Baltas, N.C. (2004), 'The Effects of the Reform on the Common Agricultural Policy' in J.A. Brox, R. Catterall and P.E. Koveos (eds), *Structural Reform and the Transformation of Organizations and Business*, Toronto, Canada: APF Press, (forthcoming).

Economic Commission for Europe (2002), *Economic Survey for Europe 2002*, New York: United Nations.

Eiteljorge, U. and Hartmann M. (1999), 'Central-Eastern Europe Food Chains Competitiveness' in R. Goldberg (ed.), *The European Agro-Food System and the Challenges of Global Competition*, Roma: ISMEA.

European Commission (1997), 'The CAP and Enlargement' *European Economy*, No. 2.

European Commission (1999), *Financial Framework of the European Union*, Europa website.

European Commission (February 2003), *Mid-Term Review of the Common Agricultural Policy – July 2002 Proposals – Impact Analyses*, Brussels: Directorate-General for Agriculture.

European Commission (March 2003), *Reform of the Common Agricultural a Policy: A Long-Term Perspective for Sustainable Analysis – Impact Analysis*, Brussels: Directorate-General for Agriculture.

European Council (1999), 'Special Berlin European Council: Conclusions of the Presidency', *Bulletin of the European Union*, No. 3, pp. 7–22.

European Council (April 2004), *Mediterranean Products Reform – Presidency Compromise* (in Agreement with the Commission), Luxembourg.

European Council (June 2003), *CAP Reform – Presidency Compromise* (in Agreement with the Commission), Brussels.

Eurostat (2002), *Statistical Yearbook*, 2002 edition, Brussels, EUR-OP

Jovanovic, M.N. (2002), 'Eastern Enlargement at the EU: A Topsy-Turvy Endgame or Permanent Disillusionment', Unedited Final Draft, Universita degli Studi di Genova, 15 November.

Mergos, G. (1998), 'Agricultural Issues in Integration of CEECs in the EU' in N. Baltas et al. (eds), *Economic Interdependence and Cooperation in Europe*, (Heidelberg: Springer-Verlag): 181–98.

4. The Impact of Enlargement on Monetary Stability

Franco Praussello

INTRODUCTION

A widespread concern surrounding the prospective economic consequences of enlargement focuses on the stability of EMU, when new entrants will be able to meet all the Maastricht criteria and join the eurozone. Indeed, new member states, unlike the UK and Denmark, have a formal duty to adopt the single currency, after completion of the nominal convergence process that the first wave of founder members underwent, since for them EMU membership belongs to the *acquis communautaire*. A different outcome in the long lasting enlargement game would have been surprising, due to the reduced bargaining power of new entrants compared with that of the Union as a whole.[1]

In addition, for at least a good number of them the option of an early entry into the eurozone seems not to be excluded, being for some even a national priority, possibly in view of the expected gains in terms of macroeconomic local stability.

Nevertheless, the Commission's official stance is more wary, reflecting perhaps the fear that current EMU rules are unfit to endure a significant widening of the number of eurozone member countries. At the same time scholars are wondering if the one-size-fits-all monetary policy managed by the European Central Bank (ECB) can be easily extended to a much more fragile economic fabric, where national divergences are larger than in present EMU, above all due to increased heterogeneity linked to enlargement to new member countries from Central and Eastern Europe.[2]

---

[1] Concession asymmetries in recent economic regional agreements are also considered as side payments from small to large partners in order to sustain the arrangements. See for instance Perroni and Whalley (2000).

[2] See, among others, Gros and Hefeker (2000), as well as Gros (2002).

The main aim of this chapter is to address two specific issues on which the future monetary stability within an enlarged EMU will rest: the degree of optimality of the latter, assessed according to the Optimum Currency Areas (OCAs) theory, on the one hand, and the possible reform of ECB functioning rules to cope with the presence of a high number of small members, on the other. The background against which these points will be treated sees the general relevance of two themes: the meaning of shock asymmetry, for the first issue, and the rule followed by the eurosystem for setting Europe-wide interest rates, for the second one.

Asymmetry of shocks or economic disturbances both of monetary and real origin, as well as on the supply and the demand side, matters a lot within a monetary union, since the common central bank has no tool for adjusting the unintended economic consequences of their occurrence. Its only instrument, the monetary policy, can help to cure a symmetric shock affecting at the same time a range of or all member countries, but is in principle helpless for coping with a disturbance affecting a single country. Think of the old days when the currencies of present EMU member countries were still in existence and could be realigned within the European Monetary System (EMS). If something went wrong and a single country was hit by an asymmetric shock, the textbook medicine of devaluation, however bitter and difficult to put into operation in a co-ordinated framework, was at hand, even though in the long term its effects were doubtful. In a currency union, this tool is no longer available, of course, and the shock absorption has to be assigned to other channels, either public – by voluntary anti-cyclical budgetary interventions, or automatic transfers deriving from a common fiscal system, if any – or passing through market mechanisms with possible sizeable adjustment costs in terms of unemployment and forgone production. When, as in the case of EMU, a fiscal union does not exist or has a negligible stabilisation impact, asymmetric shocks can be absorbed only partially and with difficulty resorting to national budgetary policies which are constrained by the 'stupid' rules of the Stability Pact.[3] All this implies a heavy cost for individual countries and a threat for the stability and viability of the currency union as a whole. Indeed, an extreme case could not be excluded, in which a single or a group of member countries could find it in their interest to avoid the costs of EMU membership by withdrawings from it: the present value of expected future benefits could fall below a cost threshold, precipitating also a possible lethal crisis for the eurozone.[4]

---

[3] The reform of the Pact rules according to a recent Commission proposal (Atkins and Parker, 2004) appears cosmetic in essence, since the fault lines of the system have not been addressed: the scarcely credible co-ordination setting of otherwise national independent budgetary policies, in the absence of a fully fledged European fiscal union, i.e. a European government.
[4] In this sense see for instance Feldstein's analysis (1998).

That is why asymmetric shock occurrence and EMU instability are two sides of the same euro coin. The overall conditions under which a generic currency union can be deemed as relatively safe from the danger of asymmetric shocks are studied by the OCAs theory, as we shall see in some detail in the next section. Here it is worth perhaps to add to this preliminary picture some thoughts about the much debated issue of shock asymmetry in the aftermath of EMU. As it is well known, on this point two conflicting arguments have long been established in literature: the Commission's view (EC Commission, 1990), according to which increased integration will reduce the number and depth of asymmetric shocks, and Krugman's view (1991), which maintains that regional specialisation effects, as in the case of the US, will enhance the probability of their occurrence. Despite the fact that we are here possibly confronted with a typical unsettled question, that will produce further research efforts on the two sides, in recent times some developments linked to the theory of endogenous currency areas seem to support convincingly the Commission's view. Indeed, there is evidence that currency unions which are *ex ante* suboptimal can turn optimal *ex post*, after their completion. In addition Krugman's argument (1991) is strongly dependent on new economic geography conditions, pertaining typically to manufactures, whereas the European economy is deepening its service features.

The second theme characterising the general background of the chapter requires fewer lines. The institutional structure of the eurosystem, which is based on the principle of equal representation for all governors, is deemed to become unworkable after enlargement. Each national governor has a preference for an interest rate taking into account the economic conditions of his country, according to the Taylor rule (1993), even though in principle his duty is to consider the eurozone economy as a whole. Nevertheless, the strategic position of the ECB board ensures that interest rate decisions mirror the conditions of the bulk of eurozone. But with enlargement, a coalition of small countries could outvote the Board, contributing to the spread of monetary instability in the greater part of EMU.

The rest of the chapter is structured in the following terms. The next section singles out a number of different tools suggested in order to test an OCA, i.e. the bundle of conditions on the basis of which a monetary union can be deemed to be viable or sustainable. The second section contains an up-to-date estimate of the optimality of EMU in its present form, employing a Weighted Optimality Index and the Hodrick-Prescott (HP) filter procedure, while the third section tests the possible increased correlation of cycles within EMU, following its completion. The fourth section deals with the eurosystem institutional reform as a prerequisite for the stability of EMU in the aftermath of enlargement. The subsequent section is devoted to the presentation of a number of exercises, with a view to checking business cycle correlations in an EMU enlarged to encompass not only the EU 15 member countries not belonging to the eurozone, but all the applicant countries, Bulgaria and Romania included, but not Turkey. The last section closes the chapter with some concluding remarks.

HOW TO TEST AN OCA

In Praussello (2003) a survey of the present state of the OCAs theory was given, in order to better evaluate the prospective stability of an enlarged EMU, including the new entrants from Eastern and Central Europe. Our aim is here to focus on the testing methods adopted in literature for identifying an OCA, as a means to carry out a battery of exercises aimed at finding a number of common links between the current EMU and the acceding countries. Yet a reminder of a recent analytical development can be useful for describing the general framework in which to set the exercises, a context in which some evolving optimality features can emerge, offsetting a number of obstacles due to the existence of possible asymmetries between incumbents and newcomers within a monetary union.

Indeed, one of the most interesting advances in the theory of OCAs has been to introduce qualification of the optimality criteria. In this vein Frankel (1999) argues that the optimum characters are not fixed but can change over time in response to policy choices and exogenous factors, whilst Frankel and Rose (1996, 1997, 1998) find that they are endogenously determined.

Karras and Stokes (2001) support Frankel's argument (1999), by showing the time variation of two parameters for a large set of EU countries: the relative size of cyclical output shocks and their degree of synchronisation. As a consequence, an optimal timing could be found for a country to join a given currency union. In their works, Frankel and Rose (1996, 1997, 1998) show that the OCA criteria are jointly endogenous, finding in particular a strong positive correlation between the bilateral trade intensity and the cross-country correlation of business cycles. It follows that the more one country increases its trade with another, the more symmetric their business cycles are. In addition, a fresh strand of literature has emphasised the strong positive effect on bilateral trade for countries included in a currency union. Engel and Rose (2000), Frankel and Rose (2000) as well as Rose (2000) estimated such an effect in the order of 300 per cent.[5]

---

[5] More recent estimates in Glick and Rose (2002) or in Levi Yeyati (2003) reduce the effect of a currency union on trade to 200 or 65 per cent, whereas Thom and Walsh (2002) find scarce evidence of a significant change in Anglo-Irish trade after the dissolution of the currency union between Ireland and the UK in 1979. In contrast with the latter, evidence of strong trade effects

These works form the basis of the so called theory of 'endogenous' or 'self-validating' currency areas (Hochreiter and Siklos, 2002; Corsetti and Pesenti, 2002), whose first hints are possibly to be found in an early intuition of Marina Whitman, according to whom an OCA is created not by birth but by experience. Thus a currency area which does not appear optimal *ex ante* can become an OCA *ex post* (von Neumann Whitman, 1967).[6] Clearly, these results could in principle improve the optimality conditions of a wider EMU, in the aftermath of EU enlargement.

Turning to the specific point of this section, it has to be remembered that the extensive empirical literature aimed at assessing the optimality of a specific currency area was based initially on a simple descriptive testing of the criteria identified in the first generation of OCAs theoretical works by Mundell (1961), McKinnon (1963) and Kenen (1969). Generally such early literature took the form of a comparison between a possible European currency union, whose optimality had to be evaluated, and the US monetary area, even though the latter could scarcely be considered as a perfect benchmark.[7] Later, optimality criteria analysis was to become more sophisticated and new approaches were developed.

Taking into account the bulk of empirical works devoted to the subject, most recent investigation has been devoted to describing relationships concerning the similarity of shocks and cycles. Among the empirical works included in the literature on the similarity of shocks and cycles, a first group of studies deal with the topic of symmetries and asymmetries of disturbances across countries, a subject that has been under scrutiny since the beginning of the OCAs theory. Bayoumi and Eichengreen (1997, 1998) consider exchange rate variability in terms of standard deviations as a proxy of asymmetric shocks, measuring at the same time output disturbances as the standard deviation of the change in the logarithm of relative output in two countries. In Bayoumi and Eichengreen (1997, 1998) exchange rate variability is measured

---

due to the existence of economic unions is given in Fidrmuc and Fidrmuc (2003), who show the sharp fall in trade intensity in the aftermath of disintegration of countries such as the former Soviet Union, Yugoslavia and Czechoslovakia.

[6] After the introduction of the theory of endogenous currency areas, this point seems currently to have gained wide acceptance. Frankel and Rose (1996, 1997, 1998) suggest for instance that countries joining EMU may satisfy OCA criteria *ex post* even though they do not *ex ante*. Similarly Alesina *et al.* (2002) emphasise the need for a country in deciding to join a monetary area to take account not of the *ex ante* situation in conditions of monetary autonomy, but of the *ex post* state of affairs, considering the economic effects of the currency union. For instance, in the aftermath of joining interest rates could decrease, if the union wide monetary policy is more credible than the single member country's. Hence, in general terms judging a country's ability to join a monetary union taking into account only historical data can be misleading. After joining, its economic structure could be transformed inducing agents and policymakers to change their behaviour, and the Lucas critique could apply.

[7] In his seminal paper founding the OCA literature, Mundell (1961) raised indeed some doubts about the optimality of the US currency union.

both on nominal and real exchange rates, producing equivalent results. Similarly Carr and Floyd (2002), in their study on the possible adoption of a currency union between Canada and the United States, identify as two possible sources of real exchange rate volatility monetary and real shocks using as a test a standard OLS analysis on a battery of variables, ranging from consumer price indexes, industrial productions and unemployment rates, to terms of trade and GNP ratios.[8]

Since the stability of a currency union depends not only on the limited occurrence of asymmetric shocks, but also on its institutional setting, an OCA test could also study the possible existence of asymmetries in the transmission mechanisms of symmetric shocks. Extending recent literature on this new subject,[9] Aksoy *et al.* (2002) analyse the effects of asymmetries in the ECB decision rules on the effectiveness of monetary policy in the eurozone. In Aksoy *et al.* (2002) optimal feedback rules for each of the EMU countries are derived from output gaps and inflation,[10] showing that if individual member countries try to follow their own optimal policy, potential sources of conflict could arise, affecting the European monetary policy. That, in turn, could put in jeopardy the stability of the currency union, through a departure from the necessary condition for OCAs.[11]

A second group of empirical studies refers to the business cycle literature, testing the symmetries of fluctuations by standard correlation techniques and specific econometric methods. The assumption is that highly correlated cyclical output movements suggest a reduced risk of asymmetric shocks, and hence a greater likelihood of the existence of an optimal currency area in the region considered.

Among the papers addressing the synchronisation of output fluctuations, some are devoted to identifying the existence of a European business cycle. Following the works of Artis and Zhang (1997, 1999), possibly the most complete study so far produced on this subject is contained in Altissimo *et al.* (2001). In it the results of a joint research project Bank of Italy-CEPR are

---

[8] The findings contained in Carr and Floyd (2002), according to which the US-Canada real exchange rate volatility is due to real and not to monetary shocks point against the setting up of a currency union between the two countries. The topic of the possible optimality of a US–Canada currency area has recently been the subject of renewed interest. See, among others, Courchene and Harris (2000), as well as Grubel (2000).

[9] See Ramaswamy and Sloek (1998).

[10] Inflation series are based on first differences of logarithm data of consumer price indexes and output gaps are obtained by detrending the industrial production series.

[11] Concerning the use of a monetary stabilisation policy in a currency union, Lane (1996) had previously shown that in the face of an asymmetric shock the common monetary authority could choose not to intervene, producing high inflation and employment fluctuations in the member countries. Besides the case considered in Aksoy *et al.* (2002), further strains could happen within a currency union with monetary–fiscal interactions. Dixit and Lambertini (2001) have recently shown that if monetary and fiscal authorities have different output and inflation targets, the Nash equilibrium output or inflation could be Pareto inferior - i.e. sub-optimal for both authorities.

presented, leading to the construction of a monthly coincident indicator of the business cycle of the eurozone, obtained by extracting the common European component of all series of monthly national GDPs.

Other inquiries are aimed at describing country specific fluctuations as in Del Negro (2002), Karras and Stokes (2001), together with Clark and Wincoop (2001). The first two papers deal respectively with business cycles in the US and Europe, whose different components are estimated by filtering methods like the Hodrick-Prescott (HP) filter usually employed in this kind of literature (Hodrick and Prescott, 1980), and whose correlations have been extensively studied. Resorting again to correlation methods, the last work compares US regional business cycles with those of European countries, finding that the former are more synchronised and that a European border effect exists, in the sense that in Europe within-country correlations are larger than cross-country ones (Clark and Wincoop, 2001).

A further type of empirical study included in this strand of literature on the business cycle addresses more general relationships between economic integration and symmetry or asymmetry of shocks within a currency union. A significant case in point is offered by Kalemi-Ozcan *et al.* (2001). Employing regression analysis they give a new contribution to the well known but largely unresolved controversy between the views of the Commission (EC Commission, 1990) and Krugman (1991) on the probability of asymmetric shocks in the aftermath of a currency union,[12] supporting the latter by finding that higher capital market integration is conducive to less symmetric fluctuations.

The last group of papers included in our taxonomy comprises studies on co-movement of relevant variables through autoregressive techniques, extending the approach followed by Bayoumi and Eichengreen (1993) in the early 1990s in estimating demand and supply shocks within a group of countries. In Alesina *et al.* (2002) co-movements of prices and outputs as a test of optimality of a currency area are estimated on the basis of a second-order autoregression, measuring the lack of co-movement by the root-mean squared error. Along similar lines Ballabriga *et al.* (1999) use a VAR approach in order to investigate the interdependence in the responses to common and specific, nominal and real disturbances in four European economies, showing that in the short run asymmetric shocks were dominant. More comprehensive works address co-movements within possible currency areas employing the tool of co-integration analysis as in Darrat and Pennathur (2002) for the Arab Maghreb countries and Haug *et al.* (2000) along with Kleimeier and Sander (2000) for the EU. In Darrat and Pennathur

---

[12] A good description of the controversy can be found in De Grauwe (2003a). References to further literature are also contained in Hochreiter and Siklos (2002).

(2002) a long-run relationship among Algeria, Morocco and Tunisia is found in terms of co-movements of their economies (as measured by their GDPs), their financial sector (as measured by their money stocks) and their monetary policies (as measured by their monetary bases). Running tests of the same kind for EMU, Haug *et al.* (2000) analyse co-integration links in the nominal convergence criteria decided at Maastricht for the 12 member countries of the eurozone, finding that a number of them could not join in the absence of major adjustments. Kleimeier and Sander (2000) in turn study co-integration in retail lending markets in six core EU countries, contrasting regional links with links through globalisation to the US and Japan.

ASSESSING THE EMU OPTIMALITY

The benchmark against which to assess the prospective stability of the eurozone after enlargement has taken place and new member countries adopt the single currency, is given by the possible, imperfect optimality of the current EMU in its present shape. As a matter of fact, even though some papers maintain that EMU has enough OCA features to be considered as a viable monetary union,[13] most of the literature shares a sceptical view about the optimality of the characteristics of the euro area, highlighting the limited sustainability of EMU – from the first inquiries in the early 1990s (Eichengreen, 1992; Bayoumi and Eichengreen, 1994), to the more recent ones (Eichengreen, 1997; Krugman and Obstfeld, 1998; Sorensen and Yosha, 1998; Ballabriga *et al.*, 1999; Swofford, 2000; Collard and Dellas, 2002).[14] The strongest criticism levelled against the establishment of EMU and the most pessimistic view about its future are to be found in Feldstein (1992, 1998, 2000).

Against this background, it is worth assessing the present EMU degree of optimality, by resorting to fresh, updated measures taking into account GDP series over the period 1979–2002. To this aim I introduce a weighted optimality index, based on cycle correlation links within the monetary union.

By definition, for EMU as a whole, optimality is achieved when the business cycles of its component regions are fully correlated with the EMU cycle:

---

[13] Recent contributions such as those of Mundell (1998), Belke and Gros (1999), Bordo and Jonung (1999), Alesina and Barro (2002), Alesina *et al.* (2002) conclude that the optimality features of the EU economies are strong enough to justify the setting up of the monetary union.

[14] Bayoumi and Eichengreen (1997) maintain that a standard result of reviews pertaining to theoretical literature consists in stating that 'Europe is not an optimal currency area', even though little attention is paid to how this situation could change or how different countries prospects could be affected.

$$C_{EMU}* = 1 \qquad (4.1)$$

where C stands for the value of the correlation matrix.

Against this benchmark, it is possible to define a simple Weighted Optimality Index (*WOI*) expressing the optimum degree of a given EMU, by considering the average of the correlation values for the different component regions:

$$WOI = C_{EMU} = \sum\nolimits^n {}_i C_i w_i /(C_{EMU}* = 1) \qquad (4.2)$$

n in our case being 12, the present number of eurozone member countries.

In (4.2) w_i identifies the average weight of the region i GDP on the EMU GDP, over the 1979–2002 time span covered by the exercise ($T = 24$):

$$w_i = \sum\nolimits^T {}_j GDP_{ij} /(\sum\nolimits^T {}_j GDP_{EMU} T) \qquad (4.3)$$

In this framework, for the union as a whole optimality implies $WOI = 1$, i.e. that cycles of the member countries and hence of the union itself are perfectly correlated, whereas $1 - WOI$ assesses its degree of suboptimality. For a single member country the cost K_i of taking part in a currency union can be measured by the difference between the situation in which the full convergence with the currency union's cycle allows to offset a shock in absence of monetary autonomy,[15] i.e. in the presence of $C_i = 1$, and the existing correlation link quantified by C_i:

$$K_i = 1 - C_i \qquad (4.4)$$

with $0 \leq K_i \leq 2$.

In order to estimate the *WOI* for EMU we need now to calculate correlations for each member country with the union as a whole, applying an appropriate technical method. This can be made resorting to the system originally employed by Hodrick and Prescott to study the US cycle (Hodrick and Prescott, 1980), and subsequently used for checking correlations between countries in the framework of OCA empirical literature. In formal terms, from the series of observed GDP values Y the trend $Y*$ in the t periods: 1, 2,..., T is extracted by minimising the following formula:

$$\text{Min } \sum\nolimits^T {}_t (lnY_t - ln\ Y*_t)^2 + \lambda \sum\nolimits^{T-1} {}_t [(lnY*_{t+1} - ln\ Y*_t) - (lnY*_t - ln\ Y*_{t-1})]^2 \quad (4.5)$$

where the parameter λ is equal to 100 for yearly data, as in our case.

---

[15] In such a state of affairs of course the shock will be symmetric.

Following the identification of the trend, the cycle component Y^c is simply given by:

$$Y_t^c = Y_t - Y_t^* \qquad\qquad (4.6)$$

In Table 4.1 the trend and cycle components of constant GDP series over the period 1979–2002, obtained by applying the HP filter are presented, as a step to cycle correlation computations for the different present EMU 12 member countries.

Table 4.1
EMU GDP, trend and cycle components, 1979–2002 (constant 1995 US$ million)

Obs	EMUGDP	EMUTREND	EMUCY
1979	5109309.00	5009445.15	99863.85
1980	5207839.00	5115886.54	91952.46
1981	5237424.00	5223326.57	14097.43
1982	5274025.00	5333683.39	59658.39
1983	5359457.00	5449016.16	89559.16
1984	5489096.00	5570787.42	81691.42
1985	5614925.00	5699564.13	–84639.13
1986	5755195.00	5835096.34	–79901.34
1987	5896563.00	5976287.72	–79724.72
1988	6140936.00	6121242.89	19693.11
1989	6378431.00	6267269.26	111161.74
1990	6566856.00	6411871.16	154984.84
1991	6696462.00	6553664.52	142797.48
1992	6799760.00	6692815.14	106944.86
1993	6744642.00	6830916.80	–86274.80
1994	6903715.00	6970632.69	–66917.69
1995	7058334.00	7113763.30	–55429.30
1996	7158707.00	7261439.92	–102732.92
1997	7326615.00	7414239.53	–87624.53
1998	7536976.00	7571711.82	–34735.82
1999	7741232.00	7732530.20	8701.80
2000	8013668.00	7895020.73	118647.27
2001	8129161.00	8057596.52	71564.48
2002	8188337.00	8219857.10	–31520.10

Source: Author's calculations based on World Development Indicators database.

The results of different correlation estimates are displayed in Table 4.2.[16] Figure 4.1 shows the correlations with the EMU cycle for Spain and Finland, the most convergent and divergent countries, with an index, respectively of 0.96 and 0.49 points.

---

[16] Detailed computations are contained in Praussello (2004).

For the union as a whole, in sum the *WOI* of EMU, considering the weighted correlations over the period 1999–2002, amounts to 0.884, not too far from the optimality condition, with a low degree of suboptimality which is equal to 0.116 points (see Table 4.2).

Table 4.2
EMU, Weighted Optimality Index, 1979–2002

EMU	w_i	C_i	$C_i w_i$
Austria	0.032745	0.76	0.024886
Belgium	0.039286	0.94	0.036929
Finland	0.019592	0.49	0.009600
France	0.222573	0.93	0.206993
Germany	0.345734	0.89	0.307703
Greece	0.017768	0.74	0.013148
Ireland	0.009085	0.57	0.005178
Italy	0.155856	0.89	0.138712
Luxemburg	0.002281	0.61	0.001391
Netherlands	0.058212	0.83	0.048316
Portugal	0.014797	0.86	0.012725
Spain	0.082072	0.96	0.078790
$\sum_{i}^{n} w_i$	1		
WOI			0.884371

Source: Author's calculations based on World Development Indicators database.

Within EMU a number of subsets can be singled out: the group of the core countries, for which $1 \geq C_i \geq WOI$, including in order of decreasing optimality Spain, Belgium, France, Germany and Italy, and that of peripheral countries. Among the latter one could also distinguish countries belonging to a second circle around the core (fixing for instance $0.75\ WOI \leq C_i < WOI$: Portugal, the Netherlands, Austria and Greece, in our case), and countries performing poorly in the union classroom ($-1 < C_i < 0.75\ WOI$: Luxemburg, Ireland and Finland).

Concerning EU member countries outside EMU, relevant computations find correlation indexes ranging from 0.07 for Denmark, to 0.64 for Sweden, with the UK reaching 0.43, over the period 1979–2002.

In interpreting these results, one has to bear in mind that the picture presented relates to the entire long period during which European countries have tried first to stabilise their exchange rate relations and subsequently to set up the monetary union, and that beginning with the years immediately preceding EMU setting up, the picture could be characterised by a higher degree of cyclical convergence.

The New Economic Setting

Figure 4.1
Finland and Spain, cycle evolutions with EMU, 1979-2002

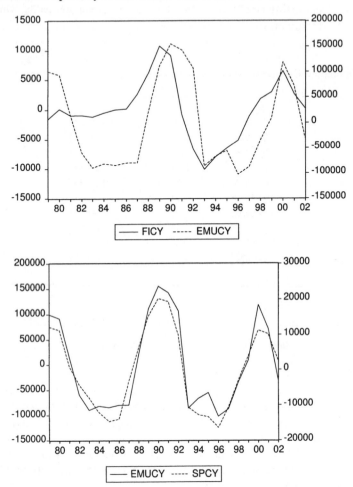

Source: Table 4.2.

POSSIBLE EVIDENCE IN FAVOUR OF THE ENDOGENOUS CURRENCY AREA THEORY

In order to test the assumption of increased cyclical correlation in recent times, our exercise continues with an investigation into the convergence process within EMU following the launch of the eurozone, by examining the links over the 1999–2002 period. By this it would be also possible to find potential confirmation of the endogenous currency area theory. However, in doing so a substantial caveat is necessary owing to the short time series which are available, in the sense that the results of this new part of our work can be at best considered only as possible clues of ongoing developments and not as robust proofs. Nevertheless, before sufficiently long series become available, a provisional exercise could provide some interesting indications. With this warning in mind, we can focus on GDP series for the period 1999–2002, obtaining the results contained in Table 4.3.

Table 4.3
EMU and EU 15 countries, business cycle correlations, 1979–2002 and 1999–2002

EMU COUNTRIES	CORRELATIONS	
	1979–2002	1999–2002
Austria	0.76	0.87
Belgium	0.94	0.98
Finland	0.49	0.90
France	0.93	0.93
Germany	0.89	0.99
Greece	0.74	-0,30
Ireland	0.57	0.94
Italy	0.89	0.89
Luxemburg	0.61	0.88
Netherlands	0.83	0.79
Portugal	0.86	0.84
Spain	0.96	0.97
EMU 12 WEIGHTED OPTIMALITY INDEX	0.884	0.915
EU 15 NON EMU COUNTRIES	-	-
Denmark	0.07	0.80
Sweden	0.64	0.89
UK	0.43	0.97

Source: Author's calculations based on World Development Indicators database.

As far as EMU member countries are concerned, for most of them, after the euro launch, convergence with the common cycle has been enhanced: two partners, Germany and Belgium, reaching a condition on the border of full optimality and others such as Ireland and Finland recording a big increase from a correlation index of half to 0.90 points compared with the optimum. By contrast, and not alone among member countries, Greece experienced a drop in convergence conditions, as well as a negative index, falling from 0.74 to –0.30 points, with an increase of the welfare cost of its participation to the European currency union from $K_{i, 1979-2002} = 0.26$ to $K_{i, 1999-2002} = 1.30$. A possible economic interpretation of such a picture would be that in principle the theory of endogenous currency areas has been confirmed, but not completely: the divergence drive followed by Greece being possibly caused by some atypical developments in intra-EMU trade flows or more probably by a deliberate anti-cyclical stance in the field of the autonomously led national fiscal policy. Indeed, whereas in 2000 the EMU cycle has peaked, before a fall, the cyclical component of the Greek GDP series has continued to expand. More precise suggestions require further investigation.

EUROSYSTEM REFORM AND EMU STABILITY

In the aftermath of enlargement, the degree of heterogeneity of the eurozone could increase to a point where the stability of a wider EMU could be imperilled. Indeed, as a matter of common knowledge, the economic conditions of new entrants are quite different from EU averages.[17] As a consequence, disparities among the different EU regions are bound to worsen, weakening the future economic fabric of the EMU.[18] However, wider income differentials within an enlarged EU do not mean that the future EMU will be necessarily unstable. Since the early 1990s a process of real convergence of applicant countries is under way that could have progressed enough to render their integration compatible with the stability of an extended EMU. Consider also the fact that in the aftermath of enlargement the convergence has to continue, as new entrants have to meet the Maastricht nominal criteria before being admitted to the eurozone (Praussello, 2002).[19]

In such circumstances an attempt to give an answer to the issue of the impact of enlargement on EMU stability requires further investigations on the economic structure of acceding countries. In general terms it is widely expected that following enlargement optimality conditions of the euzone, when the new member countries will nominally converge to the Maastricht criteria and are able to join the eurozone, will decrease, implying a more difficult stabilisation task for the governance authorities of EMU: the ECB and national governments, managing respectively the monetary and the budgetary policies.

On this topic De Grauwe (2003a) presents a clear analysis that can be considered as a provisional synthetic state of the art on the issue of the optimality of an enlarged EMU. Taking into account openness as an optimality criterion, he shows that the Central and Eastern European countries are more open towards the EU than some EU member countries such as Denmark, Sweden and the UK, which have decided not to join the

---

[17] See for example Jovanović (2000) and Kopits (2002).
[18] According to the second Commission Report on Cohesion the gaps among European regions in terms of income levels in an enlarged EU would double (EC, 2001).
[19] On the real and nominal convergence in the Central European applicant countries see Kopits (2002).

eurozone (see Figure 4.2). Nevertheless, quoting an exercise by Korhonen and Fidrmuc (2001) on the asymmetry of shocks between each of the acceding countries with those taking place in the euro area, he adds that only for a number of Central and Eastern European countries do the correlations of demand shocks have the right sign, whereas the correlations of the supply shocks are in general low. It seems therefore that the latter have a limited interest in joining the eurozone, even though they could import monetary and price stability, with a final possible positive net result.

According to De Grauwe (2003a), in a nutshell, this state of affairs can be described in the terms shown in Figure 4.3, along the axes of divergence and integration. While the present EMU 12 is not far from optimality conditions and increased economic integration is set to shift it beyond the OCA line, the prospective EMU 25 (including also Sweden, the UK and Denmark) will be further from it and placed higher up along the divergence dimension.

Figure 4.2
Exports of goods and services towards EU 15 as per cent of GDP (2000)

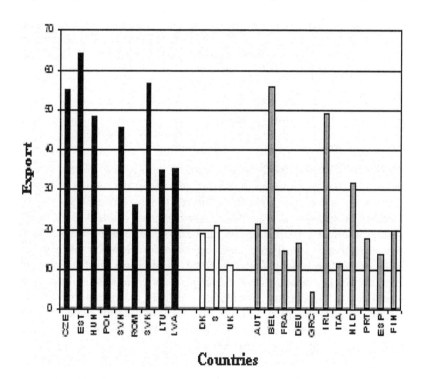

Source: De Grauwe (2003 a).

Against this background it is also possible that in an enlarged EMU the present member countries find less attractive the currency union, experiencing a worsening of their cost–benefit balance. Following a hypothetical increased asymmetry of shocks, they could more often find themselves in the position of outliers, realising that the ECB monetary policy does not take their needs into enough consideration. Indeed, in an enlarged EMU the ECB Board will lose its strategic position which ensures so far that interest rates decisions mirror the needs of the whole eurozone as such, and possible coalitions of small countries could emerge, imposing Taylor rule (1993) interest rates tailored for conditions prevailing only in a limited part of the eurozone.

Figure 4.3
Worsening of the EMU optimality conditions following enlargement

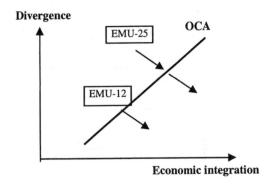

Source: Adapted from De Grauwe (2003a).

Indeed, within the present eurosystem decisions concerning monetary policy are taken by the Governing Council, which is formed by the six member ECB Board and 12 governors of national Central Banks. The Governing Council acts formally on the basis of the one-member-one-vote system, even though usually it chooses by consensus. However this happens, because of the strategic position reserved to the Board in the decision process. As already hinted, each national governor calculates the best suited interest rate for his country considering the latter's economic conditions, trying then to influence the Council in that direction, and the same holds for the Board, which takes into account however the state of the eurozone economy as a whole. The usual scheme followed by central bankers in identifying the desired interest rate r_t^* seems to be given by the Taylor rule (1993), which is essentially based on a correction made to the long–term interest rate ρ by the differences between the current π_t and the target inflation rate π^*, on the one hand, as well as between the current product and the potential output (output gap x_t), on the other:

$$r_t^* = \rho + \pi^* + a\,(\pi_t - \pi^*) + b\,x_t \tag{4.7}$$

In Table 4.4 we have calculated with 2004 data the different desired interest rates for each single country and the EMU as a whole, together with the weight of each member country's economy on the total.[20] These results are also depicted in Figure 4.4. The outcome of the exercise is enlightening: the desired rate by the ECB Board (3.40 per cent) is near to the median rate (3.65) and has therefore a very high probability of being adopted, according to the theorem of the median voter; for this it is sufficient for the Board to attract the votes of three governors with similar preferences, besides that of the Belgian central banker, whose desired rate is coincident with the median one. At the same time the Board's desired rate can be considered as representative of a vast majority of member countries' preferences.

Table 4.4
Desired EMU 12 interest rates, 2004

No	Country	Interest rate	Size
1	Germany	2.00	34.57
2	Finland	2.20	1.96
3	Netherlands	2.35	5.82
4	Austria	2.75	3.27
5	Portugal	2.90	1.48
6	EMU	3.40	100.00
	Median	3.65	-
7	Belgium	3.65	3.93
8	France	3.80	22.26
9	Italy	3.95	15.58
10	Luxemburg	4.25	0.23
11	Ireland	5.00	0.91
12	Spain	5.30	8.21
13	Greece	7.60	1.78

Source: Author's calculations based on OECD (2004).

---

[20] The value ρ has been set at 3 per cent, as in De Grauwe (2003a), and parameters a and b respectively at 1.5 and 0.5, as in Alesina *et al.* (2001), whereas π^* is equal to 2 per cent, the maximum inflation rate targeted in the medium run by the ECB.

   This efficient setting could be completely dislocated, should enlargement
be accompanied by the present formal rule of equal representation of each
governor within the Governing Council. Otherwise, as already hinted,
majority coalitions not representing the majority of the eurozone economy
could be formed, against the will of the Board, whose strategic position
would be lost, with possible negative consequences for EMU stability. De
Grauwe (2003b) finds on this point that in a EMU 27 a coalition of small
countries representing only 34 per cent of the GDP in the eurozone could
outvote the ECB Board, leading to grave conflicts within the eurosystem.
Hence the need for an institutional reform of the eurosystem, reducing the
over-representation of small countries, according to different formulas,
ranging from the US Fed system of rotating votes, to the IMF scheme of
grouping small countries in larger constituencies, to the drastic solutions of
reserving the voting right only to the Executive Board or to delegate it to a
group of apolitical technocrats.[21]

Figure 4.4
Distribution of desired interest rates and country sizes

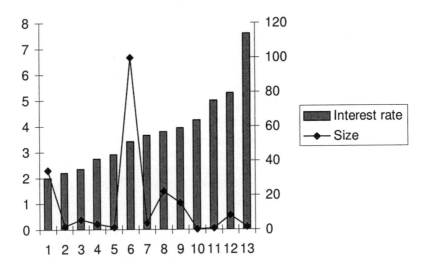

Source: Table 4.4.

---

[21] The latter proposal, which clearly does not consider the issue of ECB accountability, has been
made by Baldwin *et al.* (2001).

By the end of 2002 an official proposal of reform was presented by the ECB, considering a system combining the first two schemes: within the Governing Council three classes of rotation are forecast, with larger countries voting more often than the smaller ones (Heisenberg, 2003). After this first step, the proposal had to be approved by the European Council and by each member country.

FURTHER EXERCISES WITH THE HP FILTER

In order to get more detailed results on the issue of future EMU stability following enlargement, it is also possible to carry out exercises aimed at assessing the links between shocks taking place in the present 12 countries of the eurozone, on the one hand, and in each acceding country, on the other hand. Positive and high values in the correlation matrix would mirror a good degree of co-movement in cycles with a limited occurrence of asymmetric shocks in the acceding country, pointing to a satisfactory level of sustainability of an enlarged EMU. By contrast low or negative correlations could endanger the stability of the latter, involving at the same time possible welfare losses for the new member country.

Applying the Hodrick-Prescott filter to the series of GDP values in 1995 constant dollars for the new member countries: Cyprus, the Czech Republic, Latvia, Lithuania, Estonia, Hungary, Malta, Poland, the Slovak Republic and Slovenia, over the ten year period 1993–2002, we obtain the outcomes shown in Table 4.5. Among countries for which correlations show a positive sign, only Slovenia, Cyprus and Hungary can be deemed in condition to contribute to the stability of an enlarged EMU. For a second group of entrants (Poland and Latvia) the cycles display low reciprocal links. For Malta a positive relationship is barely perceptible.

Table 4.5
10 new member countries, correlations with the EMU cycle, 1993–2002

Positive correlations		Negative correlations	
Slovenia	0.90	Estonia	−0.08
Cyprus	0.63	Lithuania	−0.17
Hungary	0.61	Czech Republic	−0.53
Poland	0.19	Slovak Republic	−0.71
Latvia	0.15	-	-
Malta	0.01	-	-

Source: Author's calculations based on World Development Indicators database.

Conversely, the Czech and the Slovak Republics display a heavy negative correlation, whilst the negative values for Lithuania and Estonia are quite slight. On the basis of this exercise, the conclusion is therefore that the only threat posed to the stability of an enlarged EMU could come from divergences present over the period 1993–2002 in the former Czechoslovakia, even though it should not be forgotten that overall these countries, in terms of GDP produced, represent only 1 percentage point of the EMU 12. In addition, it is possible that in recent times these divergences have at least partially decreased, as we shall see in a while.

A similar exercise carried out with reference to the candidate countries to a further wave of accession makes clear that the correlation matrix contains positive values for Bulgaria and negative values for Turkey and Romania, the latter being the most divergent country in this group of economies (see Table 4.6).

Table 4.6
Bulgaria, Romania, Turkey, correlations with the EMU cycle, 1993–2002

Countries	Correlations
Bulgaria	0.31
Turkey	−0.23
Romania	−0.62

Source: Author's calculations based on World Development Indicators database.

A further step in our inquiry concerns the future optimality of an enlarged EMU, comprising not only the whole of the EU 15 but also all acceding countries, Bulgaria and Romania included (but not Turkey), i.e. an EMU 27. By doing so we carry out an intellectual experiment checking what would become the correlation network within an EMU 27, assuming that all newcomers fulfil the convergence criteria laid down in the Maastricht treaty and taking into account the period following the launch of the EMU 12. Here again, as already hinted, working on 1999–2002 series, the results of the exercise can be considered only as clues to future optimality conditions, when would-be new member countries would be ready to join. The HP filter procedure allows us to single out the EMU 27 cycle and to find its correlations with each possible member country's cycle.

The links between the EMU 27 cycle, on the one hand, and the cycles of each future member country of the enlarged European currency union, on the other, are then shown in Table 4.7, where also the result of a new *WOI* calculation is given.

Table 4.7

EMU 27 countries, cycle correlations, 1999–2002

EMU 27	Correlations
Austria	0.98
Belgium	0.99
Denmark	0.88
Finland	0.93
France	1.00
Germany	1.00
Greece	0.78
Ireland	1.00
Italy	0.96
Luxemburg	0.98
Netherlands	1.00
Portugal	0.99
Spain	0.99
Sweden	0.88
UK	0.98
Bulgaria	0.82
Cyprus	0.93
Czech Republic	0.83
Estonia	0.65
Hungary	1.00
Latvia	−0.32
Lithuania	−1.00
Malta	−0.05
Poland	0.97
Romania	−0.94
Slovak Republic	−0.97
Slovenia	0.97
EMU 27 Weighted Optimality Index	0.965

Source: Author's calculations based on World Development Indicators database.

The outcome of our test on EMU 27 cyclical links may be considered somewhat unforeseen:[22] not only does the enlarged currency union seem to be nearer to optimality conditions than the present EMU 12, with a *WOI* increasing from 0.915 to 0.965, but the number of core economies goes up as well, including now 12 countries, i.e. about half of the total. Moreover, it is not only some of the 12 founders of the EMU: France, Germany, Ireland, the Netherlands, Belgium, Portugal, Spain, Luxemburg and Austria, which are at the centre of the hypothetical currency union, but also the UK and even two new entrants: Hungary and Slovenia. Italy lies just outside the core. And what about the alleged discrepancies characterising many acceding countries? They are present indeed, mainly as Lithuania, the most divergent countries,

---

[22] Nevertheless previous literature stressed that the high intensity of trade relationships between the EU and the Central and Eastern European countries can be a basis for business cycle convergence and hence for fulfilment of OCA criteria in the medium and long run for new entrants. See for instance Fidrmuc (2001).

as well as Slovakia, Romania, Latvia and Malta (all with negative correlations), but their relative weight is negligible, as their combined economies do not total 1 per cent of the whole EMU 27 GDP. Nevertheless for these countries the welfare cost of joining the enlarged EMU is high, ranging from $K_i = 1.05$ for Malta to $K_i = 2$, the maximum possible, for Lithuania.

We find here one of the possible economic interpretations of our peculiar results, in addition to the limited significance of tests carried out over a short time span, improvement of the optimality conditions within an enlarged EMU 27 could be the consequence not only of internal developments tied to the working of built-in factors, according to the theory of endogenous currency areas, but also to deliberate efforts to follow a convergence path by would-be member countries, inside both the groups of EU 15 non-EMU countries and of the acceding ones. All this would have an impact proportional to the weight of the converging economy. From this standpoint the UK economy has played an important role, by increasing its links with the EMU cycle in the aftermath of the euro launch. In a hypothetical EMU 27 the weight of the four larger member economies (Germany, France, the UK and Italy) amounts to about 70 per cent of the area total GDP, with correlation links not inferior to 0.96 points.

In this framework the widespread assumption that, owing to past divergence characterising the new 15 would-be member countries, in the aftermath of their joining the EMU optimality will decrease seems not to be confirmed. The picture given, for instance, in De Grauwe (2003a) will therefore need to be amended, in the sense that probably an enlarged EMU will be not less optimal, as depicted in Figure 4.3, but perhaps will be shifted nearer to the OCA line, if the results of our exercise on the EMU 27 could be confirmed (see Figure 4.5).

Figure 4.5
Possible change in EMU optimality conditions following enlargement to 15 new countries

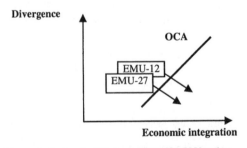

Source: Author's calculations on GDP 1999-2002 series.

CONCLUDING REMARKS

The aim of the chapter was to address the issue of the stability features of EMU in the aftermath of EU enlargement in 2004. Following their accession, the new entrants have a formal duty to join the eurozone, albeit after having successfully completed the nominal convergence process with the present member countries required by the Maastricht criteria. It is likely that in spite of the cautious stance of the Commission which advises against early entry, they will try to join EMU in a short span of time,[23] renouncing any potential gains from staying out of the currency union (Kohler, 2002).[24] During the transition period from EU to EMU, before pegging their currencies to the Exchange Rate Mechanism II, according to the Maastricht criteria, they could achieve a degree of flexibility required to adjust their economies to the occurrence of country specific shocks by means of an exchange rate mechanism not too dissimilar from the EMS.

The perspective of an early extension of the eurozone to the new member countries could in principle raise the danger to the EMU, owing to two specific risks: the possible enhanced probability of asymmetric shock occurrence, on the one hand, and the lack of appropriate timing for the necessary reform of the ECB institutional setting, on the other.

The present decision-making mechanisms of the eurosystem, where an ECB executive board and national governors co-exist on the basis of the one-man-one-vote principle, will become ineffective with enlargement, fostering conflicts and monetary instability within the eurozone. Thus, a sensible reform is needed, before the next wave of EMU member countries are ready to join. To this aim alternative new decision mechanisms have been briefly surveyed, all of which are intended to reduce the over-representation of smaller countries in the ECB Governing Council.

At the same time asymmetric shocks increasing the costs of EMU membership for divergent countries and putting the currency union in jeopardy could become more frequent, following the rise in EMU heterogeneity engendered by the admitting of countries whose economic conditions are distant from the average of the current members. In order to assess such a risk a study of the literature making use of specific tests on

---

[23] According to Gros (2002), Poland, Hungary and the Czech Republic (CEE 3) could presently be less than four years away from joining EMU. In addition, immediately after the new member countries accession' in May 2004, Estonia, Lithuania, Slovenia and Cyprus declared their will to link before the end of the year their currencies to the Exchange Rate Mechanism II, paving the way for joining the eurozone possibly two, three years later.

[24] In monetary policy co-ordination games, an outsider can play as a free-rider, successfully exporting inflation and reaping 'gains from staying out' (Kohler, 2002). By contrast, joining the EMU early would entail for an EU new member country substantial gains in terms of imported credibility (De Grauwe, 2003a), more than offsetting the loss of seigniorage (Betbèze, 2004).

optimality conditions of a currency union provided the tools for setting up a battery of empirical tests.

As a starting point for analysing the impact of enlargement on EMU stability, a new assessment of the optimality of EMU in its present form, including the cost of joining for its member countries, was carried out with the help of an Optimality Weighted Index, based on correlations between business cycles obtained employing the Hodrick-Prescott filter procedure. The latter allows us to disaggregate the trend and the cycle components of GDP series.

Subsequently a second exercise was carried out in order to determine the sign and the level of correlations between the cycles of EMU 12 and those of each acceding country, the assumption being that high correlations can be considered as evidence of low risk of shock asymmetry and hence of optimality conditions. Interestingly, the majority of the correlations proved positive, and in a number of cases also their level was quite satisfactory. Further HP filter based exercises were finally carried out with reference to a possible EMU 27, enlarged to encompass not only all of the EU 15, but also all of applicant countries, with the exception of Turkey.

Concerning in particular the impact of enlargement on EMU stability, our results seem to provide a clue that structural economic conditions in some acceding countries are not in principle incompatible with the survival of EMU in its new shape, even though the degree of optimality of an enlarged monetary union could decrease. The underlying economic interpretation could simply consist in considering these results as a consequence of the long- standing process of economic convergence with the EU followed by the candidates in the aftermath of the disruption caused by shifting from a command economy.

Moreover, according to the theory of endogenous currency areas, some of the optimality conditions of a Europe-wide currency union could improve after their accession. On the one hand, the component of the current divergence in terms of shock asymmetry due to an independent monetary stance will be offset by adhesion to the common monetary policy managed by the ECB, whereas on the other hand the national cycles will become more in phase with the EMU cycle, as reciprocal trade flows will intensify following membership of the monetary union.

The general results of our tests point to an increased convergence of business cycle movements within EMU 12 as well as to high correlations between them within a hypothetical EMU 27. Of course, whereas the former are in line with the assumption of enhanced economic integration following the setting up of a currency union, the latter could be considered as rather unexpected.

Enhanced correlations between business cycles can be the outcome of built-in stabilising factors, mainly for present member countries, which are particularly studied by the theory of endogenous currency areas, but also of deliberate efforts made by candidate countries with policies aimed at following a convergence path with the European currency union, in its different shapes. An interesting built-in factor at work for both types of countries consists in the upgrading of correlation links after the joining, due to the inclusion of the member country's GDP cycle component in that of the union. Moreover the strength of convergence effects is proportional to the weight of the member country's economy compared with the union's GDP. It follows that when large countries such as the UK adopt a policy targeted to a future adhesion to the eurozone, the impact on the overall convergence process is significant.

These preliminary results seem worthy of some interest, but have to be supported by further research, notably by taking into account other possible measures of optimality, beside those of GDP's cyclical correlations, as well as by extending time series after the EMU completion.

Coming back to the title of this chapter, my conditional conclusion is that the consequences of enlargement in terms of monetary instability within the EMU can be coped with, provided institutional reforms are carried out with a view to enhancing the functioning of the governing bodies of the eurozone.

REFERENCES

Aksoy, Y., De Grauwe, P. and Dewachter, H. (2002), 'Do asymmetries matter for European monetary policy?', *European Economic Review*, Vol. 46, pp. 443–69.

Alesina, A. and Barro, R. (2002), 'Currency Unions', *Quarterly Journal of Economics*, Vol. 117, pp. 409–36.

Alesina, A., Barro, R. and Tenreyro, S. (2002), 'Optimal currency areas', *NBER WP*, No. 9072, July.

Alesina, A., Blanchard, O., Galì, J., Giavazzi, F. and Uhling, H. (2001), 'Defining a macroeconomic framework for the euro area', *Monitoring the ECB 3*, London: CEPR.

Altissimo, F., Bassanetti, A., Cristadoro, R., Forni, M., Lippi, M., Reichlin, L. and Veronese, G. (2001), 'A real time coincident indicator of the euro area business cycle', *Temi di discussione, Banca d'Italia*, No. 436, December.

Artis, M. and Zhang, W. (1997), 'International business cycle and the ERM: is there a european business cycle?', *International Journal of Finance and Economics*, Vol. 2, pp. 1–16.

Artis, M. and Zhang, W. (1999), 'Further evidence on the international business cycle and the ERM: is there a European business cycle?', *Oxford Economic Papers*, Vol. 51, pp. 120–32.

Atkins, R. and Parker, G. (2004), 'EU critics claim "cop-out" as Prodi eases growth pact', *Financial Times*, 4 Sept.

Baldwin, R., Berglof, E., Giavazzi, F. and Widgrén, M. (2001), 'Preparing the EBC for enlargement', *CEPR Discussion Paper*, No. 6.

Ballabriga, F., Sebastian, M. and Vallés, J. (1999), 'European asymmetries', *Journal of International Economics*, Vol. 48, pp. 233–53.

Bayoumi, T. and Eichengreen, B. (1993), 'Shocking aspects of European monetary unification' in F. Torres and F. Giavazzi (eds), *Adjustment and Growth in the European Monetary Union*, Cambridge: CUP.

Bayoumi, T. and Eichengreen, B. (1994), 'Monetary and exchange rate arrangements for NAFTA', *Journal of Development Economics,* Vol. 43, pp. 125–65.

Bayoumi, T. and Eichengreen, B. (1997), 'Ever closer to heaven: an OCA index for European countries', *European Economic Review*, Vol. 41, pp. 761–70.

Bayoumi, T. and Eichengreen, B. (1998), 'Exchange rate volatility and intervention: implications of the theory of optimum currency areas', *Journal of International Economics*, Vol. 45, pp. 191–209.

Belke, A. and Gros, D. (1999), 'Estimating the costs and benefits of EMU: the impact of external shocks on labour markets', *Weltwirtschaftliches Archiv*, Vol. 145, pp. 1–47.

Betbèze, J.-P. (2004), 'Où s'arrête la zone euro', *Le Monde Economie*, 31 Mars.

Bordo M. and Jonung L. (1999), 'The future of EMU: what does the history of monetary unions tell us?', *NBER WP*, No. 7365, September.

Carr, J. and Floyd, J. (2002), 'Real and monetary shocks to the Canadian dollar: do Canada and the United States form an optimal currency area?', *North American Journal of Economics and Finance*, Vol. 70, pp. 1–19.

Clark, T. and Wincoop, E. (2001), 'Borders and business cycles', *Journal of International Economics*, Vol. 55, pp. 59–85.

Collard, F. and Dellas, H. (2002), 'Exchange rate systems and macroeconomic stability', *Journal of Monetary Economics*, Vol. 49, pp. 571–99.

Corsetti, G. and Pesenti, P. (2002), 'Self-validating currency areas', *NBER WP,* No. 8783, February.

Courchene, T. and Harris, R. (2000), 'North American monetary union: analytical principles and guidelines', *North American Journal of Economics and Finance*, Vol. 11, pp. 3–18.

Darrat, A. and Pennathur, A. (2002), 'Are the Arab Maghreb countries really integrable? Some evidence from the theory of cointegrated systems', *Review of Financial Economics*, Vol. 11, pp. 79–90.

De Grauwe, P. (2003a), *Economics of Monetary Union*, fifth edition, Oxford: OUP.

De Grauwe, P. (2003b), 'The challenge of the enlargement of Euroland', in F. Praussello (ed.), *The Economics of EU Enlargement*, Milan: Franco Angeli.

Del Negro, M. (2002), 'Asymmetric shocks among US states', *Journal of International Economics*, Vol. 56, pp. 273–97.

Dixit, A. and Lambertini, L. (2001), 'Monetary-fiscal policy interactions and commitment versus discretion in a monetary union', *European Economic Review*, Vol. 45, pp. 977–87.

Eichengreen, B. (1992), 'Is Europe an optimum currency area?', in S. Borner and H. Grubel (eds), *The European Community after 1992*, London: Macmillan.

Eichengreen, B. (1997), *European Monetary Unification: Theory, Practice, and Analysis*, Cambridge, MA: MIT Press.

Engel, C. and Rose, A. (2000), 'Currency union and international integration', *NBER WP*, No. 7872, September.

European Commission (1990), 'European economy: one market, one money', *European Economy*, No. 44.

European Commission (2001), *Second Report on Economic and Social Cohesion*, Brussels 31.1., COM (2001), 24 final.

Feldstein, M. (1992), 'The case against EMU', *The Economist*, 13 June.

Feldstein, M. (1998), 'The political economy of the European Economic and Monetary Union: political sources of an economic liability', *NBER WP*, No. 6150, February.

Feldstein, M. (2000), 'The ECB and the Euro: the first year', *NBER WP*, No. 7517, February.

Fidrmuc, J. (2001), 'The endogeneity of optimum currency area criteria, intraindustry trade and EMU enlargement', *BOFIT Discussion Papers*, No. 8.

Fidrmuc, J. and Fidrmuc, J. (2003), 'Disintegration and trade', *Review of International Economics*, Vol. 11, pp. 811–29.

Frankel, J. (1999), 'No single currency regime is right for all countries or at all times', *NBER WP*, No. 7338, September.

Frankel, J. and Rose, A. (1996), 'The endogeneity of the optimum currency area criteria', *NBER WP*, No. 5700, August.

Frankel, J. and Rose, A. (1997), 'Is EMU more justifiable ex post than ex ante?', *European Economic Review*, Vol. 41, pp. 753–60.

Frankel, J. and Rose, A (1998), 'The Endogeneity of the optimum currency area criterion', *Economic Journal*, Vol. 108, pp. 1009–25.

Frankel, J. and Rose, A. (2000), 'An estimate of the effect of currency unions on trade and growth', *NBER WP*, No. 7857, August.

Glick, R. and Rose, A. (2002), 'Does a currency union affect trade? The time-series evidence', *European Economic Review*, Vol. 46, pp. 1125–51.

Gros, D. (2002), 'Central Europe on the way to EMU', *Rivista di Politica Economica*, Vol. XCI, pp. 89–107.

Gros, D. and Hefeker, C. (2000), 'One size fits all: national divergences in a monetary union', *CEPS WP*, No. 149, July.

Grubel, H. (2000), 'The merit of Canada–US monetary union', *North American Journal of Economics and Finance*, Vol. 11, pp. 19–40.

Haug, A., MacKinnon, J. and Michelis, L. (2000), 'European monetary union: a cointegration analysis', *Journal of International Money and Finance*, Vol. 19, pp. 419–32.

Heisenberg, D. (2003), 'Cutting the bank down to size: efficient and legitimate decision-making in the European Central Bank after enlargement', *Journal of Common Market Studies*, Vol. 41, pp. 397–420.

Hochreiter, E. and Siklos, P. (2002), 'Alternative exchange-regimes: the options for Latin America', *North American Journal of Economics and Finance*, Vol. 13, pp. 195–211.

Hodrick, R. and Prescott, E. (1980), 'Postwar US business cycles: an empirical investigation', *Discussion Paper 451*, Carnegie Mellon University.

Jovanović, M. (2000), 'Eastern enlargement of the European Union: sour grapes or sweet lemon?', *Economia Internazionale, International Economics*, Vol. LIII, pp. 507–36.

Kalemi-Ozcan, S., Sorensen, B. and Yosha, O. (2001), 'Economic integration, industrial specialisation, and the asymmetry of macroeconomic fluctuations', *Journal of International Economics*, Vol. 55, pp. 107–37.

Karras, G. and Stokes, H. (2001), 'Time-varying criteria for monetary integration, evidence from EMU', *International Review of Economics and Finance*, Vol. 10, pp. 171–85.

Kenen, P. (1969), 'The theory of optimum currency areas: an eclectic view' in R. Mundell and A. Swoboda (eds), *Monetary Problems in International Economy*, Chicago: University of Chicago Press.

Kleimeier, S. and Sander, H. (2000), 'Regionalisation versus globalisation in European financial market integration: evidence from co-integration analyses', *Journal of Banking and Finance*, Vol. 24, pp. 1005–43.

Kohler, M. (2002), 'Coalition formation in international monetary policy games', *Journal of International Economics*, Vol. 56, pp. 371–85.

Kopits, G. (2002), 'Central Europe EU accession and Latin American integration: mutual lessons in macroeconomic policy design', *North American Journal of Economic and Finance*, Vol. 82, pp. 1–25.

Korhonen, I. and Fidrmuc, J. (2001), 'Similarity of supply and demand shocks between the Euro Area and the accession countries', *Focus on Transition*, Oesterreichische Nationalbank, No. 2.

Krugman, P. (1991), *Geography and Trade*, Cambridge, MA: MIT Press.

Krugman, P. and Obstfeld, M. (1998), *International Economics: Theory and Policy*, New York: Harper Collins.

Lane, P. (1996), 'Stabilisation policy in a currency union', *Economic Letters,* Vol. 53, pp. 53–60.

Levi Yeyati, E. (2003), 'On the impact of a common currency on bilateral trade', *Economic Letters*, Vol. 79, pp. 125–29.

McKinnon, R. (1963), 'Optimum currency areas', *American Economic Review*, Vol. 53, pp. 717–24.

Mundell, R. (1961), 'A theory of optimum currency areas', *American Economic Review*, Vol. 51, pp. 509–17.

Mundell, R. (1998), 'The case for the Euro-I', 'The case for the euro-II', 'Making the Euro work', *Wall Street Journal*, 24 March, 25 March and 30 April.

OECD (2004), *Economic Outlook*, No. 75, June.

Perroni, C. and Whalley, J. (2000), 'The new regionalism: trade liberalization or insurance?', *Canadian Journal of Economics*, Vol. 33, pp. 1–24.

Praussello, F. (2002), 'The Euro as a stabilisation device for the EU's neighbours' in F. Praussello (ed.), *Euro Circulation and the Economic and Monetary Union*, Milan: Franco Angeli.

Praussello, F. (2003), 'The stability of EMU in the aftermath of eastward enlargement of the European Union', in F. Praussello (ed.), *The Economics of EU Enlargement*, Milan: Franco Angeli.

Praussello, F. (2004), 'A HP test on optimality conditions within the EMU currency area', *Working Paper n. 4/2004, DISEFIN*, University of Genoa, February.

Ramaswamy, R. and Sloek, T. (1998), 'The real effects of monetary policy in the EU: what are the differences?', *IMF Staff Papers*, Vol. 45, pp. 374–402.

Rose, A. (2000), 'One money, one market: estimating the effect of common currencies on trade', *Economic Policy*, Vol. 30, pp. 7–46.

Sorensen, B. and Yosha, O. (1998), 'International risk sharing and European monetary unification', *Journal of International Economics*, Vol. 45, pp. 211–38.

Swofford, J. (2000), 'Microeconomic foundations of an OCA', *Review of Financial Economics*, Vol. 9, pp. 121–28.

Taylor, J. (1993), 'Discretion versus policy rules in practice', *Carnegie-Rochester Conference Series on Public Policy*, Vol. 39, pp. 195–214.

Thom, R. and Walsh, B. (2002), 'The effects of a currency union on trade: lessons from the Irish experience', *European Economic Review*, Vol. 46, pp. 1111–23.

Von Neumann Whitman, M. (1967), 'International and interregional payments adjustment: a synthetic view', *Princeton Studies in International Economics*, February.

PART II

Governance and Cohesion of the Enlarged
Union

5. Political Dynamics in the Enlarged European Union

Neill Nugent

INTRODUCTION

All European Union enlargement rounds have been accompanied by concerns that the increased number and diversity of member states will damage the political dynamics of the EU. In particular, there has been a concern that decision-making processes will be weakened, by becoming more cumbersome and more vulnerable to national vetoes.

Partly to allay such concerns, enlargement rounds since the 1980s have been preceded by rounds of treaty reform that have been much taken up with preparing for enlargement. The most obvious way in which rounds of treaty reform – which have been conducted via Intergovernmental Conferences (IGCs) – have been so taken up is by progressively expanding the scope for qualified majority voting (QMV) in the Council of Ministers. Successive expansions of QMV provisions – in the 1986 Single European Act (SEA), the 1992 Maastricht Treaty, the 1997 Treaty of Amsterdam, and the 2001 Treaty of Nice – have had the effect of reducing the circumstances in which national vetoes can be exercised and so also have reduced the possibilities of decisional outcomes being at the mercy of the most unwilling/reluctant member state. The 2004 Treaty on the Constitution will further extend this situation if and when it is ratified.

But recent treaty reform rounds – that is since the Treaty of Amsterdam – have had to consider a much broader range of enlargement-pressed political reforms than QMV. When it became clear in the mid-to-late 1990s that an enlargement round involving probably up to ten Central and Eastern European countries (CEECs) plus the Mediterranean islands of Cyprus and Malta would occur sometime in the early 2000s, the possibility of wide-ranging treaty reform became inevitable. It did so because it was recognised that this enlargement round would be quite unlike its predecessors and would pose unprecedented challenges for the political functioning of the Union. It would do so because the 1995 enlargement, which had raised the number of member states from 12 to 15, was viewed as having pushed the EU close to its maximum numerical limit within existing institutional rules. For example, the College of Commissioners, with a membership of 20 from 1995, was seen as having become as large as it could be without efficiency becoming seriously compromised. And for how much longer could the European Parliament (EP), with 626 members from 1995, keep growing without becoming far too unwieldly? The Amsterdam, and more so the Nice, treaties partly addressed such questions. So too did the 2004 Treaty on the Constitution. Whether, however, they did so in a wholly satisfactory manner will be one of the themes of this chapter.

But the chapter is not just concerned with the treaties and enlargement. Rather, it ranges widely over a number of key aspects of political dynamics in the enlarged EU. The analysis and discussion is organised under six main headings: the roles and influence of the EU's institutions; decision-making processes; inter-state relations; differentiation; new modes of governance; and provision of leadership.

THE ROLES AND INFLUENCE OF THE EU'S INSTITUTIONS

The roles and influence of the EU's institutions are in constant evolution. They are so via both treaty reforms and developmental custom and practice. Examples of changes brought about by treaty reform include the strengthened legislative powers that have been assigned to the EP and the increased attention the Council has had to give to foreign and defence policies. Examples of change consequent upon developmental custom and practice include the establishment of the European Council as a major decision-making institution and the role of the Council presidency as a major EU power-broker. Frequently, change brought about through custom and practice is subsequently followed up with treaty recognition and consolidation.

Many factors drive changes in the roles and influence of the EU's institutions, of which enlargement is but one, albeit an extremely important one. Other factors include:

- Unfolding policy responsibilities. Expansion of pillar one (Community) policies tends to strengthen the positions of the Commission, Council of Ministers and EP, whilst expansion of pillar two (foreign and security) and pillar three (police and judicial cooperation) policies is much more favourable to the Council since the treaty powers of the Commission and the EP are much weaker in these areas.

- Pressures from the institutions. The EU's institutions tend themselves to have attitudes about what their roles should be and this has impacted on what their roles are. Broadly speaking, institutions wish to maximise their power, and in the EU context this has been seen most clearly with the European Council and the EP. The former has increasingly wished to see major decisions either taken by it or at least passed through its hands, and because it includes all national political leaders amongst its membership and because too there are no treaty limitations on its powers it has simply been able to do just about what it likes in institutional terms. The latter has used its position as the EU's only directly elected institution to stretch its position to the maximum within the constraints of the treaties. This is seen, for example, in the way in which since the early 1990s it has extended its powers over the Commission, to the extent that in 2004 it forced the Commission President-designate, José Manuel Barroso, to change members of his College-designate.
- Evolving attitudes towards institutions. Attitudes, of both practitioners and publics, to EU institutions can evolve in such a way as to influence the roles they exercise and the influence they bring to bear. This is evidenced, for example, in the manner in which after the Santer College was forced to resign in March 1999 following criticism of its management operations, there was a widespread expectation that the Commission should shift at least some of its attention away from policy expansion towards effectiveness and efficiency of policy implementation.

It is not possible to completely disentangle the impact of enlargement on institutional change from the sort of other factors that have just been identified. For example, many EU observers are of the view that while the decline in influence and status that the Commission has suffered in recent years can be partly attributed to the increased size and diversity of ever-larger Colleges brought about by enlargement, the main reasons lie elsewhere. Amongst these other reasons are: the increased number of political actors that have become involved in EU agenda-setting; the strengthened position of the European Council; and the growing importance of second and third pillar issues and of other non Community-based policy processes that have resulted in what Helen Wallace calls 'intensive transgovernmentalism' in fields where explicit EU policies are not yet developed and hence where the role of the Commission remains modest' (Wallace, 2005).

Enlargement is thus best thought of as but one of several contributors to institutional change. In some instances the link is quite direct: as with the decision to make provision in the 2004 Constitutional Treaty for a semi-permanent president of the European Council – a decision that was influenced by a recognition of the need to give the EU of 25 a greater individual leadership focus (more on this later in the chapter); and as also with the enhancement of the Commission's implementation responsibilities in some policy areas, which has been strongly influenced by concerns in EU-15 states (pre-May 2004 members) about the administrative capacity of some EU-10 states (post-May 2004 members). More often than not, however, the link is not so direct and institutional change is a consequence of several factors which cannot easily be separated from one another.

DECISION-MAKING PROCESSES

Enlargement has posed major challenges for EU decision-making processes, not least because the increased number of member states has made for greater heterogeneity and therefore potentially less cohesiveness. The following sub-sections consider some of the implications of enlargement for EU decision-making, through the lenses of the EU's four principal political institutions.

The European Commission

Two main sets of concerns have been expressed in regard to the Commission concerning the impact of enlargement.

The first relates to the College, which has grown in size over the years in parallel with enlargements and which is now seen by many observers as being rather too large. Too large because there are only a limited number of significant College portfolios and too large also because too many Commissioners makes it very difficult for the College to act as a coherent and cohesive body. Quite what the optimal number of Commissioners is, is a matter of debate, but around 15 is a favoured number.

Problems arising from the College becoming too large have long been recognised by EU decision-makers in the context of treaty reform rounds, but the matter has been very difficult to tackle because of the political sensitivities associated with it. Until the Nice Treaty, the five largest member states were unwilling to cede their right to have two Commissioners, and most of the smaller member states were reluctant to end the principle that all member states should have at least one Commissioner. The Nice Treaty did make some progress with the size problem by ending the practice of the five largest states each having two Commissioners, but in the opinion of some observers the post-Nice 'one Commissioner per member state' principle has increased the nationality appearance – and possibly behaviour – of the College.

In the Constitutional Treaty it was agreed that from 2014 the size of the College will be equivalent to two thirds of the number of member states. This is unlikely to end the debate on the size of the College since by 2014 there could well be 30 plus states. In the meantime, the College must continue with 25, soon to be 27, Commissioners, with all the attendant problems such size can bring: some Commissioners not being satisfied with the importance of their portfolios; greater potential difficulties in proceeding by consensus (the College can take decisions by simple majority vote if necessary, but in practice it rarely does so); and fragmentation and lack of policy coordination.

Problems of fragmentation and lack of policy coordination appear to have become almost endemic in recent times, with the Prodi College being notoriously uncollegial and characterised by disputes between Commissioners: disputes that were increasingly conducted in public as the days of the College drew to a close. Barroso sought from the outset to ensure his College would not be so characterised and took a number of steps to try to promote collegiality and cohesion: key economic portfolios were mostly assigned to economic liberals; groups of Commissioners were created in key areas – including economic reform, external relations, and competitiveness – and it was made clear the groups would be expected to come forward with policy recommendations; and the former (pre-Prodi) practice of Commissioners' offices being located in the same building rather than scattered around Brussels in 'their' Directorates General, was restored. Whether such measures will have the desired effect remains to be seen, although early signs were not altogether promising following a number of 'turf' and policy disputes between Commissioners.

The second concern relates to the increased number of nationalities in the Commission's services (administration). The services are, of course, multinational in their composition, with meritocratic recruitment principles always having been offset to some extent by efforts to ensure that nationals from all member states are reasonably, though not exactly proportionately, represented throughout the services' system, especially at senior levels. This national representation principle has had both advantages and disadvantages. One advantage has been that a range of different national views have been input into EU policy-making. Another has been that member state confidence in the EU has been bolstered by the knowledge that fellow nationals are 'on the inside'. Disadvantages have been that 'the best' candidates have not always been recruited to posts, different national administrative cultures have sometimes jarred, and informal groupings of nationals have occasionally clustered in parts of the Commission.

Under the College led by Romano Prodi, a far reaching reform programme of Commission personnel policy was carried out between 2000–04, led by Commissioner Neil Kinnock. As part of this programme, less emphasis is now being attached to the nationality criterion in recruitment to the services and more is being attached to meritocracy. However, as with previous enlargement rounds, special arrangements were made for nationals from the member states which joined the EU in 2004, with provision being made for the phasing-in over a seven year period of some 3,400 permanent new Commission posts, plus 1,000 fixed-term contract staff. This will amount to about one fifth of total Commission staffing, so will have a considerable effect on the nature of the Commission and could exacerbate the disadvantages arising from the multinational nature of the services that were noted above.

Linguistic problems have been exacerbated by the 2004 enlargement, with the number of official EU languages having increased from 11 to 20. The problem does not so much concern the internal functioning of the Commission – for most business is conducted in English, French or German – but rather arises from the requirement that many documents be translated into all official languages. Shortages of financial and personnel resources have resulted in this requirement leading to delays and to the issuing by officials of shorter documents.

The European Council

Virtually all of the EU's major directional and strategic decisions are now either made by or are channelled through the European Council. Since the European Council takes nearly all of its decisions by unanimity, it is evident that in terms of its potential decision-making capacity it is the institution that is most directly affected by enlargement. This is because the larger and more diverse the membership of the European Council becomes the more difficult it is likely to be to find consensus.

Evidence of this was seen in the months immediately before and after the May 2004 enlargement of the EU when major decisions scheduled to be taken at two European Council meetings could not be agreed. The December 2003 summit, which the EU-10 attended as 'honorary' members, could not reach final agreement on the content of the Constitutional Treaty, largely because Poland and Spain refused to accept a reduction in the weighted votes in the Council of Ministers they had been assigned by the Treaty of Nice. Significantly, the December 2003 summit also demonstrated how mediation and brokerage are likely in the enlarged EU to become even more important than they have been in the past: most impartial observers attributed much of the blame for the failure of the summit to inadequate preparations by, and insufficient diplomacy on the part of, the Italian presidency.

The other European Council failure was at the June 2004 meeting, when agreement could not be reached on who should replace Romano Prodi as Commission President. The Belgian Prime Minister, Guy Verhofstadt, was favoured by most, but was adamantly opposed by the UK Prime Minister,

Tony Blair (partly because of Verhofstadt's strongly pro-integrationist views but partly too because he had been prominent in attempting to rally EU opposition to the US-led invasion of Iraq), whilst the External Relations Commissioner, Chris Patten, was also acceptable to most, but was strongly opposed by the French President, Jacques Chirac (largely because Patten was British). Significantly, post-Nice, the nomination of the candidate for Commission President is one of the (few) matters on which the European Council can decide by QMV, but no such vote was ever called on either Verhofstadt or Patten: because the political credibility of a Commission President not enjoying the confidence of all member states would be undermined even before he assumed office.

The Council of Ministers

A key feature of virtually all of the rounds of treaty reform that have occurred since the mid-1980s has been a recognition of the need to change treaty rules so as to ensure the Council of Ministers can operate effectively. In specific terms, this has particularly meant incrementally expanding the circumstances in which decisions may be made by QMV.

Enlargement has been a major, though not the only, factor in highlighting the need for more QMV and in making it acceptable to the member states. It has been so because it is clear that the more member states there are then the more difficult it is likely to be for the Council to be able to make unanimous decisions. Such has been the scale of the extensions to QMV over the years that the Council now can take the great majority of its legislative decisions in this way.

There do, however, remain important decision-making areas where the unanimity requirement still applies. These include treaty reform, membership applications, most foreign and defence policy matters, police and judicial cooperation, and all financial and budgetary issues. Since this list includes (not coincidentally) some of the most sensitive and controversial items on the EU's agenda, it can be anticipated that the continuation of unanimity will make for considerable decision-making problems. This is likely to be demonstrated as governments tussle in 2005 and 2006 with the challenge of trying to find an agreement on the EU's next multi-annual financial planning programme (technically known as the financial perspective) which is due to be applied from 2007.

Beyond problems caused by the unanimity requirement, enlargement is raising other difficulties too for Council decision-making. Many of these difficulties arise from the large number of people who are now entitled and wish to attend Council meetings. Whereas before enlargement, ministerial-level meetings would typically be attended by between 80–100 people and lower level meetings (the Committee of Permanent Representatives, Council committees, working groups) by proportionately less, in the EU-25 the numbers have been ratcheted upwards considerably. Because this means meetings have to be held in larger rooms with participants further distanced from one another, and because also in meetings attended by politicians rather than by officials more interventions have to be translated, there has been a reduction in the extent to which meetings display spontaneity and are forums of real negotiations. Participants of senior-level Council meetings complain that too often meetings are now the occasion for little more than the delivery of pre-prepared statements.

The European Parliament

Treaty reforms coupled with pro-activism on its own part have resulted in the EP making major institutional advances since the mid-1980s. The most notable advances have been in respect of the making of EU legislation, where the EP is now a co-decision maker with the Council in most legislative areas, and control over the Commission, where the resignation in 1999 of the Santer College and the changes in 2004 to the membership of the Barroso College were both directly a consequence of EP pressure. The extent to which the EP has made institutional progress is, perhaps, no more clearly seen than in the way it has become centrally involved not only in formal EU policy processes but also in the many informal processes that are such an important part of how the EU operates. For example: chairs of EP committees are now sometimes invited to informal Council meetings; informal trialogues and even conciliation meetings (meetings of Council, Commission and EP representatives) are often held at first and second legislative readings to try to resolve inter-institutional differences and speed up progress; and EP representatives play an increasingly important role in legislative planning meetings with Council and Commission representatives.

This increasing institutional importance of the EP does not, it should be emphasised, owe anything very directly to enlargement. On the contrary, indeed, enlargement rounds have created significant logistical and organisational problems for the EP as it has grown in size to become the largest democratically elected parliament in the world. More Members of the European Parliament (MEPs) means there is more in-house expertise available to the EP, but it also means the institution becomes potentially ever more cumbersome. An indication of this cumbersomeness is seen in the fact that the largest political group in the EP since the 2004 elections, the European People's Party-European Democrats, contains amongst its membership at least one MEP from each of the EU's 25 states and MEPs from 46 different national political parties!

The Amsterdam Treaty sought to deal with the increasing size problem by setting a cap on the maximum size of the EP at 700, but as part of the messy deal that was agreed at Nice on the size of the EU's institutions and voting weights in the Council this number was raised to 732 as from the 2004 elections. The Constitutional Treaty subsequently further raised the maximum size to 750, with no state to have more than 96 members or to have less than six.

A particular problem posed for the EP by enlargement has been interpretation and translation. Recruitment problems – arising from budgetary restraints and a shortage of available personnel in some languages – have resulted in a full language supporting service not always being available. MEPs from the new member states do mostly have reasonable linguistic skills and can cope with at least one of English, French or German. But not all new MEPs can so cope and, in any event, there are circumstances in which the national language must be used: for reasons perhaps of national pride, national language protection, the necessity of ensuring important matters are precisely understood, or the distribution of documents to domestic audiences. Amongst the specific difficulties to which interpretation and translation difficulties have given rise are:

- a slowing down of some policy processes, caused by waiting for documents to be translated;
- much more use of language relays in interpretation (the now 20 official EU languages means the number of possible language combinations has increased from 110 to 380), but even this is not guaranteeing that all representatives from smaller countries receive interpretation into their own language;
- MEPs from smaller countries sometimes having to choose at meetings between (reluctantly) speaking in a second language or not speaking at all.

INTER-STATE RELATIONS

In the EU-15, cleavages between the member states were cross-cutting more than they were cumulative. That is to say, where there were differences between the positions of states on particular issues they tended not to take the form of the same states being close to one another on issue after issue. The positions of states in relation to one another tended to vary rather than coincide. So, for example, states with a similar stance towards reform of the Common Agricultural Policy (CAP) might well differ sharply on, say, the opening-up of the financial services market or the desirability of Turkey being admitted to EU membership.

This system of cleavages resulted in a changing and flexible issue-based alliance system between the member states in which no states were in a permanent majority or minority across the EU agenda and in which inter-state negotiations did not, for the most part, produce festering grievances and feelings of being constantly treated unfairly. In short, it was a cleavage system that was conducive to the promotion of relatively harmonious inter-state relations. It is a system that is continuing, and seems likely to continue, in the enlarged EU. Certainly the number and nature of differences between the EU-10 states would appear to be such as to guarantee that they will not act as a coherent 'Eastern' or 'new member states' bloc in EU decision-making forums. There will, of course, be specific issues on which the new members, or at least many of them, will be drawn together, but not consistently and not across the board.

If cleavages in the EU-25 will then continue to be primarily cross-cutting, what are likely to be the key issues that will divide states and how are states likely to align on the issues? Clearly not all issues can be predicted and not all alignments of states can be anticipated. It can, however, be assumed that some key issues will feature prominently on a continuing basis and that these will be accompanied by reasonably, though not completely, consistent and persistent national positions. The issues include:

- How liberal (non-interventionist) should EU economic policies be? All EU-25 economies are, of course, market-based and all EU states have been strongly influenced by the liberal economic spirit that has prevailed in the western world since the 1980s. But significant differences can, nonetheless, be detected amongst the EU-25 regarding the extent to which, on the one hand, the EU economy should be 'managed' from both the EU and national levels and the extent to which, on the other hand, market forces should be left relatively untampered. In broad terms, the UK may be said to lead the 'non-interventionists' and Italy and France the 'interventionists'.
- What should be the size of the EU budget and what should be the spending priorities? Net contributors to EU budgetary resources – which primarily means richer EU states – favour a tight budget, whilst net recipients – which primarily means poorer states and states which greatly benefit from the CAP and the Structural Funds – favour a larger budget. This was clearly demonstrated as the negotiations on the post-2007 financial perspective got under way in 2004–05, with a group of six net contributors – Austria, France, Germany, the Netherlands, Sweden and the UK – pressing for the total size of the budget to be capped at 1 per cent of gross national income, and all CEECs pressing for the cap to be no lower than the Commission's proposed 1.4 per cent. As for spending priorities, this very   much   reflects   national   situations,   with,   for   example,   CAP

beneficiaries such as France and Poland defending this area of expenditure and Structural Fund beneficiaries, including all CEECs, defending this area.

- To what extent and in which ways should the Common Foreign and Security Policy (CFSP) and the European Security and Defence Policy (ESDP) be developed? Some states, led by France, would like to see the EU become a major global foreign and security actor, whilst others – including Ireland, Finland and Sweden, all of which have traditionally sought to be neutral in world affairs – would prefer activities to be limited to such activities as peace monitoring and humanitarian tasks. States also differ over the extent to which the CFSP and ESDP should remain intergovernmental in character, with all key decisions to be taken by unanimity, and the extent to which supranationality should be permitted.
- How Atlanticist should the EU be? All EU states attach importance to the Atlantic Alliance and to maintaining good and close relations with the US, but some are much keener than others on developing a European identity within the Alliance and on making the EU less dependent on the US. This was no more clearly demonstrated than in regard to the US-led invasion of Iraq in 2003, when the UK, Italy, Spain and all CEECs gave strong backing to the United States whilst France, Germany and Belgium were to the fore in opposing the invasion.

To these potential cleavage issues can be added others, such as divisions between large and small states and between states that are keen to proceed to further integration and those that are more cautious. There is thus no difficulty in identifying lines of division in the EU. But the divisions are not rigid and any destructive potential they may have is ameliorated by their cross-cutting nature. Enlargement does not threaten this cleavage system because the EU-10 are far from constituting a monolithic bloc. Even the issue that is most commonly identified as likely to bind the EU-10 together in the EU, their relatively poverty, will quickly lose much of its force as faster growing new member states such as Cyprus, Hungary, the Czech Republic and Slovenia narrow the gap with the EU average and indeed 'catch' poorer EU-15 states.

Enlargement has brought no signs of bringing completely new cleavages to the fore, though it has made existing ones more complex. The effect of this, as both Baun (2004) and Grabbe (2004) have noted, is to underpin the shifting and flexible nature of EU alliances. This, in turn, will prevent the emergence of permanent inter-state alliances that could endanger EU stability.

That all said, however, it is possible that enlargement could encourage more mini-alliances between states in particular issue areas. This possibility is explored in the next section.

DIFFERENTIATION

The EU has long been becoming increasingly differentiated: that is to say, characterised by policy initiatives and developments in which not all member states are fully involved. Prior to enlargement, the most prominent examples of differentiation amongst the EU-15 were EMU (with Denmark, Sweden and the UK all choosing not to become members of the single currency) and the Schengen System covering free movement of peoples across internal EU borders (with Ireland and the UK partially opting out).

It was always certain that the 2004 enlargement would increase differentiation in the short term and likely that it would do so in the longer term too. This is because the enlargement increased the range of variations between EU states in terms of their objective requirements, policy preferences, and economic, political and administrative capacities. But what sort of differentiation has the enlargement promoted, for differentiation can take different forms. Developing a framework outlined by Junge (2003), there are four main forms of differentiation:

- *Multi-speed.* All states are moving in the same direction but, for reasons either of choice or capacity, are doing so at different speeds.
- *À la carte.* All states participate in core (primarily internal market) policies, but outside the core choose the extent and nature of their involvement.
- *Overlapping circles.* States group together in different combinations in different policy areas, with overlappings occurring between the groupings.
- *Concentric circles.* All states participate in core policies, but some states (the inner circle) also participate in a wider range of integrationist policies while other states (the outer circle(s)) are less integrationist.

Only mild versions of the first two forms of differentiation occurred amongst the EU-15. EMU demonstrates both forms. Regarding multi-speed, this is illustrated by Greece: it did not join the single currency system when it was established in 1999, but rather two years later in 2001; the reason for the delay was not an unwillingness to join on the part of the Greek government but rather a judgement by the Commission and the Ecofin Council that in 1999 Greece did not meet the entry terms specified in the Maastricht criteria. Regarding *à la carte,* this is illustrated by Denmark, Sweden and the UK: in referendums the Danish and Swedish people have rejected euro membership, whilst the UK government has yet to take the issue to the people in a referendum.

The accession process of the EU-10 explicitly provided for the further development of multi-speed differentiation in the sphere of EMU. It did so by, on the one hand, insisting that all new member states explicitly commit to eventually becoming EMU members – they were not given potential opt-outs – but, on the other hand, not permitting them to become members until at least two years after their EU accession. EMU apart, however, and not including the different case of temporary derogations which EU-10 states (like their predecessors in earlier enlargement rounds) were given to enable them to meet potentially difficult demands of EU membership (as with some environmental legislation), the general thrust of the accession process was designed to ensure that differentiation would not be over-fostered.

And indeed it does appear to be the case that beyond some further modest development of *à la carte* and multi-speed integration, and perhaps limited versions of overlapping circles, differentiation is unlikely to proceed too much further in the EU-25. A key reason for this is the heavily cross-cutting nature of so many differences between EU-25 states. As has been noted above, groups of individual states do, of course, have interests and objectives in common, which enables them to ally on particular matters, but for this to lead to concentric circle differentiation, or indeed even much overlapping circle differentiation, requires accumulating rather than cross-cutting cleavages.

Beyond the absence of wide-ranging and accumulating cleavages that clearly differentiate groups of EU states from one another, there is another reason why the emergence of concentric circle differentiation – in which an inner core is surrounded by an outer core or cores – is unlikely: it is not generally desired by the member states. The case of the UK is significant here. Generally seen as being a 'slow stream' member in the sense that outside internal market policies it usually prefers an intergovernmental to a supranational approach, UK governments have sought to help lead debate on the future of Europe and to be an important player in EU circles. In this context, it has been a matter of concern to the UK government that decisions about the eurozone have increasingly come to be taken in practice by the Eurogroup of 12 EMU Finance Ministers rather than by the Ecofin Council of EU-25 Finance Ministers.

In the context of differentiation, there is speculation sometimes of the possible emergence of an EU *directoire* or *directoires*. The model for this is often seen as the Franco-German alliance, which over the years has done much to set the pace and direction of the integration process within the Community pillar. But in recent times the alliance has not proved to be as robust or an influential as it used to be, as has been witnessed, for example, with the way in which France and Germany felt smaller states did rather too well in the Nice Treaty, their failure to have their candidate for Commission President, Guy Verhofstadt, endorsed by the European Council in 2004, and the allocation to them – and especially France – of less senior Commission portfolios in the Barroso College than they judged they merited.

For reasons that are similar to why an inner core of EU member states is unlikely to be established, a single *directoire* will not emerge. The extent and nature of divisions between member states provides no bases for a *directoire*, and states that would be on the outside would resist its creation. But if a single *directoire* cannot be foreseen, *directoires* of a probably rather loose and shifting-member variety are possible in a few policy areas. Arguably there already is one of this kind within EMU, with France and Germany having taken the lead in pressing for the 'softening' of the terms of the Stability and Growth Pact that were agreed in March 2005. Justice and Home Affairs (JHA) is another policy area where there have been restricted meetings of member states which have had as their (not admitted) purpose trying to set the agenda on internal security issues. The CFSP and ESDP might also be thought of as possible policy candidate areas for *directoires*, with the larger states sharing much in terms of their capacities for foreign policy and security actions. However, there are, as the different reactions to the invasion of Iraq showed, just too many significant policy differences between the larger states for them to be able to initiate, develop and manage coordinated consistent, and broadly based CFSP/ESDP policies over time.

NEW MODES OF GOVERNANCE

Since the mid-1990s what are commonly referred to as 'new modes of governance' have become increasingly important in the EU. This term refers to a movement away in a few policy areas from traditional, hierarchical, legislation-based, forms of operation to more flexible, often network-based, and voluntary forms of policy development and practice (see Eberlein and Kerwer, 2004, on new governance). An example of new governance is the creation of European agencies such as the European Environment Agency and the European Food Safety Authority, which are extensively involved in information gathering and distribution and in making policy recommendations but which themselves have few direct executive powers. Another, and the best known, example of new governance is the Open Method of Coordination (OMC), which involves EU decision-makers identifying collective goals and then pursuing them not via compulsive regulation but via gentler mechanisms including benchmarking, league tabling, encouragement of best practice, and peer pressure. The Lisbon Process is largely based on the OMC.

New modes of governance have advantages and disadvantages. The main advantage is that they permit policy to be developed in areas where states would be very reluctant if compulsion and EU law were to be involved. The main disadvantage is that voluntarism and non-binding policy mechanisms are not always effective – as the limited progress in achieving the Lisbon goals would appear to demonstrate.

In some important respects the political dynamics of new modes of government are similar to differentiation. Both stem in part from searches to find a way in which those states that wish to proceed rapidly with further integration can do so without causing a deep rift with those states that are more Euro-cautious. And both clearly make the EU's policy and policy-making systems more varied. As Peterson (2005: 14) puts it, they are doing much to create an EU that is 'increasingly **polycentric**, or fragmented with more and more diverse centres of decision-making and control'.

Just as enlargement has promoted differentiation, so has it promoted new modes of governance. Both differentiated and new governance policy approaches have become more attractive, and arguably almost inevitable, as the EU has acquired more members. For the fact is that as the EU has grown in size then so has it become much more difficult for all member states to swim abreast in a uniform manner across all EU policies.

As also with differentiation, new governance can facilitate enlargement – in its case by providing a way in which new member states can 'slide' into what may be difficult policy areas for them. The absence of central control and compulsion gives time to adapt and adjust in a less pressurised manner than is the case where EU law applies.

PROVISION OF LEADERSHIP

In nation states, including the member states of the EU, the principal source of potential leadership is usually reasonably clear. It is a president, a prime minister, a government, or some combination of all three. This political leadership attains its position through national rules and understandings, which normally make up part of the national constitution. An important component of the rules, one way or another, is national elections, which serve to link the leadership with the people and to provide the former with legitimacy.

Of course, in some EU member states, especially those where coalition governments are common, the leadership provided is often not as sharp or as effective as is ideally desirable. But though leadership capacity and performance may sometimes be a problem, there is not normally too much difficulty in identifying where political leadership should be coming from.

This is not the situation in the EU, where neither the treaties nor political practice provide for clear and unambiguous political leadership. Rather, they provide several potential sources of leadership. These include, most notably, the President of the Commission, the Council presidency, and close and stable alliances of (especially large) states. The enormous integrationist advances the EU has made over the years, not least since the mid-1980s, suggests that leadership must in practice have been provided from these potential sources, and analysis of particular policies and events indicates that this is indeed the case. So, for example: the Commission provided much of the impetus and direction to the SEM programme from the mid-1980s; the Commission President, Jacques Delors, working closely with French President, Francois Mitterrand, and German Chancellor, Helmet Kohl, was instrumental in setting the agenda and timetable for the creation of EMU; the Commission did much from the mid-1990s to press the case for and force the pace of the enlargement of the EU to the CEECs; and from the late 1990s Prime Minister Tony Blair and President Jacques Chirac were prominent in laying the foundations for what has become the ESDP.

But the leadership that any one source can provide in the EU is always constrained by features of the EU system: the Commission can launch initiatives but it does not have the power to ensure they lead to decisions and actions; the Council presidency is only of six months duration, which is much shorter than the average policy cycle time from initiation to decision; and groups of state usually identify closely with one another only on a limited number of policy issues. Aware of these leadership limitations, EU politicians have over the years undertaken some streamlining of institutional arrangements so as to try to ensure there is not too much of a leadership deficit. So, for example, the powers of the Commission President over the College of Commissioners have been increased by treaty reform, joint planning of activities between Council presidencies has been promoted, and the rotation of Council presidencies has been arranged in such a way that larger states and smaller states are interspersed rather than following immediately on from one another.

However, such reforms have been somewhat modest in scale. Certainly in the view of many practitioners and observers they have not been sufficiently bold to provide the stronger leadership that will be required in an EU of 25 plus member states, in which there is significantly greater diversity than in the EU-15 and in which the diversity will continue to increase as more states accede. It had been anticipated that the Constitutional Treaty would provide the foundations for a more identifiable and forceful EU leadership, but in the event it hardly did so. Indeed, it arguably made it even worse, with there being four significant institutional centres of power if and when the Treaty enters into force:

- *The European Council President.* This person is to be elected by the European Council, by QMV if necessary, for a two and a half year term, which may be renewable once. The responsibilities of the post are vague, with the office holder charged, amongst other things, to 'chair and drive forward' the work of the European Council, and to 'facilitate cohesion and consensus within the European Council' *(Treaty Establishing a Constitution for Europe*: Article 1-21).
- *The Presidency of the Council of Ministers.* Provision is made for greater continuity and it is hoped for longer-term planning between still rotating Council presidencies, by assigning the presidency to groups of three member states for a period of 18 months, with each member of the group chairing for six months.
- *The Commission President.* This position is enhanced a little, notably by giving the President a greater role in the selection of the other European Commissioners. Also, as was noted above, from 2014 the number of Commissioners is to be restricted to two thirds of the number of member states, which insofar as this helps to promote College cohesion may also assist with College leadership.
- *Union Minister for Foreign Affairs.* The High Representative for the CFSP is to be replaced by a Union Minister for Foreign Affairs, who is to be appointed by the European Council acting by QMV, with the agreement of the President of the Commission. The post holder is to be responsible for the conduct of the Union's common foreign and security policy, and is to have a firm base in both the Council and Commission camps by virtue of chairing the Union's Foreign Affairs Council and being a Vice President of the Commission.

Whether these arrangements, which appear if anything to exacerbate the EU's current situation of having multiple leaderships, ever come into practice remains to be seen. They would appear, however, to do little to help resolve the leadership problem encapsulated in Henry Kissinger's famous and much quoted question of the early 1970s: who do I call when I want to call Europe?

CONCLUDING REMARKS

A central theme of this chapter has been that whilst the May 2004 enlargement has added extra dimensions to EU political dynamics and in some respects made them more complex, it has not in itself transformed them in a fundamental way. The fact is that EU political dynamics are always evolving in response to a range of factors, of which enlargement is but one.

The changing roles and influence of the EU's four main political institutions demonstrate this point. To be sure, the functioning of the institutions has been affected by enlargement in various ways, ranging from the nature of alliances in the European Council to the conduct of EP meetings arising from translation problems. But the powers and roles of the institutions have not greatly been altered. Changes of this sort in recent years – of which the most notable are the enhanced roles of the European Council and EP – are largely explained by non enlargement factors.

A particular point to emphasise and on which to conclude is that concerns expressed prior to the enlargement that the new member states would come to constitute a bloc in the EU-25, and almost an oppositional bloc to the EU-15 on some key issues, were always misplaced. They were so because both the EU-15 and the EU-10 are far too varied in both their objective situations and the political choices made by their governments to constitute anything like a bloc. Moreover, experience from previous enlargement rounds has shown that the governments of most new member states usually quickly learn 'the rules' of effective operation within the EU, and one of the most important of these rules is to have as many 'friends' as possible.

REFERENCES

Baun, M. (2004), 'Intergovernmental politics', in N. Nugent (ed.), *European Union Enlargement*, Basingstoke: Palgrave.

Eberlein, B. and Kerwer, D. (2004), 'New governance in the European Union: a theoretical perspective', *Journal of Common Market Studies*, Vol. 42, No. 1, pp. 121–42.

Grabbe, H. (2004), *The Constellations of Europe: How Enlargement will Transform the EU*, London: Centre for European Reform.

Junge, K. (2003), 'Differentiated integration', in M. Cini (ed.), *European Union Politics,* Oxford: Oxford University Press, pp. 383–96.

Peterson, J. (2005), *The Enlarged European Commission*, Paris: Notre Europe, Policy Paper No. 11, February.

Treaty Establishing a Constitution for Europe, Europa website at http://europa.eu.int/constitution.

Wallace, H. (2005), 'Exercising power and influence in the European Union: the roles of member states', in S. Bulmer and C. Lequesne (eds), *The Member States of the European Union*, Oxford: Oxford University Press.

6. Regulatory Adjustment in the Wider Europe Area

Constantine A. Stephanou

INTRODUCTORY REMARKS

Regulatory adjustment may be self-imposed or externally induced, in response to prescriptions of international organisations. Both processes may, however, be triggered by international regulatory competition. Externally induced adjustment usually leads to greater convergence of national regulations. Regulatory convergence is a broad and, to some extent, an ambiguous concept. In order to avoid confusion it is necessary to distinguish regulatory convergence from general regulatory trends. Thus, the current trend towards deregulation and elimination of administrative red-tape does not provide sufficient evidence of regulatory convergence. On the other hand, the enactment of similar regulations in order to enhance, for example, economic competition or financial stability may be considered as evidence of such convergence.

Until recently the scope of regulatory convergence was limited. Convergence occurred essentially in the field of international business law, as a result of the adoption of 'transaction standards' (Abbott and Snidal 2001, p. 351). Typical transaction standards are the uniform rules on sales contracts, bills of exchange, letters of credit, international transport law, intellectual property law, arbitration law, the goal being in this case to ensure legal certainty in business transactions. Gradually, however, the scope of regulatory convergence has expanded to areas where public interest is at stake and 'policy externalities' are involved (p.352). In most cases, demand for international standards is related to economic values, such as maintaining a level playing-field for domestic and foreign firms or ensuring systemic stability. Nevertheless, in many cases, non-economic values may also be at stake, as in the case of minimum labour standards, consumer health and safety, environmental protection.

Regulatory convergence in the aforementioned areas has often been attributed to globalisation. Thus, on the one hand, economic globalisation and capital mobility are usually perceived as the main driving forces behind the trend towards deregulation and, in some cases, the so-called 'race to the bottom'. On the other hand, it is believed that cultural globalisation has contributed to the emergence of common perceptions of risks in areas such as consumer safety and environmental protection which, in some cases, have generated a 'race to the top' (towards best practices).

Regulatory competition involving 'races to the bottom' or 'races to the top' is not an automatic outcome of globalisation or market integration and does not necessarily result in regulatory convergence. Thus, for example, globalisation has generated change in the area of corporate governance but such change has not led to substantial regulatory convergence. The basic differences remain between the Liberal Market Economies and the Organised Market Economies; according to Gourevitch (2003, p. 316) 'competition will not drive all but one system out, but rather will provide rewards to each according to its comparative advantage and may even accentuate differentiation'.

Firms seeking the so-called 'comparative regulatory advantage' (Murphy 2004) may wish, to reduce their costs by promoting competitive deregulation or decentralisation. But as pointed out by Esty and Geradin (2001, p. 31) in the real world the welfare enhancing effects of decentralisation cannot be presumed. Firms operating in relatively small markets are likely to favour regulatory heterogeneity in order to maintain entry barriers, whereas firms operating in large markets, such as the EU internal market are likely to promote regulatory convergence.

Moreover, with regard to technical standards, Sun and Pelkmans (1995, p. 84) have observed that in the EU context 'while the principles of free movement of goods and of mutual recognition of national regulations have set the stage for regulatory competition, such competition will not actually occur unless economic agents react to these differences; if they choose not to arbitrage them, these differences persist, and neither the hoped for regulatory convergence nor the level playing-field for business will occur'. Thus, mutual recognition of national regulations may actually reduce pressures towards regulatory convergence.

Regulatory adjustment, whether in the form of national deregulation or re-regulation at the EU level, is perceived as essential for ensuring the competitiveness of the European economy. Economists have offered a rather grim assessment of post-1985 regulatory reforms: despite the single market, selective sectoral regulatory reform and certain reforms at the national level, regulation in Europe still tended to discourage new entrants, impede new production methods and inhibit the exit of existing companies (Galli and

Pelkmans 2000). More recently, however, it was argued that Europe has done better than is often perceived, bearing in mind the steady process of reform in the product and financial markets, which will continue to lead to reforms in the labour market (Blanchard 2004).

The question that arises is whether the aforementioned reform process will continue and in what direction it is likely to move following the recent EU enlargement. The first part of the study aims at determining the various factors affecting regulatory adjustment processes. The second part focuses on the way in which such processes are likely to be affected by the attitudes of the new EU member States and the new neighbours towards regulatory competition and 'free riding'.

THE DYNAMICS OF REGULATORY ADJUSTMENT

Self-imposed Adjustment

As pointed out earlier, regulatory adjustment processes are affected in varying degrees by globalisation and market integration. Thus for example, although the welfare state is generally perceived as the anchor of the nation state, it is not immune to the pressures of globalisation. Sykes *et al.* (2001, p. 11) argue that globalisation processes and actors appear to play a significant role in the legitimation of welfare reforms. After reviewing the evidence from a number of case studies they draw the conclusion (pp. 203–4) that globalisation has created an agenda for change, rather than directly causing adaptations or restructuring; even between countries with similar types of welfare state regime, there have been different developments in the face of global pressures. According to another case study, welfare state reforms carried out in transition economies were enhanced by prescriptions of international financial institutions, in the form of the Washington Consensus.

As far as social protection is concerned, the prevailing view seems to be that the welfare systems of the EU-15 fit into three models: the Bismarck, the Beveridge and the Scandinavian models, the latter represented by Denmark until the accession of Sweden and Finland in 1996. In the early 1990s there was some evidence of spontaneous convergence and 'hybridisation' of the Bismarck and Beveridge models (Nicolacopoulou-Stephanou 1992). Since the mid-1990s the three models have been facing the challenge of economic sustainability but have undergone limited reforms. As pointed out by Scharpf (2002, p. 651) 'citizens in all countries have come to base their life plans on the continuation of existing systems of social protection and taxation and, would for that reason alone, resist major structural changes'. Scharpf's assessment of the literature on the comparative political economy of welfare states leads him to the conclusion that 'these studies do not provide empirical support for expectations of a general race to the bottom, but emphasize the path-dependent resistance of welfare state regimes to the downward pressures of economic competition' (p. 656).

On the other hand the revenue base of European welfare systems is eroding as a result of tax competition and the need to reduce non-wage costs (Scharpf 2002, p. 666).Recent welfare state reforms in France and Germany were accelerated by cost-cutting aimed at bringing back their public deficit to the 3 per cent ceiling provided in the Stability and Growth Pact. Notwithstanding the role of exogenous factors, reforms such as the raising of the retirement age and the introduction of flexible retirement can be identified as convergent responses to similar internal challenges, in particular the demographic challenge (ageing of populations) and the 'maturation' of pension systems (Rhodes 1997, Pierson 1998).

Spontaneous regulatory convergence has also occurred in the area of economic regulation. Thus, after the Second World War, cartels were perceived as impediments to trade and investment. Responding to the challenge the larger European economies, as well as the European Community itself, introduced antitrust legislation largely inspired from corresponding US legislation, dating back to the Sherman Act of 1890. Later, EU and US legislation inspired national antitrust legislation, including, more recently, the antitrust legislation of the acceding countries. There remain, however, essential differences in respect of enforcement, to the extent that in the USA infringement of antitrust law entails criminal liability, whereas in Europe such infringement is dealt with as an administrative offence, without implications for company directors. Finally, convergence trends can also be detected in the application of antitrust law, expressed in the form of guidelines, communications or regulations on mergers, vertical restraints, etc.

Regulatory convergence in the field of antitrust should not dissimulate, however, the fact that in many countries regulations exist in the rule-book but are wilfully not enforced. A typical example is that of Russia. As pointed out by Stiglitz (2002, p. 156) in Russia's case 'the IMF chose to emphasize privatization, giving short shrift to competition … The consequences of IMF's mistake here were far more serious than just high prices: privatized firms sought to establish monopolies and cartels, to enhance their profits, undisciplined by effective antitrust policies'. Moreover, although privatisation is supposed to eliminate the role of the State in the economy, in Russia's case 'privatization did reduce the power of central government, but the devolution left the local and regional governments with far wider discretion' (p. 158).

Convergence trends can also be detected in the areas of corporate and financial governance. Although the OECD corporate governance principles of 1999, revised in 2004, and EC regulation 2157/2001 on the European Company may help diffuse 'best practices', there is no evidence of convergence towards a single model of corporate governance. In the area of banking and finance, the recent repeal by the USA of the Glass Steagal Act requiring the separation between commercial and investment banks provides evidence of convergence towards the model of universal banking. On the other hand, as pointed out earlier, substantial regulatory convergence has not occurred in the area of financial governance. Nevertheless, the Enron debacle in the USA and the Parmalat debacle in Europe have set in motion a convergence dynamic. A number of European countries have enacted legislation along the lines of the Sarbanes-Oxley Act of 2002, broadening internal controls, disclosure requirements and the duties and obligations of auditors and supervision authorities. At the EU level, the Commission has recently outlined an agenda of measures to prevent and combat corporate and financial malpractice [COM (2004) 611].

At the Lisbon European Summit in March 2000 the Open Method of Coordination (OMC) was adopted for the purpose of ensuring convergence towards the goals of the European knowledge economy, in the absence of Community competence to adopt compulsory measures. Although in the framework of the OMC member states are free to choose the appropriate means in order to achieve the common goals and related 'indicators', the OMC provides for the exchange of best practices, enhancing thereby regulatory convergence.

Adjustment to Prescriptions of International Organisations

Voluntary adjustment

State adjustment. International standards are perceived as a means to enhance *free* trade in goods and services, thereby generating economic gains. Moreover, in areas such as social and environmental regulation, international standards may contribute to the goal of ensuring *fair* trade and a level playing-field for business. Often, these concepts are contested by developing and transition economies which regard them as new forms of protectionism. Moreover, the implementation of new standards may involve substantial industrial restructuring and costs in terms of resulting unemployment.

a) Technical standards. According to a recent OECD study on *Regulatory Reform and International Standardization* (1999, p. 4), 80 per cent of international trade is affected by mandatory regulations and non-mandatory standards. Although they are often referred to as behind-the-border barriers to trade, they may be related to consumer health and safety and/or environmental protection and thereby reflect legitimate non-economic goals and needs. International action in the field of technical regulations and standards has followed four courses:

- commitments to apply national treatment to imported goods covered by technical standards;
- commitments regarding the mutual recognition of technical standards;
- adoption of international uniform standards;
- regulatory cooperation between national authorities.

Regulatory convergence is the outcome of the third and fourth processes.

Technical standards have been at the centre stage of multilateral trade negotiations. Already at the Tokyo Round (1973–79) the EC was driven by its desire to enhance the competitive position of European firms vis-à-vis their US and Japanese rivals by means of European standards. In his study of the aforementioned negotiations Joseph Grieco applied the distinction between absolute and relative economic gains. In respect of the Standards Code (subsequently the Agreement on Technical Barriers to Trade or TBT agreement) he observed that although both the EC and the USA stood to gain from the strengthening of the agreement, the EC reasoned in terms of relative gains (Grieco 1990, p. 182–209). The EC believed that the USA would gain more than itself from the strengthening of the TBT agreement and the elimination of technical barriers. The EC priority was the elimination of such barriers at the EC level, in order to enhance the capacity of European firms to compete vis-à-vis American firms. Subsequently, Community-wide standards were developed in areas where European firms were lagging behind US and Japanese rivals (Austin and Milner 2001), although the opposite is true in the case of the European GSM standard (Pelkmans 2001).

International standards emanate from:

- intergovernmental or non-governmental organisations;
- world-wide or regional organisations.

Regional regulation has been perceived as a 'second best' option, in comparison to world-wide regulation. In practice there has been, however, intensive interaction in standard-setting between international and regional organisations, as well as between intergovernmental and non-governmental organisations (NGOs). On the one hand, at the intergovernmental level, the 55 member United Nations Economic Commission for Europe (UNECE) where the USA, Canada and Israel, as well as the former CIS countries participate and, on the other hand, NGOs, such as ISO and IEC, have laid down numerous standards for implementation by State and non-State actors.

Under the Agreement on Technical Barriers to Trade (TBT) Members are encouraged to adopt international uniform standards. Thus, article 2.4 provides that 'Where technical regulations are required and relevant international standards exist or their completion is imminent, Members shall use them, or the relevant parts of them, as a basis for their technical regulations...' Moreover, article 2.5. provides that 'Whenever a technical regulation is prepared, adopted or applied for one of the legitimate objectives explicitly mentioned in paragraph 2, and is in accordance with relevant international standards, it shall be rebuttably presumed not to create an unnecessary obstacle to international trade.' A similar – but arguably stronger – presumption is laid down in the Agreement on the Application of Sanitary and Phytosanitary Measures (SPS). Article 3.2 provides that SPS measures 'which conform to international standards, guidelines or recommendations shall be deemed to be necessary to protect human, animal or plant life or health, and presumed to be consistent with the relevant provisions of this Agreement and of GATT 1994.' Commenting on this provision Juliane Kokott, Advocate General at the Court of Justice of the European Communities (2005, p. 35), rightly stresses the 'factually binding effects' of the above standards.

Regulatory convergence is further promoted by the Code of Good Practice for the Preparation, Adoption and Application of Standards, annexed to the TBT Agreement. Moreover, in 2001, the UNECE which includes transition economies which are not members of the WTO, adopted Recommendation L embodying the International Model for technical harmonization based on good regulatory practice for the preparation, adoption and application of technical regulations via the use of international standards (Romanovska 2003).

In the context of the Transatlantic Business Dialogue (TABD) initiated in 1995, priority was been given to the negotiation between the EU and the US of a Mutual Recognition Agreement (MRA) covering testing, inspections and conformity assessments. Initial reluctance on both sides was overcome when each side became convinced about the comparability of economic gains resulting from improved market access in the sectors where the MRA would apply. A framework agreement was finalised at the EU–US summit in May 1998 and was published in the Official Journal of the EC on 4 February 1999. At the same summit the two sides adopted, moreover, a Declaration on the Transatlantic Economic Partnership and, in November of the same year, the relevant action plan which, in its section 3.1.1, provides for regulatory cooperation in the field of technical regulations and standards. On the basis of this plan the European Commission services and the US administration finalised in February 2002 a set of Guidelines on Regulatory Cooperation and Transparency. At the EU–US summit in May 2002 it was decided – in the context of the 'Positive Economic Agenda' – to pursue regulatory convergence in the areas of cosmetics, automobile safety, food labeling and metric systems.

b) Social regulation. Maintaining low labour standards in order to attract foreign direct investment is often viewed as a valid policy option for developing and transition economies. Nevertheless, a major OECD study (1996, p. 105) notes that 'the view which argues that low-standard countries will enjoy gains in export market shares to the detriment of high-standard countries appears to lack solid empirical support'. States are free to subscribe to International Labour Conventions and Recommendations aimed at improving working conditions. These instruments also aim, however, at creating a level playing-field for business and avoiding practices known as 'social dumping'. The relevant standards are implemented by means of national legislation. Most developing countries have been unwilling to implement the ILO conventions and recommendations. They fear that any raising of labour standards will lead transnationals to shift their production to other countries where there is less regulation. Interestingly, some European countries have refused to be bound by the ILO minimum wage convention.

The International Labour Conference adopted on 18 June 1998 a Declaration embodying four fundamental principles stemming from ILO conventions, namely: the freedom of association and the effective recognition of the right to collective bargaining; the elimination of all forms of forced or compulsory labour; the effective abolition of child labour; the elimination of discrimination in respect of employment and occupation. The obligation to implement these principles applies to all ILO members, including those who have not ratified the relevant ILO conventions. Developing countries were offered assistance by the EU for their implementation [COM (2001) 416]. On the other hand, under EU and US foreign trade legislation, the benefits of the Generalised System of Preferences (GSP) may be refused to countries which do not implement the core social rights embodied in the 1998 ILO Declaration; furthermore, additional benefits may be provided to countries which observe the said principles.

c) Banking and financial regulation. International standards in the areas of banking and finance aim, primarily, at ensuring international financial stability. States are keen to implement international financial and accounting standards embodied in instruments of 'soft law' (recommendations, codes of conduct, etc.) in order to demonstrate their commitment to sound financial management and financial stability. These standards are adopted by international bodies such as the Basle Committee on Banking Supervision, the International Organisation of Securities Commissions (IOSCO), the Financial Action Task Force (FATF) and NGOs such the International Accounting Standards Board (IASB). The instruments of 'soft law' are transposed into domestic law by the relevant regulatory authorities and become mandatory.

Business adjustment. In the period stretching from 1972 to 1992 efforts at regulating multinational / transnational corporations by means of voluntary codes of conduct adopted in the framework of international organisations had limited success (Haufler 2003, p. 235–41). Nevertheless, in 1976 the OECD adopted the Guidelines for Multinational Corporations, revised in 2000. These guidelines increased pressures on MNCs to behave responsibly. On the other hand, the ILO Tripartite Declaration of Principles concerning multinational enterprises and social policy adopted in 1977 and revised in 2000, gave some leverage to trade unions. Their position was further strengthened with the adoption of EC directives 94/45 on European Workers Councils and 2002/14 on the information and consultation of workers, which also apply to foreign based transnationals.

Trade unions and NGOs in developed countries have exerted pressure on governments of developing countries and on transnational corporations operating in these countries to ensure the correct implementation of the four fundamental principles embodied in the 1998 ILO Declaration. Non-implementation is reported to international organisations and the media, and respective governments and transnational corporations are named and 'shamed'. In response to the aforementioned pressures major transnational corporations have adopted self-regulatory strategies based on corporate codes of conduct developed within the corporations (Haufler 2003, p. 243–4),

The most striking development in the area of social and environmental governance has been the adoption of non-governmental systems of labour standards and monitoring (O'Rourke 2003); there are currently 30 codes of conduct that transnational corporations have concluded with trade unions, which commit the respective firms and their subcontractors worldwide to observe certain labour standards. On the other hand, a few hundred transnational corporations participate in the Global Reporting Initiative and implement the 2002 Sustainability Reporting Guidelines laying down common reporting standards on economic, social and environmental performance; a significant number also participate in the Global Compact Initiative and are committed to observe nine principles – which include the four core principles of the aforementioned ILO Declaration and the precautionary principle embodied in the Rio Declaration. Furthermore, numerous multi-stakeholder partnerships are dedicated to sustainable development goals. Commenting on these developments, Haufler (2003, p. 250) notes that 'corporate leaders view the threat of further regulation, especially traditional "command and control" type, as having the potential to hobble them in international competition. They prefer to adopt voluntary mechanisms that would avoid legal liability and preserve their flexibility in the face of rapidly changing technologies and markets'.

At the EU level as such, incentives for responsible business conduct regarding environmental protection have been introduced by the provisions on the Community eco-label award scheme (Regulation 880/1992 replaced by Regulation 1980/2000) and the provisions allowing voluntary participation by organisations in a Community eco-management and audit scheme (EMAS) (Regulation 1836/93 replaced by Regulation 761/2001). The latter adopted ISO 14.001 as a standard of reference. Recently the EU has called for new measures to promote the goal of sustainable development, in the context of corporate social responsibility [COM (2002) 347].

Adjustment to conditionalities of international organisations

Adjustment is often related to the prerequisites and conditionalities for membership of international organisations. The two most hotly debated cases are those related to EU and WTO accession. As far as EU membership is concerned, aspiring members are required not only to take up the Community 'rule book', commonly known as *acquis communautaire*, but also to comply with the so-called Copenhagen criteria, i.e. a set of political and economic conditionalities laid down at the Copenhagen European Council meeting of June 1993. Progress by candidate states is monitored by the European Commission which is required to submit a progress report each year.

An interesting distinction has recently been made with respect to countries aspiring to become members of the EU. Thus, Hughes *et al.* (2004, p. 526) distinguish between 'formal conditionality which embodies the publicly stated preconditions as set out in the broad principles of the Copenhagen criteria and the legal framework of the *acquis* and informal conditionality which includes the operational pressures and recommendations applied by actors in the Commission to achieve particular outcomes during interactions with their CEEC counterparts...' The issue area examined by the aforementioned authors was regional policy. The decentralisation policies recommended by the Commission were seen as evidence of informal conditionality.

Transition economies experienced conditionalities when they applied to become members of international economic organisations. Most had started their adjustment spontaneously, by transposing western norms for the protection of property rights, corporate and financial governance, etc. Nevertheless, there seem to be problems in some transition economies with the enforcement of the aforementioned norms. The recommendations of the Round Table on Industrial Restructuring in European Transition Economies (UNECE 2002, pp. 33–4), indicate that

> Restructuring of the existing enterprises and the creation of new competitive industries depend in large measure on the regulatory and institutional environment created by Governments... Macroeconomic stabilization, undistorted price and tariff structure, competitive environment neutral to all resident companies, both domestically and foreign owned, sustainable enforcement of property rights, including the rights of minority shareholders and intellectual property rights, transparent rules governing new firm formation, and clear regulations allowing for an orderly market exit (bankruptcies) are the key preconditions of successful restructuring and attracting investment to the restructured enterprises, including the strategic direct investment from abroad.

In order, however, to be accepted as functioning market economies transition economies had to introduce further reforms. Reforms related to WTO accession are dealt with in a separate section.

Conditionalities are also imposed by international organisations to members seeking their assistance. Thus, conditionalities related to economic policy are imposed to State borrowers by the IMF; some were perceived as 'shock therapies' and were strongly criticized. Thus, Stiglitz (2002, p. 187) points out that 'In my judgment the successes in countries that did not follow IMF prescriptions were no accident. There was a clear link between the policies pursued and the outcomes, between the successes in China and Poland and what they did, and the failure in Russia, and what it did. The outcomes in Russia were, as we have noted, what the critics of shock therapy predicted – only worse.' Another example of conditionalities is that of the covenants subscribed by borrowers seeking project financing by the World Bank. Conditionalities are also instrumental in the area of EU external relations. Political and economic conditionalities have been incorporated in Association Agreements with developing countries, Partnership and Cooperation Agreements with transition economies, Stabilisation and Association Agreements with countries of the Western Balkans, etc.

Mandatory adjustment

In the EU, the *Cassis de Dijon* ruling of 20 February 1979 imposed the mutual recognition of the norms and standards of member States, allowing however exceptions for reasons of consumer health and safety, etc., in accordance with article 30 (ex-36) of the EC Treaty. In such cases, free trade depended on the adoption of European standards. Member States had accepted the idea of European standard-setting in the original text of the EC Treaty. Until the mid-1980s, however, standard-setting was practised by means of detailed directives adopted by unanimity at the Council.

The challenges of globalisation and competitiveness led the Council to adopt on 7 May 1985 a resolution on the so-called 'new approach' in the field of technical standards, combining mandatory recognition of national standards with more expedient mechanisms for the adoption of European standards. Under the 'new approach', national standards compatible with EU requirements were henceforth automatically recognised by member States; moreover, EU directives, adopted by qualified majority since the entry into force of the Single European Act in 1987, were limited to essential requirements of consumer and environmental protection. Most importantly, however, EU-wide standardisation was facilitated by the enhanced role of European NGOs in standard-setting. Thus, technical standards adopted by CEN, CENELEC and ETSI, in conformity with essential requirements laid down by EU directives, receive automatic recognition in member States. The 'new approach' has entailed, on the one hand, a shift from national to regional (Europe-wide) regulation and, on the other, a shift from centralised to decentralised regulation, involving the main stakeholders (Mattli 2003).

At this stage, it is worth noting that the 'new approach' also inspired regulatory action in the area of services; the principle of mutual recognition and its emanation, the country of origin or 'home country' control principle is not, however, conducive to regulatory convergence. In the realm of banking and insurance services the aforementioned principle was accompanied by regulatory approximation in areas such as capital adequacy, deposit insurance, etc. Recently, a controversial directive, known under the name of its sponsor, former Commissioner Bolkenstein, aims at extending the country of origin principle to the provision of a large array of services where liberalisation was incomplete due to regulatory discrepancies [COM (2004) 2]. The basic criticism addressed to the proposed directive is that regulations of some CEEs affecting labour costs are below standard and are likely to generate social dumping and 'races to the bottom' in the provision of services. The directive aims at ensuring legal certainty to service providers, to the extent that the obstacles to be eliminated have already been declared incompatible with EU law by the European Court of Justice.

Reference to regulatory approximation can also be found in bilateral agreements concluded by the EU with third countries. Thus, article 53 of the Partnership and Cooperation Agreement (PCA) between the EC and Russia lays down rules regarding competition law, including state aids, state monopolies and state enterprises; article 54 confirms the commitments under the international conventions for the protection of intellectual property and, finally, under article 55, Russia undertakes to progressively ensure the compatibility of its legislation to that of the EU, in practically all the areas where the EU has enacted legislation. The 'Common Spaces' agreement signed in Moscow on 10 May 2005 provides, among other things, a road map for establishing the Common European Economic Space between the EU and Russia, with commitments by the latter to harmonise its laws with EU legislation.

THE CHALLENGES OF REGULATORY COMPETITION AND 'FREE RIDING' IN THE WIDER EUROPE AREA

The Impact of the Accession of CEE Countries on Regulatory Adjustment in the EU

Policy dilemmas

One of the motives behind international and regional standard-setting is the need to avoid destructive regulatory competition among member States, also referred to as the 'race to the bottom'. Concerns, however, for such a race have often been exaggerated. Thus, for example, there is no evidence of such destructive competition taking place in the field of environmental standards (Vogel 1997, 2001; Scharpf 1999, p. 96). International regulatory diversity in this area can help promote the gradual tightening of regulations, as each trading partner raises its standards in response to actions of the other, the classic example being that of the gasoline emissions regulations of California. Moreover some environmental process regulations may be maintained although they may drive certain types of production out of the country (Scharpf 1999, p. 99).

In contrast to environmental standards, considerations of regulatory competition seem to play an important role in social and fiscal policies. Heavy taxation of capital income or company income, or too demanding social standards, may be self-defeating, in the sense that they may deter private investment and job creation. Shifts to lower taxation on capital income or company income may attract private investment but may also entail negative externalities; thus a greater part of the tax burden may fall on workers rather than on capital; or public investment in infrastructures may be reduced, thereby deterring private investment. On the other hand, shifts to lower labour standards, such as longer working time, are likely to enhance competitiveness but may also generate social unrest. In the EU context, although old and new member States supposedly share the same values, it is far from certain that they would adopt similar responses to the aforementioned policy dilemmas.

Social policy coordination

Labour standards. Developed countries have implemented most ILO Conventions setting minimum standards. Moreover, European countries are bound by the European Social Charter and other instruments concluded under the auspices of the Council of Europe. In the EU region directives have been successfully elaborated and implemented in some areas of social policy, such as health and safety at work and employment conditions. Nevertheless, the British opt-out from EU social policy from 1993 to 1999 may be seen as evidence of social dumping, to the extent that British policy aimed at enhancing the competitiveness of British firms by exempting them from European standards. In actual fact, UK policy may have contributed to the decline of the regulatory output during that period. There is reason to believe that the UK attitude has restrained the other member States from enacting additional European standards which would have put their firms at a disadvantage in comparison to British firms, including US and Japanese subsidiaries in the UK. Furthermore, during the post-Maastricht period, very few directives were elaborated by the social partners, under the innovative provisions on social dialogue introduced by the Maastricht Treaty. More importantly, these directives reflected the current situation in most member States and only in marginal cases did they raise labour standards.

Related to the issue of minimum labour standards is that of minimum wages. Interestingly, the UK had stayed out of the relevant ILO Convention until the advent of the Blair government. On the basis of econometric evidence demonstrating that the unit labour cost is roughly comparable between the USA and India, (Irwin 2002, pp. 210–12) draws the conclusion that 'low wages reflect low labour productivity' and that "the growth in domestic wages tracks the growth in domestic productivity". Other studies have shown that in the EU-12 (Bouigues *et al.* 1990) and in the EU-14/15 (O'Mahony and Van Ark 2003) there were considerable differences in wages but unit labour costs were comparable, with the exception of Ireland (less than half the EU average for 1999–2001).

Enlargement gave new salience to the issue of wage competition in the European region: average Polish wages are a quarter of French wages; average Romanian wages are a tenth of French wages. Thus, unit labour costs of Polish and Romanian labour intensive industries may be significantly lower than those in the EU-15. The recent Report of the High Level Group chaired by Wim Kok on the Lisbon strategy for growth and employment (Kok 2004, p. 9) argues that

> Europe did not want to compete both internally as an economic union and externally, by initiating a race to lower real wage and non-wage costs so that Member States would find their systems of social cohesion, partnership in the workplace and protection of the environment undermined. The more Europe could sustain itself as high productivity, high value-added, high employment economy, the better able it would be to create the wealth and jobs that would allow it both to sustain its vital commitment to open markets and to social and environmental Europe

The Report adds in respect of enlargement that CEE countries 'as they replace redundant ageing technology with state of the art processes they will jump a generation in terms of their technological capacity. There is every prospect of their growth in output and productivity continuing. Nonetheless, their low tax and wage rates attracting inward investment from the rest of the EU are likely to be a source of growing friction' (Kok 2004, p. 15). In this respect, it should be noted that article 137 para. 5 of the EC Treaty explicitly excludes Community competence on wages.

A hotly debated issue in the EU is the recent proposal of the Commission on the amendment of directive 2003/88 on the organisation of working time [COM 2004 (607)]. The UK had challenged unsuccessfully the initial directive adopted in 1993 (before the entry into force of the British opt-out provision). UK opposition to the directive continued ever since and the amended directive of 2003 included two review provisions. In the aforementioned proposal the Commission took into account the views expressed during the pre-legislative phase by eight EU member States, including five new members, in favour of greater flexibility. The proposal allows for opting-out from the 48 hour week. The European Parliament rejected the provision but the relevant amendment is unlikely to be adopted by the Council, making highly probable the recourse to the conciliation procedure. The new coalition of eight liberal-minded member States may not be strong enough to erode existing standards, but it may successfully oppose the adoption of stricter norms. Thus, in respect of labour standards the prospect is that of a stalemate, rather than a movement towards regulatory convergence or divergence.

Social protection. EU involvement has been minimal in the field of social protection. Unanimity is required under article 137 of the EC Treaty for exercising Community competence in the area of social security and social protection. MISSOC and cooperation initiatives undertaken by the Commission in accordance with article 140, have contributed to the diffusion of best practices. Convergence has also been enhanced by 'soft law', namely the Council recommendations on social protection of 1992. More recently, the conclusions of the Lisbon European Council meeting in March 2000 included a commitment to 'modernising the European social model'. There is much ambiguity regarding this concept, but it appears to cover social welfare in the wider sense. At any rate, progress achieved in the areas of employment and social inclusion may, to some extent, be attributed to the implementation in these areas of the 'open method of cooordination' (OMC), whereby member States set common goals and common indicators of achievement and assess national performances by means of benchmarking and peer review.

The Treaty of Nice which entered into force in February 2003 has introduced in article 137 a reference to the 'modernisation' of social protection; the Commission had already used this term to describe efforts aimed at ensuring the sustainability of pension systems [COM (1999) 347].

On the other hand, the aforementioned treaty has facilitated resort to 'enhanced cooperation', which can henceforth take place with eight member States. Scharpf (2002, pp. 660–63) has observed that in social and employment policies closer cooperation would be issue-specific. Rather than creating solid blocks of countries it would result in overlapping clusters; it would also support CEE countries 'in developing economically and politically viable institutions of social protection without being required to conform to a European blueprint' (Scharpf 2002, p. 603, quoting Muller 1999). Nevertheless, should this course remain unavailable, Scharpf recommends a combination of two modes of governance: on the one hand, the adoption and implementation of framework directives setting differentiated standards 'that take account of differences in countries' ability to pay at different stages of economic development and of existing institutions and policy legacies of member States' (p. 663); on the other hand, implementation of the Open Method of Coordination "within sub-groups of member states with roughly similar welfare institutions and policy legacies" (p. 665). Thus, under this scheme, rather than being excluded from convergence initiatives, CEE countries would be required to converge, with due regard, however, to their capabilities.

Fiscal policy coordination
The conceptual framework. In this section we are concerned with direct taxes on capital income and company income. A recent assessment of tax competition by the World Bank, after acknowledging that fiscal competition may have a disciplining function on government spending, questions the theoretical models suggesting that tax competition might result in a race to the bottom. Thus, 'although marginal corporate tax rates have fallen over the past decade, bases have often been broadened. As a result, corporate tax revenues have increased or remained steady on average, except in European transition economies, where the decrease of revenues was more from privatization than from economic integration' (World Bank 2004). Moreover, a study commissioned by the European Parliament observed that 'tax competition has effectively "capped" the tendency for taxes to rise in relatively high-tax countries, and produced convergence within the EU' (European Parliament 2001, p. xiv). In a resolution of 18 June 1998 the European Parliament welcomed 'beneficial tax competition among member States as a tool to increase the competitiveness of the European economy confronted with the challenges of globalisation'. The new CEE member states are, nevertheless, accused of using low tax rates and preferential tax bases in order to attract foreign investment in key economic sectors. The question that arises is not so much whether these accusations are well

founded but, rather, whether the slow process of tax coordination is likely to be deadlocked following the recent EU enlargement.

For many years capital income tax and company income tax were considered by the EC (and the OECD) from the point of view of double taxation, rather than fiscal competition. Although the EC lacks explicit authority for the approximation of direct taxes, past initiatives have been based on the general provisions requiring unanimity at the Council for the adoption of approximation directives. There was, furthermore, opposition to the granting of exemptions or opt-outs, because it was felt that countries exempted from harmonisation would function as tax havens. Although the 1985 White Book on the establishment of the Single European Market appealed to the member States to eliminate tax obstacles, harmonisation in the field of capital income tax and company income tax has proceeded very slowly. In the course of 1997 the Commission proposed a package of measures to handle harmful tax competition [COM (97) 495]. These were deemed too far-reaching and the Commission proposed a revised package [COM (97) 567] which included: a Code of Conduct for business taxation; the elimination of distortions to the taxation of capital income (minimum withholding tax on bank interest); measures to eliminate withholding taxes on cross-border interest and royalty payments between companies. The central proposal of this package was the Code of Conduct for business taxation which took the form of a Council Resolution adopted on 1 December 1997. The Code covers 'those business tax measures which affect, or which may affect, the location of business activity in the Community in a significant way', also identified as 'those tax measures which provide for a significantly lower effective level of taxation, including zero taxation, than that which generally apply in the country in question'. Thus, the Code aims at combating preferential tax treatment, some forms of which may constitute State aids and be liable to prosecution by the Commission. In 1998 the Commission issued a notice on the application of State aid rules to measures relating to direct business taxation (OJ 1998, C 384) and has since enforced the rules in individual cases. Interestingly, the view that some forms of preferential tax treatment may constitute state aids was upheld in the WTO context, where the Appellate Body determined in its decision of 14.2.2002 (case DS 108) that the US system of corporate tax was discriminatory and incompatible with the Agreement on Subsidies.

Capital income tax. The fundamental issue is whether low-tax jurisdictions should agree to repeal their privacy laws and surrender their fiscal sovereignty so that high-tax nations can more easily enforce their tax laws – including taxation of income earned outside their borders. The situation before the entry into force of the EU directive on the taxation of capital income, also known as savings directive has been, in a nutshell, that competition took place on the basis of comparative tax advantages, rather than on the basis of comparative costs of the financial intermediation industry. Thus, as pointed out by Kanavos (1997, p. 281), as a result of the distinction in fiscal treatment between residents and non-residents, the ongoing competitive process threatened to degenerate into a situation where each country acted as a tax haven for financial asset holders residing in the 14 other member States, given the free movement of capital in the EU. In actual fact, Britain and Luxembourg were the prime beneficiaries of the system, because they combined the favourable tax treatment with an efficient financial intermediation industry. These two countries were concerned that harmonisation would lead to capital flight to non-EU countries.

After a long gestation period the EU adopted on 3 June 2003 Directive 2003/48 on the taxation of income in the form of interest from savings. According to article 10 of the directive, entry into force is subject to the conclusion of bilateral agreements with Switzerland and the European micro-States. Switzerland refused to participate in the automatic exchange of information but agreed to apply a withholding tax on the aforementioned income of non-residents, at the rates agreed within the EU for countries maintaining bank secrecy, namely the UK, Austria and Luxembourg. Accordingly, the directive entered into force on 1 July 2005.

As far as competition by non-European countries is concerned, it is worth noting that in 1998 the OECD issued a report and recommendations on 'harmful tax competition' (OECD 1998) and, since then, has been pursuing efforts aimed at the elimination of tax havens. The success of these initiatives is, however, far from certain, in view of the ambiguous US position. The OECD, branding the threat of retaliation by affected member States, convinced some low-tax countries in Asia and the Caribbean to sign 'commitment letters' indicating that they would take the aforementioned steps, but these countries stated that the letters were not binding unless all OECD nations agreed to abide by the same rules. Although the EU savings directive was adopted and the requirement of Swiss participation was achieved, several OECD nations, as well as tax havens in Asia and the Caribbean, would be exempt from any requirement to share information, meaning that the so-called level playing-field does not exist. Free market proponents observe that more and more nations are lowering tax rates and therefore pressure to attack low tax jurisdictions will abate. They expect that the number of nations interested in tax harmonisation will shrink and the process will collapse.

Company income tax. In contrast to the above, EU efforts aimed at the approximation of tax rates and tax bases have not borne results. The Ruding

Committee report (1992) had recommended the introduction of a minimum rate of 30 per cent and a maximum rate of 40 per cent, bearing in mind that the Community average at that time was 35 per cent. The Commission's views were recently expressed in a publication on 'Company taxation in the internal market' (2002), based on the communication *Towards an Internal Market without Tax Obstacles* [COM (2001) 582], which in turn, supplements and builds on a Commission Services Study [SEC (2001) 1681].

According to the Commission's Services Study, as economic integration in the internal market proceeded, taxation systems only adapted to this process very gradually. The pattern of international investments is therefore likely to be increasingly sensitive to cross-border differences in corporate tax rules, in an environment now characterised by the full mobility of capital. From the point of view of economic efficiency, tax systems should ideally be neutral in terms of economic choices. The choice of an investment, its financing and its location should in principle not be driven by tax considerations. The analysis by the Commission does not provide evidence of the impact of taxation on actual economic decisions, although empirical studies show that there is a correlation between taxation and location decisions.

The Commission's estimates of effective corporate tax rates builds on the methodology involving the calculation of the effective tax burden for a hypothetical future investment project in the manufacturing sector. It calculates effective tax rates at a given post-tax rate of return, whereas other studies compute the effective tax rate for a given pre-tax rate of return. The most important features of taxation systems such as the rates, major elements of the taxable bases and tax systems are included in the study. Finally, effective tax rates are calculated for marginal investment projects (where the post-tax rate of return just equals the alternative market interest rate) and infra-marginal investment projects (which earn extra profits).

With regard to domestic investments the Commission Services Study concludes that the different national nominal tax rates on profits can explain many of the differences in effective corporate tax rates. The Commission cites with approval the findings of a study by Baker Mackenzie which concluded that, in general, the composition of the tax base does not have a great impact on the effective tax burden and that the level of the tax rate is the truly important factor for the difference in the tax burden.

With regard to transnational investments the Commission Services Study observes that the effective tax burden of a subsidiary depends on where that subsidiary is located. Similarly, subsidiaries operating in a given country face different effective tax burdens depending on where the parent company is located. Moreover, outbound and inbound investments are more heavily taxed than otherwise identical domestic investments. To the extent, however, that companies are free to choose the most tax-favoured form of finance, then through international tax planning foreign multinationals operating in a host country are likely to face a lower effective tax burden than domestic companies.

The Commission Services Study concludes that that the most relevant tax component which provides an incentive to locate across the border and to choose a specific form of financing is the overall nominal tax rate – except in specific situations when, for instance, a country applies particularly favourable depreciation regimes. Interestingly, in its subsequent communication the Commission refrained from proposing the harmonisation of nominal tax rates, while also asserting that the scenario of a common tax base would 'tend to increase the dispersion in effective tax rates if overall nominal tax rates are kept constant'. The Commission added, however, that 'in a dynamic context it is possible that the transparency associated with the harmonisation of the taxable base would induce a convergence of the statutory corporate tax rates, thus implying a reduction in the dispersion of effective tax rates'.

Although the harmonisation of nominal tax rates would go some way towards reducing locational inefficiencies in the EU, priority was given to the harmonisation of savings tax, to the extent that competition in the area of portfolio investment does indeed take place on the basis of comparative tax advantages. In fact, opposition to the harmonisation of company taxes has grown since the recent EU enlargement. The coalition of States opposed to tax harmonisation is actually larger than in the case of social policy harmonisation, because it includes the small Mediterranean member States. On the other hand, the pressures in favour of harmonisation are far more intense. France and Germany have made it known that they would oppose the increase of the resources of the Community structural funds demanded by the CEE member States, as long as these countries reject harmonisation of company tax. These countries were accused of siphoning jobs from France and Germany, an accusation that is not corroborated by evidence on investment flows. According to the annual report of UNCTAD for 2003 on foreign direct investment, no large-scale diversion of FDI from the older EU members to CEE countries occurred during 2003. Moreover, in absolute terms FDI in these countries slipped from a record high of $31 billion in 2002 to $21 billion in 2003, compared to a decline from $310 billion to $280 billion in Western Europe. Some CEE countries also argue that they have a lower tax rate (for example 19 per cent in Poland) but also a broader tax base, and that the effective tax burden is as high as that of countries with 25 per cent or 30 per cent tax rates. Others argue that the most effective way to measure the corporate tax burden is to measure the ratio of corporate tax earnings to GDP. Thus, Poland's corporate tax revenue amounted to 2 per cent of GDP, whereas that of Germany amounted to 0.7 per cent of GDP. Competition from CEEs recently led Germany to reduce its rate from 25 per cent to 19 per cent.

At this stage, the Commission is not likely to submit proposals for the harmonisation of tax rates. It might be possible, however, to make progress on a common tax base. Such a measure would enhance the transparency of national taxation systems and increase pressures for the harmonisation of tax rates, in accordance with the neo-functionalist expectation of 'spill-over'. As a last resort, it may be possible to overcome the unanimity requirement by making use of the mechanism of 'enhanced cooperation' for the adoption of the relevant directives [COM (2003) 726, 24 November 2003]. This, however, makes more sense in respect of the common tax base than regarding the harmonisation of tax rates where the problem of 'free riding' is likely to undermine the logic of harmonisation.

Adjustment of Transition Economies to the Prerequisites of Membership of the WTO

Nature of adjustments

In some transition economies there is an ongoing discussion on the merits of acceding to the basic international trade regime, namely the WTO. Accession to WTO entails abandoning some of the aforementioned policy options. Countries have to adjust not only their foreign trade legislation, but also their domestic legislation in areas such as taxation, technical standards, sanitary and phytosanitary measures, government procurement, investment laws in accordance with the TRIMS agreement, intellectual property rights in accordance with the TRIPS agreement, etc.

Special difficulties arise in relation to the commitments regarding State trading enterprises. As pointed out by Ognitsev *et al.* (UNCTAD 2001, pp. 201–2), under Article XVII of GATT the criterion is not ownership but rather how and under what conditions the enterprise operates. Thus, privatising an enterprise, transforming it into a joint stock company or having it operate within special funds does not change its position as a state trading enterprise if it still enjoys exclusive or special rights or statutory or constitutional powers through which, with its purchases or sales, it influences the level of imports or exports. State-owned enterprises which do not enjoy special rights or privileges do not fall within the disciplines of Article XVII. Moreover, WTO members have paid special attention to all types of monopolies that the acceding countries may have in the areas of production, distribution and/or foreign trade – relating these questions often to state trading but also to government procurement, state subsidies, etc. Commitments are included in a country's accession protocol.

Capacity to fulfil obligations

Newly acceding countries, including transition economies, are required to comply with WTO rules upon accession or within a very short period of time. As observed by the former Hungarian Ambassador to the WTO, Peter Naray, (UNCTAD 2001, pp. 148–9), their political, social, institutional problems are routinely disregarded. 'Systemic inconsistencies' with multilateral rules and obligations as was the case with some Eastern European countries when they joined GATT in the 1960s and 1970s cannot be sustained. Because of the great outside pressure to undertake liberal commitments and the substantial interest of acceding countries in WTO accession, they accept the accession conditions even if they are not sure of being able to implement them fully. Therefore, there is a danger that the present accession policy will produce members which are WTO compatible only on paper. Naray (UNCTAD 2001, p. 150) rightly points out that acceding countries should not be requested to accept more commitments than they can fulfil. Thus, WTO accession should not entail liberalisation, but rather sustainable liberalisation should be the objective.

From the above inquiry it became apparent that candidates for WTO membership had to adjust not only their foreign trade legislation, but also their domestic economic regulations. Thus, for countries seeking WTO membership the challenge of regulatory adjustment is almost as important as adjustment for EU membership. In contrast, however, to WTO accession, EU accession is often accompanied with transitional periods and pre-accession aid which facilitate adjustment. Commenting on the EU negotiating position in respect of Russia's accession to the WTO, Shemiatenkov noted that 'as a result of the EU requests to the Russian Federation became overloaded with issues, which are either unrelated to the WTO membership or simply untenable' (Shemiatenkov 2002, p. 148). Nevertheless, at the EU–Russia summit in May 2001 the two parties approved a related project, that of creating a Common European Economic Space (CEES), whose overall aim 'is to link the EU and Russia in a privileged relationship, focusing on regulatory and legislative convergence and trade and investment facilitation' (Report of the High-Level Group, quoted by Shemiatenkov 2002, p. 149). At the EU–Russia summit in May 2004 an agreement was finally reached on Russia's accession to WTO; similar negotiations have also taken place with the USA. Nevertheless, the slow progress of Russia's WTO accession negotiations, in comparison to those leading to China's accession, remains a puzzle. Perhaps as Shemiatenkov pointed out, the West is demanding too much. At any rate, in terms of 'relative economic gains', Russia may gain less than its partners from free and fair trade and it may be in its interest to remain a 'free rider'. On the other hand, to the extent that WTO accession is a prerequisite for building the Common European Economic Space with the

EU, in accordance with the road map adopted in the May 2005 summit, it may be in Russia's interest to conclude WTO accession negotiations by accepting, among other things, to repeal the dual pricing of energy. The final decision, however, is likely to be based on political considerations.

CONCLUSIONS

The first part of the study aimed at determining the conditions under which regulatory adjustment occurs, by distinguishing self-imposed adjustment from externally induced adjustment in response to prescriptions of international organisations. Evidence of self-imposed adjustment is provided by similar measures adopted in the context of welfare state reform, antitrust law and corporate and financial governance. Externally induced adjustment is essentially related to the 'conditionalities' and prerequisites for membership of international organisations. The countries concerned often face difficult policy dilemmas, including the temptation to behave as 'free riders'. Mandatory adjustment is typical of the EU process of approximation of national laws but, under the so-called 'new approach' is limited to essential requirements of consumer and environmental protection.

The second part of the study dealt with the issue of regulatory adjustment in the wider Europe context. The first case study aimed at determining to what extent the accession of CEE countries will affect perceptions and responses in respect of regulatory competition. The case study on social policy concluded that a new coalition of eight liberal-minded member States may not be strong enough to erode existing standards, but it may successfully oppose the adoption of stricter norms.

In comparison to social policy, pressures for harmonisation are far more intense in the area of fiscal policy. The directive on income from savings entered into force in July 2005, in view of the fact that European tax havens had agreed to cooperate in its implementation. On the other hand, as in the case of labour standards, a coalition of old and new member States is likely to block progress on the harmonisation of company taxation, although it might be possible to introduce a common tax base in consenting member States by resorting to the mechanism of 'enhanced cooperation'. More generally, however, the benefits that non-participants are likely to secure from 'free riding' may restrain regulatory approximation in the areas of social and fiscal policy.

From the subsequent analysis regarding the prerequisites for WTO membership it became apparent that transition economies which are candidates for WTO membership have to adjust not only their foreign trade regulation, but also their domestic economic regulation. Thus, for countries seeking WTO membership the challenge of regulatory adjustment is almost as important as adjustment for EU membership. In contrast to WTO accession, however, EU accession is often accompanied by transitional periods and pre-accession aid which facilitate adjustment. As far as Russia's bid to join the WTO is concerned, in terms of 'relative economic gains', Russia may gain less than its partners from free and fair trade and it may be in its interest to remain a 'free rider'. The final decision is likely, however, to be politically motivated.

In conclusion, there is reason to believe that the varying perceptions of new member States and new neighbours in respect of economic and social reforms associated with regulatory approximation are likely to impede substantially regulatory convergence in the wider Europe area.

REFERENCES

Abbott, K. W. and Snidal, D. (2001), 'International standards and international governance', *Journal of European Public Policy*, Vol. 8, No. 3, pp. 345–70.

Austin, M. and Milner, H. (2001), 'Strategies of European standardization', *Journal of European Public Policy*, Vol. 8, No. 3, pp. 411–31.

Blanchard, O. (2004), *The Economic Future of Europe*, MIT Dept. of Economics, Working Paper Series, Working Paper 04-04.

Bouigues, P., Ilzkovitz, F. and Lebrun, F. (1990), 'The impact of the internal market by industrial sector", *European Economy*, Special Edition.

Commission of the European Communities (2001), *Company Taxation in the Internal Market*, [SEC (2001) 1681].

Commission of the European Communities (2001), *Promoting Core Labour Standards and Improving Social Governance in the Context of Globalisation*, COM (2001) 416, 18.7.2001.

Commission of the European Communities (2001), *Towards an Internal Market without Tax Obstacles. A Strategy for Providing Companies with a Consolidated Corporate Tax Base for their EU-wide Activities*, COM (2001) 582, 23.10.2001.

Commission of the European Communities (2002), *Company Taxation in the Internal Market*, Luxembourg: Office for Official Publications of the EC.

Commission of the European Communities (2002), *Corporate Social Responsibility. A Business Contribution to Sustainable Development*, COM (2002) 347, 2.7.2002.

Commission of the European Communities (2003), *An Internal Market without Company Tax Obstacles. Achievements, On-going Initiatives and Remaining Challenges*, COM (2003) 726, 24.11.2003.

Commission of the European Communities (2004), *Preventing and Combating Corporate and Financial Malpractice*, COM (2004) 611, 27.09.2004.

Commission of the European Communities (2004), *Proposal for a Directive of the European Parliament and the Council on the Amendment of Directive 2003/88/EC Regarding some Elements of the Organisation of Working Time*, COM (2004) 607 final, 22.9.2004.

Esty, D. and Geradin, D. (eds.), (2001), *Regulatory Competition and Economic Integration*, Oxford: Oxford University Press.

European Parliament (2001), 'Tax co-ordination in the European Union', Working Paper, *Economic Affairs Series*, ECON 125 EN, 03-2001.

Galli, G. and Pelkmans, J. (eds), (2000), *Regulatory Reform and Competitiveness in Europe*, 2 vols., Cheltenham, UK and Northampton MA, USA: Edward Elgar.

Gourevitch, P. (2003), 'Corporate governance. Global markets, national politics', in M. Kahler and D. Lake (eds), *Governance in the Global Economy*, Princeton, NJ: Princeton University Press, pp. 305–31.

Grieco, J. (1990), *Cooperation among Nations. Europe, America and the Non-tariff Barriers toTtrade*, Ithaca: Cornell University Press.

Haufler, V. (2003), 'Globalization and industry self-regulation', in M. Kahler and D. Lake (eds), *Governance in the Global Economy*, Princeton, NJ: Princeton University Press, pp. 226–52.

Hughes, J., Sasse, G. and Gordon, C. (2004), 'Conditionality and compliance in the EU's eastward enlargement: regional policy and the reform of sub-national government', *JCMS*, Vol. 42, No. 3, pp. 523–51.

Irwin, D. A. (2002), *Free Trade under Fire*, Princeton, NJ: Princeton University Press.

Kanavos, P. (1997), 'Tax harmonisation: The Single Market challenge', in S. Stavridis, E. Mossialos, R. Morgan and H. Machin (eds), *New Challenges to the European Union: Policies and Policy-Making*, Aldershot: Dartmouth Publishing, pp. 269–96.

Kok, W. (2004), *Report of the High Level Group chaired by Wim Kok on the Lisbon Strategy for Growth and Employment*, Luxembourg: Office for Official Publications of the European Communities.

Kokott, J. (2005), 'Soft law standards under public international law', in P. Nobel, *International Standards and the Law*, Berne: Staempfli, pp. 15–41.

Mattli, W. (2003), 'Public and private governance in setting international standards', in M. Kahler and D. Lake (eds), *Governance in the Global Economy*, Princeton, NJ: Princeton University Press, pp. 199–225.

Muller, K. (1999), *The Political Economy of Pension Reform in Central-Eastern Europe*, Cheltenham, UK and Northampton, MA, USA: Edward Elgar.

Murphy, D. (2004), *The Structure of Regulatory Competition*, Oxford: Oxford University Press.

Nicolacopoulou-Stephanou, I. G. (1992), *Convergence of Social Security Systems in Western Europe*, Athens: Sideris Publications (in Greek).

O'Mahony, M. and Van Ark, B. (eds), (2003), *EU Productivity and Competitiveness: An Industry Perspective*, Luxembourg: Office for Official Publications.

O'Rourke, D. (2003), 'Outsourcing regulation: analyzing non-governmental systems of labor standards and monitoring', *The Policy Studies Journal*, Vol. 31, No. 1, pp. 1–29.

OECD (1996), *Trade, Employment and Labour Standards. A Study of Core Workers' Rights and International Trade*, Paris.

OECD (1998), *Harmful Tax Competition: an Emerging Global Issue*, Paris.

OECD (1999), *Regulatory Reform and International Standardization*, Paris.

Pelkmans, J. (2001), 'The GSM standard: explaining a success story', *Journal of European Public Policy*, Vol. 8, No. 3, pp. 432–53.

Pierson, P. (1998), 'Irresistible forces, immovable objects: post-industrial welfare states confront permanent austerity', *Journal of European Public Policy*, Vol. 5, No. 5, pp. 539–60.

Rhodes, M. (1997), 'The welfare state: internal challenges, external constraints', in M. Rhodes, P. Heywood and V. Wright (eds), *Developments in West European Politics*, Basingstoke: Macmillan.

Romanovska, L. (2003), 'Regulatory convergence and technical standards', Paper presented to the UNECE Workshop on *EU Enlargement: Regulatory Convergence in Non-Acceding Countries*, Athens, 7–8 November 2003.

Ruding, O. (1992), *Report of the Reflection Committee of Independent Experts on Company Taxation*, Luxembourg: Office for Official Publications of the European Communities.

Scharpf, F. (1999), *Governing in Europe: Effective and Democratic?*, Oxford: Oxford University Press.

Scharpf, F. (2002), 'The European social model: coping with the challenges of diversity', *JCMS*, Vol. 40, No. 4, pp. 645–70.

Shemiatenkov, V. (2002), 'EU–Russia: the sociology of approximation', in *Peace, Stability and Security*, Proceedings of the 6th ECSA-World Conference, Brussels 5–6 December 2002, European Commission, Jean Monnet Project.

Stiglitz, J. (2002), *Globalization and its Discontents*, London: Allen Lane – The Penguin Press.

Sun, J. M. and Pelkmans, J. (1995), 'Regulatory competition in the Single Market', *JCMS*, Vol. 33, No. 1, pp. 67–89.

Sykes, R., Palier, B. and Prior, P. (eds), (2001), *Globalisation and European Welfare States*, Basingstoke: Palgrave.

UNCTAD (2001), *WTO Accessions and Development Policies*, UN Sales No. E.02.II.D.19.

UNCTAD, *World Investment Report* (annual).

UNECE (2002), *Industrial Restructuring in European Transition Economies. Experience to Date and Prospects*, UN Sales No. E.02.II.E.11.

Vogel, D. (1997), *Barriers or Benefits: Regulation in Transatlantic Trade*, Washington D.C.: Brookings Institution Press.

Vogel, D. (2001), 'Environmental regulation and European integration', in Esty, D. and Geradin, D. (eds.), *Regulatory Competition and Economic Integration*, Oxford: Oxford University Press, pp. 330–347.

World Bank (2004), *World Development Report 2005: 'A Better Investment Climate for Everyone'*, New York: World Bank & Oxford University Press.

7. Economic and Social Cohesion in the Enlarged Union

Panagiotis Liargovas

INTRODUCTION: ENLARGEMENT AND THE NEW FACE OF THE EU

The recent eastern enlargement of the EU to include 25 (and soon 27) Member States represents a historical moment that puts an end to the technical division of Europe. The new, wider and stronger Union creates an internal market of around 500 million consumers. Starting from six founding members in 1950, the European Union reached 15 members in 1995 and 25 members at the beginning of the new millennium. The enlarged Union has created a new economic reality which puts new challenges for its competitiveness and internal cohesion. This new economic reality could be described as follows.[1]

Larger size, smaller GDP per head: The EU increases its surface area by 34 per cent, its population by 28 per cent. At the same time GDP per head falls by 15 per cent.

New income groups between Member States: Three groups of countries can be distinguished in an enlarged Union (PPS, 2001): (a) The first group includes the eight accession countries (21 per cent of the EU-25 population) with the lowest income per head, averaging 42 per cent of the EU-25 average and ranging from 65 per cent in Czech Republic to 37 per cent in Latvia (for comparison in Bulgaria and Romania figures are 27 per cent and 26 per cent respectively). (b) In the second group income per head (13 per cent of the EU-25 population) ranges from 71 per cent of the EU average in Greece to 92 per cent in Spain; it includes the two remaining accession countries, Slovenia and Cyprus, as well as Portugal. (c) The third group includes the remaining current Member States, with income at least 11 per cent above the EU-25

---

[1] See Commission of the European Communities (2003a).

average (115 per cent for the group as a whole), and accounts for almost 66 per cent of the EU-25 population.

An unprecedented widening of economic disparities within the Union: The gap in per capita GDP between the 10 per cent of the population living in the most prosperous regions and the same percentage living in the least prosperous ones will more than double compared with the situation in EU-15.

More Europeans will live in less developed regions: In EU-25, 116 million people – representing some 25 per cent of the total population – will live in regions with a per capita GDP below 75 per cent of the EU average as against 68 million people, or 18 per cent of the total, in EU-15. Of these, four out of ten citizens will be living in regions belonging to the existing Member States while the other six will be nationals of the candidate countries.

A less advantageous employment situation: In 2001, the employment rate for the candidate countries was almost 6 percentage points lower than that of the EU-15. Only Cyprus and Slovenia registered a higher employment rate than the EU average. In most candidate countries, the employment rate for women developed more favourably than for men, either falling more slowly or rising faster. Three million jobs will have to be created if the average level of employment in the new Member States is to be aligned with that of the rest of the EU on account of the trend of decline in the rate of employment and a higher long-term youth unemployment rate. Within the enlarged EU, appreciable employment gaps will persist according to age, gender and the level of qualifications and skills.

Increase in regional disparities as regards unemployment: Disparities in employment and unemployment would rise as well. While the unemployment rate in the top 10 per cent of regions of an enlarged EU would average 2.4 per cent, it would average 22.6 per cent in those where rates were highest. The top group of regions would almost exclusively consist of regions located in the current Member States, whereas the majority of regions in the bottom group would be located in the candidate countries.

A shift in the sectoral composition of employment: Enlargement will also have a stronger impact on the sectoral composition of employment of an enlarged EU. Agriculture accounts for a much higher share of employment in the candidate countries as compared to the EU-15 – 13.2 per cent for the ten acceding countries, 20.8 per cent if data from Bulgaria and Romania is added. Enlargement would increase the share of employment in agriculture from 4.1 per cent in EU-15 to 5.5 per cent in EU-25 (and 7.6 per cent in EU-27), while the share in the service sector would decrease and that of the industrial sector would stay the same. The agricultural sector of most candidate countries is expected to undergo a significant restructuring process in the coming years (with or without enlargement), leading to structural pressures on rural areas in these countries.

The purpose of this study is to discuss the main impact of enlargement on the future EU Cohesion policy. The next section presents Cohesion policy up to 2006, while the third section raises the main questions regarding Cohesion policy for the period 2007–2013. The fourth section presents the proposed reforms regarding the future shape of EU Cohesion policy by the Commission, while the fifth section makes a critical assessment of these reforms. Finally the last section offers some conclusions.

EU COHESION POLICY UP TO 2006

There is no doubt that EU Cohesion policy does not represent a simple budgetary transfer, but a policy that has had a profound European value added. This is proved by the fact that it has assisted convergence between Member States and regions. Thus, GDP per capita in the four Cohesion countries Greece, Spain, Ireland and Portugal increased from 68 per cent of the EU average in 1988 to 80 per cent by the year 2000 (Figure 7.1). By the same token, the growth of GDP, employment and productivity of Objective 1 regions has exceeded that of the rest of the EU over the past 15 years (Figures 7.2–7.3). As a result of structural intervention, GDP is expected to increase by 6.2 per cent in Greece, 6.0 in Portugal and 2.4 per cent in Spain over the period 2000–06 (Figure 7.4).

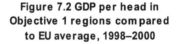

Figure 7.1 GDP per head in GR/ESP/IRL/POR compared to EU average, 1988–2000

Figure 7.2 GDP per head in Objective 1 regions compared to EU average, 1998–2000

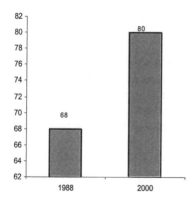

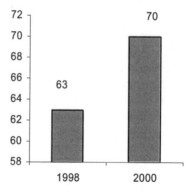

Figure 7.3 Employment
rates in Objective 1
regions

Figure 7.4 Total expected
addition to GDP as a result
of programmes, 2000-06

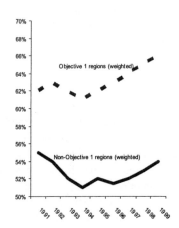

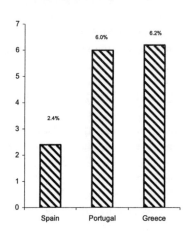

Source: Eurostat

EU resources for structural action have steeply increased since 1989. Thus, from EUR 8 billion per year in 1989 then went up to 32 billion in 1999 (1999 prices) or from 20 per cent of EU budget (1987) to above 35 per cent (1999). For the period 2000–06 a package of 211 billion Euro was agreed for MS-15 (Table 7.1).[2]

The main decision regarding the amounts and the functions of Structural Funds for the period 2001–06 was taken in the Berlin European Council in March 1999.[3] The Council initially opted for 16.78 million Euro for the financing of the six new countries that would join the EU in 2002; but after a period of negotiation, the Council accepted the method of allocating appropriations proposed by the Commission based on a strict application of the acquis communautaire. The Copenhagen Council finally opted for an envelope of almost €21.7 billion for the Structural Funds and the Cohesion Fund for the period 2004–06.[4] In 2006 that amount will result in total aid of €117 per person, compared with €143 per person that was granted for Objective 1 in the first programming period, 1989–93, which rose to an

---

[2] See also EU Commission, COM (2003a).
[3] More   details   regarding   the   Berlin   Council   can   be   found   in: http://europa.eu.int/abc/doc/off/bull/en/9904/p106001.htm.
[4] More   details   regarding   the   Copenhagen   Council   can   be   found   in: http://europa.eu.int/comm/enlargement/communication/pdf/report_december_2002.pdf.

average of €217 per person for objective 1 regions in the 15 Member States in 2000–06. Aid from the Structural Funds will be concentrated chiefly on Objective 1 eligible areas in accession countries. The regions eligible under Objectives 2 and 3 (Prague, Bratislava and Cyprus if there is no political settlement) will enjoy a per capita aid intensity identical to that of the EU-15. The Community Initiatives will be reduced to two (Interreg and Equal) while the measures eligible under the other Initiatives (Leader and Urban) could be incorporated into Objectives 1 and 2. One third of the allocation will go to the Cohesion Fund.

Table 7.1
EU resources committed to structural action, 2000–06.
Breakdown according to Member State and objective (million €, 1999 prices)

	Objective 1	Objective 2	Objective 3	Cohesion Fund	Com. Initiat.	Total
Germany	19,958	3,510	4,581		1,608	29,657
Greece	20,961			3,060	862	24,883
Spain	38,096	2,651	2,140	11,160	1,958	56,005
Ireland	3,008			720	166	3,974
Italy	22,122	2,522	3,744		1,172	29,560
Portugal	19,029			3,300	671	23,000
Other	12,700	13,771	13,585		3,844	43,900
EU-15	135,954	22,454	24,050	18,240	190,281	210,979

Source: EU Commission, COM (2003) 34 final, Brussels

THE MAIN POLICY QUESTIONS REGARDING COHESION POLICY AFTER 2006

Enlargement represents a major challenge for Cohesion policy. The future shape of Structural Funds is presently under discussion at the European level and decisions will be made at the end of 2006. The final outcome will be the result of negotiations between the 25 EU Member States. Some of the most critical questions that both Member States and the EU officials have to consider are the following:

Question 1: Should Cohesion policy continue to focus on economic convergence in the less developed regions? According to the current philosophy of Cohesion policy, the less developed areas are those with the lowest GDP per head or those that have a GDP per head below the criterion of 75 per cent of the EU average (Objective 1 regions). For the period 2000–2006, 64 per cent of the total package goes to Objective 1 regions.[5] Together with the Cohesion Fund this percentage goes up to 74 per cent. If all of the

---

[5] See Commission of the European Communities (2001).

new Member States fall under Objective 1 and the amount foreseen for them represents approximately 50 per cent of the package, then there could be only 24 per cent of the package available for the remaining objective 1 regions and phasing out of (ex) Objective 1 regions of the current 15 Member States. This issue raises a lot of concerns since the EU budget does not seem to increase. Countries with a net contribution to the EU budget are not willing to accept an increase in their contributions beyond the current ceiling of 1.27 per cent of EU GDP (when national budgets reach around 47 per cent of GDP). On the other hand, the remarkable faster growth of GDP per head in Objective 1 regions compared to the other European regions offers the best justification that economic convergence can be a viable target for EU Cohesion policy.

An issue related to the above question has to do with the criterion of 75 per cent of EU GDP. If the Commission continues to retain this criterion, then enlargement will create a statistical effect in a large number of European regions. It could be estimated that 18 of the current 48 Objective 1 regions will lose their status of Objective 1 region. A possible solution to this 'statistical effect' is to add more criteria to the GDP criterion. The question is then which criteria can and should be used and how can one ensure sufficient objectivity in criteria and concentration of financial means.

Question 2: Should there remain Objective 2 regions or rather horizontal thematic priorities? Linked to the discussion on (extension of) the criteria for Objective 1 regions there are several options for reform of the Objective 2 aid. Implementation problems in Structural Funds occur especially in Objective 2 regions.[6] When applying a multitude of criteria there is a risk of competition between the regions in a country or possible thinning of aid over many regions. Where to strike the balance? Horizontal thematic priorities, as for Objective 3, could be an alternative.

Question 3: Should Community Initiatives continue to be incorporated in the Structural Funds or should they be separated? Community initiatives have been recognized for their high level of value added by the Union to measures concerning co-operation, the exchange of experiences and good practices.[7] Nevertheless, the concept of 'Community initiatives' means that the EU assumes responsibility for all issues which are of major importance for the Community as a whole and for its future development. With enlargement the EU border and cross-border regions will gain importance as border areas account for 66 per cent of the new Member States' total surface and for 58 per cent of their population.[8] Therefore the EU has many reasons to continue and extend Community Initiatives. But integration of the Community Initiatives into the national mainstream programmes entails two major risks.

---

[6] See Commission of the EU (2003b) and Commission of the EU (2003c).
[7] Commission of the EU (2003d) and Commission of the EU (2003e).
[8] According to Eurostat.

First every Member State would be free to decide or not to incorporate cross border, transnational or interregional issues. As soon as one country opts to do so while the neighbouring country does not or sets different priorities, cross-border co-operation would become nearly impossible. Second, ember States would lose interest in genuine cross-border programmes and projects. A possible separation of Community Initiatives from Structural Funds will enable the EU to reach citizens and regions all across Europe and to implement the principles of 'subsidiarity' and 'partnership' while being close to citizens. But such a separation would require additional EU funds which might not be available. An intermediate solution could be to consider Community Initiatives as independent political objectives.

Question 4: What are the most appropriate rates of EU co-financing? An extension of the previous discussion is related to the use of different maximum levels of support within the enlarged EU as a whole: (a) high and targeted levels of support in Central and Eastern Europe (e.g. 50–80 per cent), according to the different regional situation in and between these countries; (b) a reduced level of support within the EU-15 Member States (e.g. for a short period 75 per cent, then 30–50 per cent). Alternatively, if Objectives 2 and 3 were to be altered one could imagine different rates of EU co-financing depending on the European value added of the projects. For example, to overcome regional disparities it would be possible that Member States' co-finance is around 50 per cent. For some cross-border projects and projects that are of importance for the EU as a whole, but which may not be able to attract sufficient public and/or private financing (e.g. because of national administrative rules which differ and are difficult to reconcile), higher EU co-financing rates could be envisaged.

Question 5: How to strengthen 'partnership', 'additionality', implementation and administration? Local authorities, NGOs and social partners are still not always adequately involved at all stages of the procedures. How could the Commission bring about a bottom-up approach? Could a system of calling for proposals open to social, economic and environmental factors be an alternative, e.g. in the case of horizontal priorities? How best to adapt programming procedures without creating too much of an administrative and bureaucratic burden? What kind of contracts? Bi- or tri-partite? The underlying principle of European Cohesion policy is that EU expenditure should not take the place of national expenditure. Member States should not save on their national budgets because of the funds they get from the EU budget. The application and control of this principle seems difficult to implement and currently there exists no sanction to enforce it. How can it be upheld when national budgets are under restraint and there are new Member States which have very limited national budgets compared to the current Member States?

National co-financing problems and differences between European and national priority setting may be among the reasons for low implementation of Objective 2 programmes. Apart from them, perceivable differences as regards legal and administrative systems or structures, legislation relating to taxation, social issues and economic promotion, rescue systems, industrial law and workforce skills create additional difficulties for the implementation of EU policy.

Structural Funds measurement is often inflexible and counts on 'quick-wins'. Output is measured in jobs created, jobs safeguarded, additional turnover and turnover safeguarded and must be counted by the end of six months after the official end of the project. Problems arise in that it can take years from the inception of a project within a business for it to bear fruit and create jobs and improve turnover. But if these cannot be counted within six months of the end of the project they are not counted as outputs. This can lead to targets being missed and money clawed back. A more flexible approach is needed here.

Question 6: What is the future of rural development? Rural development is now divided between the EAGGF Guarantee and the EAGGF Guidance section. Part of the funding falls under category 1 of the Financial Perspective (agriculture and rural development), part of it under category 2 (Structural Operations). For the period 2000–06 in total 52.2 billion is foreseen under the various instruments (on average 7.5 billion per year).[9] The Commission apparently foresees grouping rural development together with agriculture, fisheries and the environment and the assisted amount for the year 2011 would be 9.8 billion. It is not clear at this moment whether this would include rural development measures now financed under Cohesion policy. We would have to consider possible advantages and disadvantages of placing rural development under one heading and to be managed by one Fund and determine in such case whether or not it should go together with agriculture Cohesion policy.

THE PROPOSED REFORMS BY THE COMMISSION

The Commission has already outlined its thinking in its Third Report on Economic and Social Cohesion.[10] According to the Report, the Commission retains a budgetary envelope of 1.24 per cent of EU GNI. This means that the funds available for Structural and Cohesion Funds will be 336 billion Euro. Annual spending on EU Cohesion Policy would rise by 31 per cent, from 39

[9] See Commission of the EU (2004).
[10] See Commission of the EU (2004).

billion in 2006 to 51 billion in 2013. The current nine Objectives and Community Initiatives (Cohesion Fund, Objectives 1, 2 and 3, INTERREG, URBAN, LEADER+ and rural development and restructuring of the fisheries sector outside Objective 1) would be replaced by three new Objectives: (a) Convergence and Competitiveness, (b) Regional Competitiveness and employment and (c) Cooperation of Regions (Table 7.2).

Table 7.2
Instruments and objectives

2000–06		2007–13	
Objectives	*Financial instruments*	*Objectives*	*Financial instruments*
Cohesion	Cohesion Fund	Objective 1:	Cohesion Fund
Objective 1	ERDF	Convergence	ERDF
	ESF	and	ESF
	EAGGF Guidance	Competitiveness	
	FIFG		
Objective 2	ERDF	Objective 2:	ERDF
	ESF	Regional	ESF
		Competitiveness	
		and	
Objective 3	ESF	Employment	
		regional level	
		national level:	
		European	
		Employment	
		Strategy	
INTERREG	ERDF	Objective 3:	ERDF
URBAN	ERDF	European	
EQUAL	ESF	Territorial	
LEADER+	EAGGF Guidance	Cooperation	
Rural development	EAGGF Guarantee		
and restructuring of			
the fisheries sector	FIFG		
outside Objectives 2			
and 3			
9 objectives	6 instruments	3 objectives	3 instruments

Source: Commission of the EU (2004), p. xiii.

About 78 per cent of total Structural and Cohesion Funds (€262 billion) would be devoted to the Convergence Priority. This compares to the 73 per cent currently devoted to Objective 1 and Cohesion funding in the current programme. This convergence would be addressed through: (a) a Cohesion Fund, allocated to Member States whose GDP per head is below 90 per cent of the EU-25 average. According to the Report, it should 'represent a third of the financial allocation for the new Member States concerned'.[11] Transport and environmental infrastructure should remain the main priorities of the

---

[11] See Commission of the EU (2004), p. xxix.

Cohesion Fund; (b) convergence funding, available to all NUTS II regions whose GDP per head is below 75 per cent of the EU-25 average; and (c) convergence funding to 'statistically affected' regions – that is, to regions which have GDP per head below 75 per cent of the EU-15 average (but above 75 per cent of the EU-25 average). This funding would be in the interest of equity, and to allow the regions concerned to complete the process of convergence. The Report makes it clear that this funding would be temporary, lasting until 2013, and would not be followed by a further phasing out period. Finally, there would also be a specific programme for outermost regions under this Objective.

About 18 per cent of total funds (€60.5 billion) would be devoted to the Regional Competitiveness and Employment strand. This roughly corresponds to Objectives 2 and 3 of the current regime, which currently accounts for 22 per cent of total funds. It would consist of: (a) transitional phasing-in funding for regions that currently receive Objective 1 funding but which, due to economic growth, would no longer have GDP per head below 75 per cent of the EU-15 average; and (b) competitiveness and employment funding to regions which are not eligible for Convergence or Transitional funding. The Commission proposes a two-fold approach:[12] First, through regional programmes, Cohesion policy will help regions and the regional authorities to anticipate and promote economic change in industrial, urban and rural areas by strengthening their competitiveness and attractiveness. Second, through national programmes, Cohesion policy would help people to anticipate and adapt to economic change, in line with the policy priorities of the European Employment Strategy (EES) by supporting policies aimed at full employment, quality and productivity at work and social inclusion.

According to the Report, the resources for the Regional Competitiveness and Employment Objective would be allocated by the EU to Member States on the basis of 'economic, social and territorial criteria'.[13] It does not specify what the specific criteria or indicators would be. It would then be for Member States to distribute the funds to their regions.

About 4 per cent of total funds (€13.5 billion) would be devoted to the Territorial Cooperation strand. In the current programme, the Community Initiatives account for 5 per cent of total funds. However, the 4 per cent of total funds going to the Territorial Cooperation strand certainly implies growth compared to the current INTERREG III Community Initiative which it most closely resembles. All NUTS III areas along external and internal borders (land or sea) would be eligible for cross-border Territorial Cooperation funding, while all NUTS III regions could be eligible for

---

[12] See Commission of the EU (2004), p. xxix.
[13] See Commission of the EU (2004), p. xxx.

funding for translational cooperation (depending on evaluations of the performance of current translational Interreg IIIB Programmes). The size of their populations and their socio-economic conditions could guide the distribution of funds.

The implementation of these Objectives, will be based on the key principles of Cohesion policies – multi-annual programming, partnership, co-financing, shared responsibility and evaluation. The Commission will retain the system of payments (advances and reimbursements) as well as the essential principle of automatic de-commitment ($n + 2$ rule).

A CRITICAL ASSESSMENT OF THE PROPOSED REFORMS

The guidelines proposed by the Commission are in line with the main targets of the European Union (Lisbon and Gothenburg), they are designed according to a territorial approach and they are open to the idea of partnership. Compared to the current regime, the proposed Structural Funds regime would have more of a 'focus regime' on Convergence funding, the main source of funding in the proposed reforms, territorial as well as social and economic cohesion, and would make all regions eligible for funding under one or other of the proposed objectives. Convergence funding would favour new Member States as well as parts of Greece, Portugal, Spain, Italy and Eastern Germany. Cohesion funding would include the new Member States as well as Portugal and Greece. The recipients of statistical effect funding would ultimately depend on the statistics at the time when decisions are made, but in the basis of current data would mainly include regions in Germany, the UK and Spain. However, statistical-effect funding would be temporary. As noted earlier, it would end in 2013 and not be followed by a further period of funding. The continuation or otherwise of such funding after 2013 might more appropriately be determined by examining the statistical indicators of need nearer the time.

The Commission is proposing (Regional Competitiveness and Employment Objective) that the future EU Cohesion Policy should focus on a limited number of objectives that reflect the Lisbon and Gothenburg agendas such as innovation and the knowledge society, accessibility and services of general interest, environment and risk prevention. These would be complemented by the Commission's employment strand – based on European Employment Strategy – adaptability of the workforce, job creation and accessibility to the labour market for vulnerable persons. The reform proposals would entail an allocation of funds from the EU to Member States and from Member States to regions. In neither case is the detail on how these allocations would be determined known. The expectation is that 'financial envelopes' would be allocated to Member States on the basis of the economic, social and territorial criteria and Member States would then have the responsibility for allocating resources within their territories to address the Competitiveness themes. However, for Competitiveness funding, the Commission has not yet specified adequate details on how the 'financial envelopes' would be derived for Member States; second, it is not known how the Member States would decide to allocate their envelope for Competitiveness, nor whether Member States would have total autonomy, or if the Commission might ultimately seek to influence the process in some way. Allocation of funding by region will be made up to each Member State, in accordance with the Treaty and the principle of subsidiarity, to determine which regions will or will not be eligible under this priority, both in respect to the national component (employment and training) and the regional component (competitiveness), and to fix its own rules on how funding will be shared out between the regions under each of these two components. Regarding the national component there are plenty of criteria which could be used such as the unemployment rate, the medium term growth in employment, the educational attainment, etc. Regarding the regional component it is important for Member States to uphold the principle of eligibility for all regions and for the Commission to draw up an indication of funding allocation taking into account certain criteria to ensure fairness in terms of Community aid. Such criteria might include GDP per capita in a region, jobs in research and innovation, information and communication technologies, percentage of population living in sparsely populated areas, island regions or mountain areas, etc.

Territorial Cooperation is not seen any more as an instrument, but as an objective. For Territorial Cooperation funding, it would be for Member States and regions to propose cross-border and transnational cooperation areas and for the Commission then to agree these with the Member States. For transnational cooperation, this would be on the basis of evaluated current performance of existing programmes, but it is not possible to know at this stage what programme areas would be agreed. The integration of Community initiatives into the mainstream programmes does not entail the risk that countries would lose interest in cross-border programmes and projects or that countries would be free to decide whether or not to incorporate cross-border, transnational or interregional issues.

The Commission's special provision for allowing a higher rate of EU co-financing in Regional Competitiveness and Employment areas with geographical handicaps could benefit a number of European regions. It is not clear, however, how eligibility would be determined, but population scarcity could be an indicator. If so, qualification would depend on how low the population scarcity threshold was set.

The proposed changes to rural development planning (concentrating on supporting the agricultural and farm diversification sectors) could be less flexible than current programmes. Furthermore, the proposed Regional Competitiveness and Employment themes do not seem to offer rural partners the same scope as is currently available to promote rural development. While it is not clear at this stage what will be in the new rural development regulation, it is likely that the scope for, for example, LEADER+ activities under this could be limited. Similar uncertainties about activities in support of fishing communities also exist with regard to the proposed single instrument for actions in the fishing industry. It is inappropriate to review the Structural Funds separately from the Common Agricultural Policy when these are the two most significant sources of European funding and when there is scope for some synergy between the rural elements of the Structural Funds and the rural development elements of the Common Agricultural Policy as the Common Agricultural Policy moves away from a simple price support system towards meeting the real needs of our communities.

Regarding the implementation, the proposed simplification of the plethora of funding schemes is positive. The Commission's new design of 'one programme, one fund' is a first step into the right direction and should be pursued. The Commission's intention to devolve more responsibility to Member States regarding audit accountability is a positive move. The development of functional and practical tripartite agreements with national governments as accountable bodies would help to allow a less bureaucratic approach to programme delivery. Tripartite contracts will make the principle of 'subsidiarity' clearer. It represents a way to bring the policy closer to citizens and to provide regional decision makers with greater influence in terms of the preparation and implementation of the Cohesion policy. This is best done through tripartite contracts formed between EU–state–region for the application of structural fund programmes. Also a high degree of transparency is needed to assure the general public as well as the business communities that funds are not embezzled, misallocated or cause distortion of competition.

CONCLUSIONS

The recent eastern enlargement has brought considerable changes in the economic and demographic picture of the EU. It represents a major challenge in a number of policies, such as Cohesion policy, Common Agricultural Policy, etc. As regards Cohesion policy, enlargement raises a number of important questions. The Commission has made public certain elements of the future Cohesion policy in its Third Cohesion report. Although a large number of these elements are seen as positive, many have to be negotiated. First, the final budget agreements that will allow credible substance to be given to the current proposals; second, the criteria that will serve as the basis for allocating funding between states and European regions. This issue concerns Objective 2 of the proposal focusing on competitiveness and employment. Objective 1-based funding will probably continue to be allocated on the basis of GDP and population. Finally, the large number of synergies that might exist between Structural Funds as well as other EU Funds implies that in future, e.g. in 2011/2013, all European policies should be reviewed together.

REFERENCES

Commission of the European Communities (2001), *Unity, Solidarity, Diversity for Europe, its People and its Territory, Second Report on Economic and Social Cohesion*, Brussels.
Commission of the European Communities (2003a), *COM 34 final*, Brussels.
Commission of the European Communities (2003b), *Ex-post Evaluation of 1994–99 Objective 2 Programmes*, DG Regional Policy, Brussels.
Commission of the European Communities (2003c), *Analysis of the Impact of Community Policies on Regional Cohesion*, DG Regional Policy, Brussels.
Commission of the European Communities (2003d), *Ex-post Evaluation INTERREG II Community Initiative (1994–1999)*, DG Regional Policy, Brussels.
Commission of the European Communities (2003e), *Ex-post Evaluation Urban Community Initiative (1994–1999) – Final Report*, DG Regional Policy, Brussels.
Commission of the European Communities (2004), *A New Partnership for Cohesion, Convergence, Competitiveness, Cooperation, Third Report on Economic and Social Cohesion*, Brussels.

PART III

External Relations of the Enlarged Union

8. Challenges of Adjustment: Economic Integration in a Wider Europe

Carol Cosgrove-Sacks[*]

INTRODUCTION

The geopolitical and economic framework as it existed in Europe over the last 50 years has undergone a dramatic transformation with the enlargement of the European Union (EU) on 1 May 2004. The Union expanded from 15 to 25 members, now including Cyprus, the Czech Republic, Estonia, Hungary, Latvia, Lithuania, Malta, Poland, the Slovak Republic and Slovenia. Another three candidate countries, Bulgaria, Romania and Turkey, are waiting in the wings.

This latest enlargement will obviously have a significant impact on the region as a whole. It is, however, only one step, be it a big one, in the journey of continuing European integration. Several measures are in place, including the European Commission's 2003 Wider Europe Initiative, that seek to strengthen relations between EU Member States and their neighbours in the east and in the south of the Mediterranean.

This chapter comments on the challenges of adjustment confronting those countries in the region which do not have a current perspective to join the EU and in particular on the efforts of harmonisation in the Commonwealth of Independent States (CIS): Armenia, Azerbaijan, Belarus, Georgia, Kazakhstan, Kyrgyzstan, Russia, Tajikistan, Turkmenistan, Ukraine and Uzbekistan. In order to strengthen economic cooperation with the enlarged EU, there is a need for these countries to adopt and implement standards and legislation that are not necessarily identical to the EU's but that comply with

---

[*] The comments expressed in this paper are the sole responsibility of the author and do not necessarily reflect the views of the United Nations.

the *acquis communautaire*. The United Nations Economic Commission for Europe (UNECE) is strongly committed to the European integration project throughout the region and has the expertise and willingness to assist the CIS in developing the norms, standards and regulatory instruments required to trade efficiently in the 21st century.

IMPACT OF ENLARGEMENT ON NEW MEMBERS

The 2004 enlargement of the EU has significantly increased its geographical, economic and political weight in the world. Having embraced another 75 million people, the Union now has a total population of 450 million citizens, fewer than China or India, but far more than for example the United States, Russia or Japan. Its common market, which is based on a single set of trade rules and an open economy, is the largest in the world, accounting for some 20 per cent of world trade and more than 25 per cent of world GDP. In 2003, the EU accounted for nearly half of the world's outward foreign direct investment (FDI) and received a more than a fifth of inward investment. In political terms also, the enlarged EU is a major international actor. It is the largest contributor to the World Bank and the IMF and, through its Common Foreign and Security Policy and Common Strategies in external relations, it exerts an increasingly significant influence in the international arena, particularly when its Member States succeed in speaking with one voice.

The new EU states will benefit significantly from their membership status, they receive net direct EU financing and participate fully in all aspects of the *acquis communautaire*, profiting in particular from the provisions related to trade, regulatory convergence and standards. In general, they now have tariff free access to the whole EU market for their goods and services, which is also expected to make them more attractive as a destination for foreign investment. Increased competition is expected to improve business transparency and corporate accountability and economies of scale should drive down prices and transactions costs, while productivity of labour and capital increase.

IMPACT OF ENLARGEMENT ON THE CIS

While enlargement will also affect the EU's neighbours in the southern Mediterranean and the countries in the south-east of Europe that are assumed to be in line for EU accession in the coming years, the focus of the following analysis is on the 12 CIS countries, the EU's new neighbours in the east. This enormous region has a combined population of 385 million people, most of whom have a nominal GDP of less than EUR 2,000 or less than 10 per cent of the EU average. The total share of world FDI going to the CIS is just 1.65 per cent as opposed to the 21.3 per cent that flows into the enlarged EU. Considering the historic ties of the region to the new EU members, enlargement is likely to have a profound effect on the CIS countries.

Before enlargement, the EU was already a major trading partner for the majority of CIS countries and has only become more important since. The EU-15 represented an important market for the CIS as the destination of 29 per cent of total exports from the region. Adding trade with the new Members, the EU-25 is the destination of 62.7 per cent of its exports. Among the CIS countries, Russia and Ukraine are likely to be particularly affected by the recent enlargement, due to their more developed economic and social connections with both the old and new EU Members. Before enlargement, Russia was already the EU's fifth largest trading partner (after the US, China, Switzerland and Japan), while the EU was Russia's main trading partner, accounting for some 40 per cent of its total trade. Indeed, Russian trade with the EU in 2002 amounted to some EUR 78 billion with a EUR 17 billion surplus at the Russian side. A similar picture can be drawn for Ukraine, with EU–Ukraine trade exhibiting steady growth over the past years, adding up to around EUR 10 billion in 2002.

Two questions regarding the implications of enlargement are of particular importance. First, how will adoption of EU trade rules by the new Member States affect trade between these countries and the countries of the CIS? Second, what impact will EU enlargement have on flows of FDI into the CIS? In general, enlargement is expected to have a positive influence on trade between the EU and non-member states, particularly in the CIS. Important factors that lead to this conclusion are the adoption of the Common External Tariff (CET) by the new EU members; simplified access to a unified market; better protection of property rights in the new Member States; and expectations that expansion will lead to greater support for regulatory reforms in the EU's new neighbours. Some issues that may have a negative impact on CIS–EU trade should also be considered, namely the tariff free access of the new Members to the EU-15's market for agricultural products; the extension of EU export subsidies to the new Member States; the loss of pre-enlargement preferential trade agreements between CIS countries and new EU Members; and the introduction of the new EU visa regime. The impact of enlargement on FDI is less clear and will, particularly in the short term, strongly depend on the investment environment the CIS countries manage to create.

The main positive effect on CIS trade with the enlarged EU arises from the adoption of the CCT by the new EU Member States. This allows non-member states to benefit from lower tariffs in their trade with these countries as average tariffs decreased from 9 per cent to 4 per cent. An exception may be agricultural products, which, with a rise of 37.8 per cent in exports to the EU over the 1995–2001 period are increasingly important for the CIS countries. Although, on average, tariffs on agricultural products before enlargement were higher in the new Member States than in the EU-15, a few products now receive higher protection than before May 2004. This is particularly the case for fish and fish products. The rise of the tariffs on these products in the new Member States could be a reason for concern for net exporters of these products, such as Russia. A related aspect is the fact that the CIS countries, apart from Armenia and Georgia, are not yet members of the World Trade Organisation (WTO). According to WTO rules, raising tariffs over and above their bound levels entitles net exporters to the market in question to claim compensation. Countries that are not members of the WTO, however, have few options in the event of a tariff increase.

Other positive effects on CIS trade are expected from simplified and enhanced access to the markets of the new Member States as well as the EU as a whole. A single set of trade rules, norms and standards, a single tariff and a single set of administrative procedures apply across the enlarged EU. This should greatly simplify the dealings of third country operators. When, for example, the products of a Russian exporter comply with the safety or health protection requirements of, say Slovenia, those goods can also be sold on the Swedish or Spanish markets or anywhere in the Union, because the same rules apply across the EU market.

Another advantage for the CIS is that their national companies, if already established in a new Member State, will also be able to open branches in other EU Member States. Further, third countries should receive enhanced levels of Intellectual Property Rights protection in the acceding countries due to their adoption of EU directives and, finally, but very importantly, EU enlargement should raise support for further regulatory reforms in CIS countries, but more on this later.

Whereas the new EU Member States already had unrestrained access to the EU-15's market for manufactured goods in the years before enlargement and thus little change is expected where trade in these products is concerned, they only received free access to the market for agricultural products after accession. Obviously, this will pose a disadvantage for CIS producers that do face tariffs over their exports to the EU. The fact that EU enlargement also means an extension of EU export subsidies to the new Member States may have a further negative impact on the CIS countries. Due particularly to agricultural subsidies, new Members may increase their exports of these products to non-member states, potentially distorting their production and trade possibilities. In addition, previous preferential trade agreements between new Member States and non-member states have been terminated.

These include for example bilateral agreements between Estonia and Ukraine, Latvia and Ukraine, Lithuania and Ukraine, and Hungary and Yugoslavia. Yet another factor that could disrupt cross-border trade in a number of cases is the introduction of the new EU visa regime.

How EU enlargement will affect flows of FDI to the CIS countries will depend crucially on future investment decisions. In the short term, rising income in the new Member States may create new comparative advantages as well as export opportunities for countries beyond the enlarged EU. Nevertheless, for non-member states to attract FDI they need political stability, positive macroeconomic developments, progress in the transformation process and a friendly business climate together with active implementation of a trade facilitation environment. If they are not able to achieve these prerequisites, efforts to mobilise investment will be less than successful.

In the longer term, EU enlargement is likely to make supply networking easier in the new Member States, since the supply chain is no longer disrupted by border formalities. At this point, the gap between the new members and the CIS countries could increase, making it more difficult for firms from non-member states to update their capabilities through industrial cooperation. Research to date, however, suggests that the enlargement will not cause a dramatic fall in the amount of FDI going to non-member states. Rather, the danger is that it will affect the structure of investment, reinforcing the sectoral imbalances that are already present and tighten, rather than loosen, the constraints on future growth of the CIS countries, leaving them even more dependent on the export of raw materials.

NEW NEIGHBOURS, NEW POLICY

Closely linked to the recent enlargement, the European Commission has launched its Wider Europe Initiative[1] to enhance the EU's relations with its neighbours and to ensure a 'ring of friends' in Eastern Europe and the Mediterranean. In particular, the initiative is aimed at strengthening relations with those countries that do not currently have membership prospects.[2]

At the moment, bilateral Partnership and Cooperation Agreements (PCAs) regulate political, economic and cultural relations between the EU and most of the CIS countries. Such agreements came into force in 1997 for Russia,

---

[1] Based on the Communication from the Commission to the Council and the European Parliament *Wider Europe – Neighbourhood: A New Framework for Relations with our Eastern and Southern Neighbours,* (Brussels, 11 March 2003, COM (2003) 104 final).

[2] Due to its location, the Southern Caucasus also falls outside the geographical scope of this initiative.

1998 for Ukraine and 1999 for the other CIS countries with the exceptions of Belarus and Turkmenistan, with whom the PCAs have been signed but are not yet in force, and Mongolia, with whom there is only a 1993 Trade and Cooperation Agreement.

The PCAs aim to stimulate the countries' participation in a wider Europe by creating a closer relationship with the EU, thus ensuring a more stable climate for traders and investors. They offer the business community numerous benefits: trade is carried out within the most favoured nation treatment and national treatment, subject to exceptions for regional trade agreements and preferences to developing countries. The Agreements also help to create the conditions necessary for the establishment of future trade areas between the EU and its partners. A party may not apply quantitative restrictions on imports from the other party, although special provisions are made for separate agreements on 'sensitive' products (textiles and clothing and iron and steel products). A final important aim of the PCAs is to promote convergence of the standards and certification frameworks of the CIS countries with international norms, thus facilitating the two-way flow of goods.

The European Commission's 2003 Wider Europe Initiative intends to supplement and deepen the PCAs and other existing contractual relations and arrangements. Its main objectives are the reduction of poverty and the creation of an area of shared prosperity based on increased integration. Its basis will be a differentiated framework for providing concrete benefits in the form of increased market access as well as other advanced forms of cooperation in fields of mutual interest, for those countries that demonstrate shared values and concrete progress in the implementation of political, economic and institutional reforms. Common objectives and benchmarks will be negotiated, as well as a timetable for achievements, which will be reviewed annually. The long-term goal of the Initiative is for the EU's neighbours to align their legislation with the *acquis communautaire*, creating as close political and economic links as currently enjoyed between EU Members and non-EU members in the European Economic Area.

In order to maintain the momentum needed to ensure the support of both EU Member States and the other countries concerned, the Commission decided to create a Wider Europe Task Force and drew up plans for the creation of a New Neighbourhood Instrument within the overall Wider Europe Initiative to promote cross-border cooperation with a focus 'on ensuring the smooth functioning and secure management of the future Eastern and Mediterranean borders, promoting sustainable economic and social development of the border regions and pursuing regional and transnational cooperation' (COM (2003) 393 final). The Instrument, which again would be building on existing agreements and differentiated by country and region, should help avoid new divisions within Europe and 'promote stability and prosperity within and beyond the new borders of the Union'. Its objectives include promoting sustainable economic and social development in border areas; addressing common challenges in fields such as the environment, public health and the prevention of and fight against organised crime; ensuring efficient and secure borders; and promoting local 'people to people' type actions.

TRADE ISSUES IN THE CIS

In the CIS, contrary to in the EU, goods that cross borders for export or in transit to a third country also move from one legal system to another. Legal systems on both sides of a border can be so different that they create a 'legal wall' that prevents the smooth transit of goods. They may be particularly incompatible if each system's legal tradition and historical or socio-economic legacies have different roots and have taken different directions. In many border areas, distribution and transit centres have been built not because they have a particular economic relevance in the logistics process, but simply because they mark the furthest point a truck can legally travel and where new legal conditions have to be complied with, for example legal documents such as bills of lading or insurance policies. To tackle these problems, harmonised approaches are the only logical way.

According to the World Bank, whose consultants reviewed the factors affecting trade and transport issues in several CIS countries (UNECE, 2003), transport costs often amount to at least three times those in developed countries. Unofficial payments exacerbate this situation and further deteriorate the international competitiveness of CIS countries. Truckers that transit Caucasus or central Asian countries, for example, pay up to US$ 2,000 in unofficial payments or for semi-compulsory guard services. Depending on world market prices of the commodities carried, total transport costs (official and unofficial) can add up to 50 per cent of the value of the goods, far exceeding the comparable costs of competitors outside the CIS. Extremely high unofficial fees in transport and customs arrangements and unreliable transport in general have almost certainly caused much of Uzbekistan's loss of market share and contributed to trade diversion, notably to China. The same also applies to Turkmenistan, which accounted for 0.7 per cent of the world's output in November 2002, down from approximately 3 per cent in 1988/1989 .

The geographic position of the country, its economic power and its location in the transport chain further influence the total costs of impediments. The landlocked central Asian countries are particularly disadvantaged where their location is concerned, as will be discussed below in more detail. The origin of the cargo and the flag under which the goods are transported also influence delays and charges incurred. The value of the goods and the mode of transport are other relevant factors, as higher value goods and road transport are more expensive than bulk goods or goods transported by rail. Containerised goods perform better, both in terms of speed and additional charges, but the use of this method in the CIS is still underdeveloped .

Another important issue is the incompatibility of existing border procedures[3] in the region with all the principles of the Revised Kyoto Convention and countries' failure to meet the obligations contained in many of the multilateral and bilateral agreements that have been signed, including the agreements on the TRACECA project discussed below. Although most of these agreements present commitments to simplify and harmonise border procedures, in reality no significant improvements have been implemented over the last ten years. Customs systems based on that of the former Soviet Union overly rely on physical inspection and often change, leaving room for arbitrary interpretation and application. Besides, customs rules are interpreted in many different ways and there is evidence that the procedures themselves are not fully understood by those who have to execute them. In breach of international conventions, customs officers regularly break seals because they doubt the integrity of a previous customs authority, making effective control of transit traffic even more difficult.

A final problematic issue concerns immigration services. At most border crossings, drivers and passengers must leave their vehicles to have their passports checked, slowing the border process. There is a lack of equipment so checks have to be performed manually and even though visa requirements based on bilateral or CIS - wide agreements are increasing, few border posts are able to issue full or transit visas. Visa arrangements for professional drivers are cumbersome and time consuming. It may take so long for a driver to be issued a visa that, by that time, the cargo has already been collected by a foreign haulier. The International Road Transport Union has called for a special visa regime with multiple entry rights, specifically for professional drivers in the framework of international road transport. With traffic increasing, border delays will worsen and the improvement of border procedures and border facility layout becomes more and more urgent.

---

[3] Possible inspections/checks related to the cargo on the road: normal customs formalities (guarantee documents such as CMR, T1, TIR), import/export permits, seals; detailed customs controls (origin, quantity, value, goods inspections, sampling, payments of duties); veterinary and phyto-sanitary inspections, etc.

SPECIAL PROBLEMS OF THE CENTRAL ASIAN CIS COUNTRIES

In contrast to the central European countries, the central Asian countries that make part of the CIS are both landlocked and far from markets. This has had negative consequences for their economic performance, especially since the beginning of the region's economic transition.

One of the most prominent features of landlocked countries is their dual vulnerability: they are vulnerable on their own account because they are deprived from access to the sea, but also because they depend on neighbours that often have little interest in making the flow of goods across their borders easy for them. Furthermore, whereas coordinating infrastructure in one country is not an easy task, coordinating across borders is even more difficult. High transport costs caused by infrastructure deficiencies, delays, fees and procedures both internally and in the transit country are the single most important obstacle to equitable access to global markets and competition with other countries. In a statement to the United Nations General Assembly in October 2000,[4] the Permanent Representative of Kazakhstan noted that transport costs in central Asia can amount to up to a prohibitive 60 per cent of the value of manufactured imports.

Particularly relevant to the extent to which the situation of being landlocked affects a country is its closeness to markets and the composition of its exports. European landlocked countries, such as Austria and Switzerland, have main markets 'just across the border' and have been able to specialise in the export of high-value and, more importantly, high value-added goods, making transport costs less of an issue. The central Asian countries do not have this proximity to markets, nor does their dependency on the export of raw materials work in their advantage.

In contrast to central Asia's history of booming trade, located along the ancient Silk Route (UNECE, 2002), during the 20th century the region's geopolitical situation limited the exchange of goods and services following a strict Soviet-centred trading pattern. Because international borders only became effective after the dissolution of the Soviet Union, many cross-border issues are relatively recent. Suddenly, highways and railways that link central Asia to Moscow run across active national boundaries. The recent fortification of borders in central Asia has turned many of these boundaries into real barriers to the movement of people, goods and services[5].

---

[4] Statement by HE Mrs Madilna B. Jarbussynova Ambassador, Permanent Representative of the Republic of Kazakhstan to the United Nations, New York, 26 October 2000.
[5] *Cross-border Trade Facilitation Issues in the Central Asia Region*, Liliana Annovazzi-Jakab, UNECE International Consultant, ICT Publication for the Technical Roundtable Meeting on Central Asia.

During the past ten years, central Asia has been able to develop and negotiate a number of transit routes, including important pipelines for energy exports through Russia. China and Iran can be transited by rail and road, the trans-Caspian ferry routes offer transit by rail and road, and roads can be accessed towards the south through China to Pakistan and India. These main transport corridors have already significantly opened landlocked central Asia to trade, although much remains to be done, especially in terms of infrastructure maintenance and upgrading. Several transport assistance projects are in place to deal with these issues, supported by a long list of international organisations, including UNECE and the United Nations Economic and Social Commission for Asia and the Pacific (ESCAP)'s United Nations Special Programme for the Economies of Central Asia (SPECA), the EU (which initiated the TRACECA project discussed below), the World Bank and the Asian Development Bank.

Apart from problems with the state of basic infrastructure, central Asian countries lack efficient basic legal and regulatory standards that would allow them to trade much more efficiently. Existing rules are diverse and inefficient. In Kazakhstan for example, there are over 1,000 customs-related laws, instructions, decrees and amended and overruled orders. Lack of transparency, information and resources are other major concerns. Kyrgyzstan and Tajikistan still lack computer terminals and process the bulk of their customs declaration manually. The Kyrgyz customs authority processes about 60,000 customs declaration per year by hand . On top of this, customs authorities, government agencies and the private sector in these countries have little experience in dealing with the far-reaching implications of international borders. The low wages of public servants and limited transparency of rules and regulation create inefficient systems vulnerable to fraud and corruption leading to other major bottlenecks and security issues .

Harmonising rules on all these issues would considerably lower transport and transit costs and time. To date however, only Kazakhstan and Uzbekistan, the countries with the largest customs force, have adopted the Harmonised System of Commodity Codes and the WTO Valuation Code, even though substantial efforts are being made by adopting major international transport and transit conventions including the TIR convention. It is however not enough to sign and ratify conventions, they must also be implemented, which will take time and cost money. With good intentions, central Asian governments have signed many bilateral and multilateral agreements seeking to facilitate trade and transit with lending and donor agencies and international organisations in addition to the many international conventions. Unfortunately, these agreements sometimes set forth different or contradicting sets of rules, procedures, mandates and institutional arrangements for the various projects or transit corridors, leading to less rather than more efficiency.

COOPERATION AND HARMONISATION SOLUTIONS

Implementing common rules and standards can assist economic operators of non-EU member states such as the CIS countries to compete in their own markets, the EU market and international markets. Essentially, the goal of the introduction of standards is to protect the health of consumers, to keep costs of research, information, negotiation and transport low for both processors and consumers and to safeguard honest trade practices. The benefits of common standards are manifold. In short, standards facilitate trade because all the parties involved in the transaction speak a common language. But many more arguments can be brought forward. Harmonisation of regulatory measures, such as technical regulation, standards and legislation can increase economic cooperation and facilitate trade between the enlarged EU and non-member states and among non-member states themselves. Simplification and standardisation should particularly benefit small and medium-size enterprises for which the costs of compliance with trade procedures are proportionally higher.

The most desirable for the CIS, would be an integrated regional approach that addresses all issues concerned, but that develops tailor-made measures and technical assistance projects for each country/region based on proximity to the EU market and takes into account any geographical constraints (e.g. land-locked countries). Inter-country agreements are an important prerequisite as they address access to and maintenance of transit corridors and potentially streamline and harmonise regulation. Cross-border cooperation between agencies, such as customs administrations, is an efficient means to implement and enforce harmonised regulation in the region. Such cooperation can even include transport operators so that transit procedures are more closely followed and monitored, as in the case of the Transit Contact Group under the umbrella of the European Convention on Common Transit.

As mentioned, one area in which much progress has been made to date is that of transport corridors, which maximally enhance profitable interregional cooperation. The Transport Corridor Europe Caucasus Area (TRACECA) project, for example, initiated by the EU, was launched in 1993 to develop a transport corridor on a west–east axis from Europe, across the Black Sea, through the Caucasus and the Caspian Sea to central Asia. A very interesting approach taken in the development of the corridor was to attempt in the first phase to establish a common legislative base in the transport and transit sector. The rationale for such an approach was the lack of a single legislative framework in the participating states structures, which made a coordinated approach to the concept of international freight traffic difficult if not impossible. The legacy of the former Soviet Union was a unique transport system, difficult to adapt to the principles of a free market economy and to international transport operations. The EU, therefore, proposed highly customised draft laws and draft multilateral agreements to the states participating in the development of regional transport corridors. It was agreed that laws should be systematically harmonised and amended to meet international principles and new laws should be adopted to regulate international freight traffic. Another interesting aspect of the TRACECA project is its spill-over effects on other countries as the project stimulated the signing of bilateral treaties with countries such as Romania and raised interest in the Republic of Korea, China, Italy, Poland and Estonia to explore the construction of possible rail corridors .

One important factor where trade facilitation is concerned must be kept in mind: the best agreement can only work if backed by political will and the capacity of governments to actually control their agencies. If a government does decide to make the commitment to trade facilitation, the form and execution of the commitment still remain very important. Governments can implement a regime based purely on enforcement, with the potential result of over-regulation and excessive control. A preferred option however, would be to establish a policy based on enforcement and cooperation with the business community. This approach will have more effect as both government and businesses have a common interest in improving the trade environment. Facilitation will not hamper governments from implementing the necessary controls. By consulting with business, however, on how the institutional and legislative process could be improved, compliance can be enhanced. Being party to the consultations, the trade community will be more inclined to comply with predictable and transparent rules and procedures that do not interfere with its logistical organisation. Indeed, the public/private sector trade facilitation bodies already established in many countries could play a key role in the process.

THE ROLE OF THE UNITED NATIONS ECONOMIC COMMISSION FOR EUROPE

Since its establishment in 1947, the United Nations Economic Commission for Europe (the United Nations regional commission for Europe and North America) has supported greater economic cooperation among its members and provided a regional forum for governments to develop conventions, regulation and standards. During the cold war, the UNECE was the only official bridge between East and West, a neutral meeting-place where two diametrically opposite systems could discuss economic cooperation. Following the break-up of the Soviet Union, all the successor states became members of the UNECE, which continues to support the economic integration of the European continent in the 21st century.

The UNECE has been a major player in trade facilitation development for over 20 years. The United Nations Centre for Trade Facilitation and Electronic Business (UN/CEFACT), hosted by the UNECE, developed the UN Layout Key for Trade Documents, which is the foundation for the EU's Single Administrative Document; the United Nations Directories for Electronic Data Interchange for Administration, Commerce and Transport (UN/EDIFACT), the only international standard for electronic commerce; and over 30 major trade facilitation recommendations. Further, the UNECE developed the UN/LOCODE, a listing of three-letter codes for cities and international ports used all over the world to allow easy identification of each location in support of the efficient movement of goods.

In addition to its own programme to develop and promote trade facilitation, the UNECE works closely with the United Nations Conference on Trade and Development (UNCTAD) to promote and implement UN/CEFACT recommendations through technical assistance projects in many countries. Thus, the UNECE and the UNCTAD together contribute to future negotiations on trade facilitation by sharing expertise with members, by contributing to the policy debate on trade facilitation and by providing technical assistance to developing and transition countries.

As set out above, trade facilitation is an important issue in the CIS countries. In fact, the removal of procedural and regulatory inefficiencies may often be more beneficial to these countries' industries than the removal of tariff barriers. Reduced transaction costs can help them become more competitive in international markets and increased transparency, simplification and harmonisation of trade procedures and information flows will promote greater security, which in turn will help to fight corruption and improve revenue generation. Trade facilitation is also a major factor in attracting foreign investment, especially investment related to supply chains where efficient import and export processes are essential (Butterly 2002, p. 36).

The existence of standards is particularly important where agricultural products are concerned. They allow for their long-distance trade, with the buyer able to acquire goods based on a description according to accepted standards. Furthermore, a common standard can encourage farmers to improve the quality of their produce, especially when the technical description is broken down into different categories. For example, by moving from a class B to a class A quality of product, the producer can earn a better return. Finally, standards can reduce waste; when produce is sent long-distance and is not marketed for quality reasons, it will spoil.

The UNECE's agricultural quality standards are widely implemented in international trade and therefore very important in the operation of the international food supply chain. The UNECE has developed 85 standards for fresh fruit and vegetables, dry and dried produce, early and ware potatoes, seed potatoes, meat and cut flowers. Of these, 36 form the basis for EU standards covering around 90 per cent of the market volume of agricultural trade in Europe. The texts of the EU standards are almost completely harmonised with UNECE standards and efforts are being made to reach full harmonisation. In practice, the EU accepts produce coming from non-EU countries that are marked and controlled according to UNECE standards for purposes of quality. Additionally, a total of 52 UNECE standards have been adopted by the Organisation for Economic Cooperation and Development and are promoted internationally through their Fruit and Vegetables Scheme and, in addition, a number of Codex Alimentarius standards are based on UNECE standards for fresh fruits and vegetables.

The UNECE has thus had a profound influence on the development of norms, standards and regulatory instruments to facilitate international trade and continues to make valuable contributions to the field. If non-EU members such as the CIS countries would adopt standards set forth by the UNECE and compatible with the *acquis communautaire* this would be a large step in their further integration with Europe and most positively affect their economic relations with each other, with an enlarged EU and with the world as a whole. The UNECE has the expertise and willingness to help these countries develop and implement such regulation through technical assistance projects

CONCLUSIONS

On 1 May 2004, the EU entered a new and historic phase. EU enlargement and measures such as the Wider Europe Initiative that seek to strengthen relations between EU Member States and their neighbours create opportunities and challenges for non-member states such as the CIS countries. Specific implications of EU enlargement for these countries depend to a large extent on whether they will benefit from a trade-creating effect or suffer from trade diversion. The UNECE expects that the economic implications of EU enlargement for the region as a whole should be generally positive. The view is that if enlargement boosts the economic performance and particularly the rate of growth in the new Member States, it will have an expansionary effect on imports from, and hence on GDP, of non-member states. The extent of this effect however will mainly depend on their capability to take advantage of increased demand both due to enlargement and through the other opportunities for increased access to the EU market.

The EU and its neighbours have a mutual interest in cooperating, both bilaterally and regionally, to ensure that their migration policies, customs procedures and frontier controls do not prevent or delay people or goods from crossing borders for legitimate purposes. Infrastructure, efficient border management and interconnected transport, energy and communication networks will become more vital to expanding mutual trade and investment. Cross-border cultural links, not least between people of the same ethnic/cultural affinities, gain additional importance in the context of proximity. Equally, threats to mutual security, whether from the trans-border dimension of environmental and nuclear hazards, communicable diseases, illegal immigration, trafficking, organised crime or terrorist networks, will require joint approaches in order to be addressed comprehensively.

The EU says it is determined to avoid drawing new dividing lines in Europe and to promote stability and prosperity within and beyond the new borders of the Union. It reaffirmed that enlargement will serve to strengthen relations with its neighbours. The UNECE similarly seeks solutions to avoid the emergence of new divisions in the region and to bridge the gaps between the enlarged EU and the rest of Europe, especially the CIS countries. The UNECE will, to the extent possible, assist its member states in their integration within the European region and try to ensure that all the countries of the region enjoy full benefits within the international trading system. In order to strengthen economic cooperation with the enlarged EU and to increase competitiveness in general, there is a need for non-member states to adopt and implement standards and legislation that are not necessarily identical but comply with the *acquis communautaire*. The fact that the CIS recently agreed to adopt the UNECE 'International Model for Technical Harmonisation' will significantly contribute to regulatory convergence in the region.[6] The UNECE is willing and prepared to further assist countries in developing the necessary norms, standards and regulatory instruments.

Both the EU and the UNECE suggested that this contribution could be reinforced through joint activities and cooperating within the 'Wider Europe' initiative. Active collaboration between the EU, the UNECE, the CIS countries and the various other actors involved, will be an important contribution to meeting this challenge. In conclusion, the enhanced regional, sub-regional and cross-border cooperation will contribute significantly to

---

[6] Note for the Press, *CIS Countries to Adopt UNECE Legal Instruments to Boost Regional Trade*, ECE/TRADE/03/N05.

overcoming disparities in the region and is vital for achieving sustainable peace and prosperity in Europe.

REFERENCES

Butterly, T. (2002), *Trade Facilitation in a Global Environment, Trade Facilitation: The Challenges for Growth and Development*, United Nations Economic Commission for Europe.

European Commission (2003), Communication from the Commission to the Council and the European Parliament, *Wider Europe – Neighbourhood: A New Framework for Relations with our Eastern and Southern Neighbours*, Brussels, 11 March 2003, COM (2003) 104 final.

European Commission (2003), Communication from the Commission: *Paving the Way for a New Neighbourhood Instrument*, Brussels, 1 July 2003, COM (2003) 393 final.

UNECE   (2002),   *Landlocked   Countries: Opportunities,   Challenges, Recommendations*, Committee for Trade, Industry and Enterprise Development, United Nations Economic Commission for Europe, document number UNECE TRADE/2002/23,14 March 2002.

UNECE (2003), Note for the Press, *CIS Countries to Adopt UNECE Legal Instruments to Boost Regional Trade*, ECE/TRADE/03/N05.

UNECE (2003), *Transport and Trade Facilitation Issues in the CIS-7, Kazakhstan and Turkmenistan*, Eva Molnar, World Bank and Lauri Ojala, World Bank consultant, reprinted by the United Nations Economic Commission for Europe under document number ECE/TRADE/NONE/2003/18, 22 April 2003.

UNECE, *Cross-border Trade Facilitation Issues in the Central Asia Region*, Liliana Annovazzi-Jakab, UNECE International Consultant, ICT Publication for the Technical Roundtable Meeting on Central Asia.

9. A Major Challenge for the EU's External Action: The European Neighbourhood Policy

Christian Franck

In the seminar held in Leuven in mid-September 2004 in expectation of taking up its duties in November, the Barroso Commission pointed out that the new European Neighbourhood Policy (ENP) would become a key element and a central stake for its external action (Agence Europe, 2004). It was the December 2002 Copenhagen European Council which gave the kick-off for this new policy, stressing the Union's determination to avoid drawing new dividing lines in Europe and to promote stability and prosperity within and beyond the new borders of the Union. It reaffirmed that enlargement will serve to 'strengthen relations with Russia' and called 'for enhanced relations with Ukraine, Moldova and the Southern Mediterranean countries to be based on a long term approach promoting reform, sustainable development and trade' [COM (2003) 104 final].

A few days before, in a speech to an academic audience in Brussels, the president of the Commission, Romano Prodi had pointed to the same direction. He wanted to see 'a ring of friends surrounding the Union and its closest European neighbours from Morocco to Russia and the Black Sea'. These would be offered a proximity policy consisting of 'more than partnership and less than membership, without precluding this latter...'; referring to the concept of 'sharing everything with the Union but institutions', R. Prodi explained that 'the aim is to extend to this neighbouring region a set of principles, values and standards which define the very essence of the European Union; (Prodi, 2002).

FROM ENLARGEMENT TO NEIGHBOURHOOD: A SPILL-OVER EFFECT

At the same time as it settled the final package of the accession's negotiations with the ten new members who joined the EU on the 1st May 2004, the December 2002 European Council opened the prospect for a new policy with the neighbour countries of the EU of 27 with Bulgaria and Romania which are to accede by 2007. The simultaneity of completing enlargement negotiation with the kick-off for the neighbourhood policy was not only coincidental: it actually expressed the continuation of the same goals but in a wider context and with lower leverage. In the above mentioned speech, president Prodi declared that 'the current enlargement is the greatest contribution to sustainable stability and security on the European continent that the EU ever made. It is one of the most successful and impressive political transformations of the twentieth century, (Prodi, 2002).

Through its enlargement policy, the EU aimed at sharing common values, promoting political stability and diffusing well-being and prosperity by offering membership to 12 candidate countries. The European Neighbourhood Policy (ENP) is to achieve the same goals beyond the new Union's border through a privileged relationship with the new neighbouring countries but setting apart the issue of a prospective accession. The March 2003 Commission's communication stresses the connection between both processes:

> Over the coming decade and beyond, the Union's capacity to provide security, stability and sustainable development to its citizens will no longer be distinguishable from its interests in closer cooperation with the neighbours ... closer geographical proximity means the enlarged EU and the new neighbourhood will have an equal stake in furthering efforts to promote transnational flows of trade and investment as well as even more important shared interest in working together to tackle transboundary threats – from terrorism to air-borne pollution. The neighbouring countries are the EU's essential partners to increase our mutual production, economic growth and external trade, to create an enlarged area of political stability and functioning rule of law, and to foster the mutual exchange of human capital, ideas, knowledge and culture. [COM (2003) 104]

The ENP is not only presented as the continuation of the enlargement policy. Commissioner Günter Verheugen also suggested that a 'spill-over effect' binds the two processes, making ENP necessary for the full completion of the enlargement. In a speech in October 2003 at the Diplomatic Academy of Moscow, he stated 'that if the successful story of enlargement has expanded the area of stability and prosperity in Europe, this area can only be sustainable if it is also extended to our neighbourhood.

Achieving this is a crucial EU interest, just as it is of crucial interest to our neighbours' (Verheugen, 2003).

By leaving aside the prospect for accession, the ENP raised however a crucial question: can the objectives of sharing common values, promoting stability and bringing greater prosperity be achieved without offering the main incentive which has driven the Central and Eastern European Countries on the path of reforms? Will the ENP be attractive enough to stimulate the neighbouring countries to make strong efforts to approximate to the EU without the prospect for joining? A German ENP expert, Heinz Timmermann, estimates that this 'policy lacks the stimulant which the prospect of membership ... would offer the elites in implementing the difficult structural reforms [of these countries] ...' (Timmermann, 2004, p. 47). A statement delivered in Brussels in March 2003 by the Prime Minister of Ukraine Viktor Yanukovich gives weight to this assessment. After having been briefed by president Prodi about the new neighbourhood policy which is removing the prospect for Ukrainian accession, Yanukovich stated that this new context would deprive the Ukrainian government of part of the needed incentives to progress with reforms (Yanukovich, 2003). That the ENP will balance obligations with incentives is far from being guaranteed.

In his 5 December 2002 speech, president Prodi openly addressed this objection: 'the goal of accession is certainly the most powerful stimulus for reform we can think of. But why should a less ambitious goal not have the same effect? A substantive and workable concept of proximity would have a positive effect' (Prodi, 2002). To make his prognosis convincing, the president of the Commission argued:

> you can improve the climate for direct investment without being a member of the EU. You can align legislation on the EU's without being a member. You can have limited or unlimited access to the internal market without being a member. You can tighten budget controls and boost economic growth without being a member. But ... these benefits can only be obtained if and when the process is well structured, when the goals are well defined and the framework is legally and politically binding. And only if the two sides are clear about the mutual advantages and the mutual obligations. (Prodi, 2002)

THE PRACTICAL ISSUES

The March 2003 Commission's communication stresses too that 'a response to the practical issues posed by proximity and neighbourhood should be seen as separate from the question of EU accession' [COM (2003) 104, p. 5]. Of what do these 'practical issues' consist?

By 2007, when Bulgaria and Romania will have joined, the EU's eastern border will stretch over more than 5000 km from the Barents Sea to the Black Sea, adjoining four countries: Russia, Belarus, Ukraine and Moldova, to which southern Caucasus Countries – Georgia, Azerbaijan and Armenia have been added later. In 1995, when Finland acceded, the common border with Russia was only 1300 km. The maritime border with the Southern Mediterranean covers a length of 5,500 km, with ten countries facing it: Syria, Israel, Lebanon, Jordan, Occupied Palestinian Territory, Egypt, Libya, Tunisia, Algeria and Morocco. Both areas contain around 400 million inhabitants. Their standard of living is far below the EU's. In 2000, these countries had a GDP per capita less than 10 per cent of the EU (Tunisia has 9.9, Russia 8.3), except Israel (79.7) and Lebanon (19.1). Their exports were largely dependent on access to the EU market. In 2000 again, Maghreb countries directed more than 70 per cent of their exports to the EU 15. For Syria, Egypt and Israel, the figures were 61, 31.5 and 26.7 per cent. The share of the eastern countries' exports to the EU 15 was 39 per cent for the Russian Federation, 20.5 for Ukraine, 21.4 for Moldova and 11.1 for Belarus. This share is expected to increase with the EU.25 and will reach 50 per cent, for example, of Russian exports.[1] This also reminds us that more than 50 per cent of Russian oil exports and 60 per cent of gas exports go to the EU.

This concerns not only economic and trade interdependence but also immigration, internal security and regional crises. Immigration from these countries represented around 14 per cent of all non-EU immigrants in 1999 (8.4 per cent from the Southern Mediterranean and 5.4 per cent from Russia and the other Western New Independent States); a larger share came from Turkey, Central and Eastern candidate countries and ex-Yugoslavia. Regarding immigration to the acceding countries, Russia and Western NIS accounted for 23 per cent of non-national immigrants, with Southern Mediterranean countries accounting for 1.9 per cent [COM (2003) 104].

Proximity raises also the risks of illegal immigration, trafficking in drugs and people, organised crime and terrorism which affect the EU's internal security. Regional crises like those of Chechnya, Transniestra, Ossetia or Nagorny Karabakh may also damage political stability at the EU's border. For challenging these new elements, risks and potential threats, will the Union draw a dividing line, shut out its frontier and set up a 'Fortress Europe'? Or will it create a special cooperative regime which will allow it to tackle the 'practical issues' of the new proximity? As William Wallace has pointed out, 'the choice for the EU is therefore whether to export security and

---

[1] All these figures come from Tables in the annex of the March 2003 Commission's communication.

stability to these neighbours or risk importing instability from them'
(Wallace, 2003, p. 4).

Through its ENP, the EU opts for an enhanced cooperative relationship
and for exporting security and greater prosperity by offering to its neighbours
a stake in its internal market and participation in its policies and programmes.
Even if there cannot be completely free movement of people and labour, the
ENP is to combine reliable safeguards of the borders with their significant
openness. As Heinz Timmermann estimates 'that this is not necessarily an
illusion is demonstrated by the well functioning border regime on the
Finnish–Russian border with more than five million crossings every year'
(Timmermann, 2004, p. 47).

OUTLINING THE ENP

Before outlining further the geographic scope and the sectors of the ENP, let
us recall how this has come about.

As William Wallace writes, it was 'to translate the rhetorical commitment
of the Copenhagen European Council into practical measures' (Wallace,
2003, p. 6) that the Commission framed the concept of Neighbourhood
Policy and spelled out a wider range of measure in its already mentioned
March 2003 Communication: *Wider Europe – Neighbourhood: A New
Framework for Relations with our Eastern and Southern Neighbours.*

This communication was to be followed by two others, each of them
receiving positive endorsement by the Council. On the 1st of July 2003, the
Commission issued a document: 'Paving the Way for a Neighbourhood
Instrument'. The term 'Wider Europe' which mainly concerns Eastern
Europe and the new EU borders, was dropped. It was not an appropriate
name for a policy which includes also the Southern Mediterranean region.
This second Communication displayed a two phase project: the first,
covering the 2004–2006 period would construct a Neighbourhood
Programme on the basis of allocations already earmarked for existing
programs. The second phase should be post-2006 and would be provided
with a special new Neighbourhood Instrument which should have its own
budget line in the next Financial Perspectives 2007–2013.

After the Commission had delineated the Neighbourhood approach and
revealed a two phase programme, it drafted a third Communication, that of
12 May 2004, entitled 'Strategy Paper', proposing that the ENP should
consists of two kinds of acts: Actions Plans encompassing all the dimensions
of the enhanced partnership would first be set up for the next three to five
years, using existing means as well as the new post-2006 instrument. These
Actions Plans would be defined by common consent with each partner,

expressing the 'Joint Ownership' of the ENP. The second step 'could consist in the negotiation of European Neighbourhood Agreements, to replace the present generation of bilateral agreement, when Action Plan priorities are met' [COM (2004) 373]. After the Commission had issued its Strategic Paper, it drafted on 29 September 2004 a 'Proposal for a Regulation laying down general provisions establishing a European Neighbourhood and Partnership Instrument', which was submitted to the co-decision of the European Parliament and of the Council [COM (2004) 628 final]. The Regulation should have its legal basis in the EC Treaty, in particular in its article 179 (multi-annual programmes for Developing Countries) and 181a (Economic, Financial and Technical Cooperation with Third Countries). It describes the types of programmes (country and multi-country, thematic and cross-border cooperation programmes) and stresses complementarity with national measures and co-financing. The Neighbourhood and Financing Instrument will have a dual nature, mixing external policy and economic and social cohesion. To manage its ENP, in July 2003 the Commission established a task force under the authority of the Commissioner for Enlargement, G. Verheugen (Harris, 2004, p. 109). Headed by Michael Leigh, Deputy Director General in DG External Relations, it is staffed by around 30 civil servants. In the new Barroso Commission, it will depend on Mrs Ferrero-Waldner, who is in charge of External Relations and of Neighbourhood Policy. It should be noted that the acceding countries have been associated in the shaping of the ENP. The Polish 'Non-Paper' concerning new Eastern neighbours after enlargement illustrates the interest the new Eastern European members are giving to this issue (Republic of Poland, 2003).

THE MAIN OBJECTIVES

The global political goal of the Neighbourhood Policy is to bring political stability and economic prosperity at the borders of the Union, by diffusing and promoting the fundamental values of Human Rights, Democracy, Market Economy and social solidarity. To quote the March 2003 Communication, 'the EU should aim at developing a zone of prosperity and a friendly neighbourhood – a ring of friends – with whom the EU enjoys close, peaceful and co-operative relations [...] In return for progress demonstrating shared values and effective implementation of political, economic and institutional reforms, including in aligning legislation with the acquis, the EU's neighbours should benefit from the prospect of closer economic integration with the EU.' This could consist of getting 'the prospect of a stake in the EU's Internal Market and further integration and liberalization to promote the free movement of persons, goods, services and capital (the freedoms)' [COM (2003) 104, p. 4]. By organizing proximity and diffusing prosperity, the ENP is also to tackle the challenge of poverty and several exclusion.

The Strategy Paper elaborates more about the main sectors of the new policy. The Neighbourhood approach is trans-pillar, encompassing possible integration in the internal market, foreign and security policy issues and home and justice affairs activities.

As for the CFSP, exploring 'involvement of partner countries in aspects of CFSP and ESDP, conflict prevention, crisis management, possible participation in the EU-led crisis management operations' [COM (2004) 373, p. 13] is envisaged. The Justice and Home Affairs dimension will focus on the border management. The goal is 'to facilitate movement of persons whilst maintaining a high level of security' (p. 16). A local border traffic regime will be established to allow border area populations to maintain traditional contacts.

The economic and social development dimension aims at enhancing preferential trade relations and at increasing financial and technical assistance. For trade, greater market opening, gradual elimination of non-tariff barriers and for agricultural products, convergence with EU standards for sanitary and phyto-sanitary controls, are to enhance reciprocal trade between the partners and the EU. Free trade in services and improvements in the regime of investments in the neighbouring countries are also part of a closer integration in the EU internal market (p. 15).

Particular emphasis is put on energy: 'Enhancing our strategic partnership with neighbouring countries is a major element of the ENP. Russia, the Caspian Basin, North Africa are important suppliers of oil and natural gas. The Southern Caucasus countries are also important on this respect. For their part, Ukraine, Belarus, Morocco and Tunisia are transit countries. The Action Plans will contain concrete steps to increase energy dialogue ... and to foster gradual convergence of energy policies and the legal and regulatory environment' (p. 17). Transport, Environment, Information Society and Research are also included in the ENP. For the 'people to people' dimension, the Strategy Paper suggests 'the gradual opening of certain Community programmes, like YOUTH, Tempus and Erasmus Mundus'. The Commission proposes creating a specific 'Tempus Plus' which would address the education and training needs of the neighbouring countries.

Promotion of regional cooperation on the EU eastern borders will be one of the main objectives of the new European Neighbourhood Instrument which would support cross-border projects and wider trans-national cooperation. As mentioned above, the Commission issued in late September 2004 a proposal for the creation of a specific ENP instrument which will globalize the MEDA and TACIS activities.

A TWO STEP STRATEGY

According to the Strategy Paper, forming and then implementing the ENP will be carried out in two main stages. The first step will consist of defining Action Plans with every neighbouring partner. Even if the new Policy delineates common orientations and guidelines, it will give place to differentiated treatments which will be adapted to the partner's situation. Action Plans will define the actions to be undertaken in the various fields of the Neighbourhood Policy. Regarding financial assistance, the existing instruments will be used until the end of 2006 and the new European Neighbourhood and Partnership instrument will operate after 2006 to fund activities inside and outside the Union. These are to be Cooperation and Association Councils. Once Action Plans will have been progressively carried on, new contractual links in the form of European Neighbourhood Agreements are to replace the existing agreements.

Even if the ENP begins to tap the full potential of existing agreements and instruments, they will be replaced afterwards by a new generation of specific agreements based on art. I. 57 of the Constitutional Treaty. Action Plans will succeed to Common Strategies for Russia and Ukraine. The ENP will establish a global framework encompassing both Russia and the other Western N.S, Southern Caucasus and Southern Mediterranean. This new approach is raising two main questions, the first one about differentiation, the second one about added value.

DIFFERENTIATION AND ADDED VALUE

The whole official literature on ENP stresses differentiation. 'It is obvious that our neighbours differ largely. So do their relations with us. Hence differentiation is a key notion in our neighbourhood policy,' said Commission Verheugen in Tunis.

> Different Action Plans will reflect different sets of common interest and different magnitudes in sharing values ... The initial political intention or the European Union [is] to elevate its relationship with neighbours to a status as close as economically and politically feasible to the status of in coming members. How close a given neighbour want to be to the European Union will, in the end, be its own political decision. (Verheugen, 2004)

Verheugen's speech made it clear that the ENP will run at different speeds according to the situation and the will of the partners. In the heterogeneous group of neighbours, Russia will be a special case: 'The Russian Federation is of course more than a neighbour to the Union. Its geography, its size and potential, and its role in would affairs make that one relationship with Russia has developed into a far-going strategic partnership', declared G. Verheugen in his January 2004 speech in Moscow (Verheugen, 2004). This strategic partnership will be developed through the creation of four common spaces, which were defined at the St Petersburg Summit in May 2003: a common European economic space (CEES), a common space of freedom, security and justice, a space of cooperation in the field of external security and a space of research and education, including culture. Moreover, Russia and the EU sustain a dialogue on energy.

While the strategic partnership is between two equal powers, the ENP which implies approximation to the EU legislation may give the impression of imbalance to the detriment of Russia. If the ENP, like the Association agreements, means that the EU is the policy-maker and Russia a policy taker, 'it is difficult to imagine that such an arrangement would be politically acceptable', Marius Vahl emphasises, explaining: 'a central feature of Russian Cold-War foreign policy is the emphasis on Russia being acknowledged as a great power and cooperator with other major powers taking place on the basis of equality' (Vahl, 2004, p. 196). Moreover, Moscow cannot perceive itself as a participant in a ring of EU friends which would run from the Russian–Finish border up to Morocco. The ENP could also face competition from the will Moscow shows to keep close contact with and even control over its 'near abroad', as is indicated by the creation of multilateral agreements like the 'Eurasian Economic Community', created in 2000 and grouping Russia, Balkans, Kazakhstan, Kyrgyzstan, Tajikistan, with Moldova and Ukraine joining as observers, or the 'Unified Economic Space' between Russia, Belarus, Ukraine and Moldova. In its approach towards Russia and the Western NS, the EU should avoid the two extremes pointed out by Heinz Timmermann: 'it should not treat the New Neighbours as a dependent variable of its partnership with Russia, which would be tantamount to the recognition of Russian claims of hegemony and would revive the old theses of "limited sovereignty". On the other hand, the intensification of relations with these countries should not be pursued in confrontation with Russia' (Timmermann, 2004, p. 51).

While Russia does not feel it belongs to an EU ring of friends extending up to Morocco and sticks to its equal to equal power status, other European neighbour countries fed expectations which targeted beyond the ENP framework. Not only Ukraine but Moldova, Georgia and Armenia too had already expressed the hope of being offered a long-term perspective of accession through a process similar to the Stabilisation and Association Pact which paves the way for the Western Balkan countries becoming EU members in a not too distant future. Even if the ENP does not definitively rule out but sets aside their accession, it can mainly be deemed as second best for the Western New Independent and Southern Caucasus countries. Through its ENP, the EU bids for a better trade regime which is to lead towards preferential treatment, from which they did not benefit under the Partnership and Cooperation Agreements (except for some goods under the Generalized System of Preferences). With this preferential access to the EU market, cross-border facilitations (at term, visa free travelling) for the people living at the outside of the new enlarged EU border and an increase in investments and financial assistance may represent the main attractive advantages those countries could gain from the ENP replacing PCA.

Differentiation not only separates Russia and the other Eastern European countries but also and mainly the latter and the Mediterranean neighbours. Apart from accession being ruled out for Southern Mediterranean countries, two major differences separate the two groups. In terms of economic conditionalities, the Eastern European partners, which are also members of the Council of Europe, will have to show a better record in human rights, rule of law and pluralist democracy than the Maghreb and Mashrek countries to which the EU could hardly apply the same standards and which 'have only subscribed to the weaker UN conventions on human rights', as Michael Emerson observed (Emerson, 2004, p. 15). If the ENP may require less from the Mediterranean countries for political conditionality, it will also appear less attractive to them in terms of trade, seeing that free trade is already planned by 2010. The question of whether it will bring substantial added value to what these countries are already offered through the Barcelona Process remains unanswered. With the Southern Mediterranean area, the ENP seems to be more the continuation of the same trend under a new label than a new stage in the approximation of the two sides of the Mediterranean Sea. The ENP will probably be more significant in managing a Wider Europe than in organizing a global neighbourhood from the Barents Sea to the Strait of Gibraltar.

REFERENCES

Commission of the European Communities (2003), *Communication from the Commission to the Council and the European Parliament: Wider Europe – Neighbourhood: A New Framework for Relations with our Eastern and Southern Neighbours*, COM (2003) 104 final, 11 March 2003.
Commission of the European Communities (2004), *European Neighbourhood Policy Strategic Paper*, COM (2004) 373, 12 May 2004.
Commission of the European Communities (2004b), *Proposal for a Regulation of the European Parliament and of the Council laying down general provisions establishing a European Neighbourhood and Partnership Instrument*, COM (2004) 628 final, 29 September 2004.

Emerson, M. (2004), 'EU neighbourhood policy too low gear', *European Voice*, Vol. 10, No. 19, 27 May-2 June 2004.

Harris, G. (2004), 'The wider Europe', in Fraser Cameron (ed.), *The Future of Europe*, London and New York, Routledge.

Prodi, R. (2002), 'A wider Europe – a proximity policy as the key to stability', *Speech delivered to the Sixth ECSA-World Conference*, Brussels, 5 December 2002.

Republic of Poland, Ministry of Foreign Affairs (2003), *Non-Paper with Polish proposals concerning policy towards new Eastern Neighbours after EU enlargement*, January 2003, reproduced in Stefan Batory Foundation, *European Union Enlargement and Neighbourhood Policy*, Warsaw.

Timmermann, H. (2004), 'The European Union and its new neighbours: Ukraine, Belarus and Moldova', *The Federalist Debate*, Year XVII, No. 2, July 2004.

Verheugen, G. (2003), 'EU enlargement and the Union's neighbourhood policy', *Speech at the Diplomatic Academy*, Moscow, 27 October 2003.

Verheugen, G. (2004), 'The neighbours policy of the European Union: an opportunity for Tunisia', *Speech at the Institut Arabe des Chefs d'Entreprises*, Tunis, 21 January 2004.

Vahl, M. (2004), 'Whither the common European economic space?', in Tanguy de Wilde d'Estmael and Laetitia Spetchinsky (eds), *La politique étrangère de la Russie et l'Europe, Enjeux d'une proximité*, Chaire Interbrew – Baillet Latour Union européenne – Russie, UCL – KUL, Bruxelles PIE – Peter Lang.

Wallace, W. (2003), 'Looking after the neighbourhood: responsibilities for the EU-25', *Notre Europe, Policy Papers*, No. 4, July 2003.

Yanukovich, V. (2003), Speech by the Prime Minister of Ukraine to the TEPSA Friends, Brussels, Fondation Universitaire, 23 March 2003.

10. The EU's Enlargement and Euro-Mediterranean Relations

Dimitris K. Xenakis

INTRODUCTION

European integration has been a cumulative and incremental enterprise, both in terms of membership and of the scope and level of integration. The post-1989 shift in the vocation of the European international system has resulted in the countries of Central and Eastern Europe becoming part of the European Union's (EU) zone of democracy, stability and prosperity. Ten new member countries have recently joined the EU. It took courage, determination and considerable effort from the people and political forces in the new members to get this far. At the same time, it took vision and generosity from the people and leaders of the older EU members to support this process.

Apart from the serious questions regarding the future of the Union itself after this massive enlargement, there are also concerns regarding the Mediterranean dimension of the European project. No doubt, this enlargement has also a small Mediterranean dimension. *Prima facie*, the accession of Cyprus and Malta suggests a serious change in the European involvement in Mediterranean security affairs, which are of great importance for the international European system. Yet, it is also no secret that the Euro-Mediterranean Partnership (EMP) and the so called Barcelona Process, in place since 1995, face serious obstacles, such as its own structural and functional problems, and the continuing conflict in the Middle East, and will now have to adapt to the new politico-economic difficulties that the enlargement poses. In addition, contemporary Euro-Mediterranean affairs are also clearly affected by the formation of the new European crisis-management tool – a new development that enhances the role of the Union in regional security affairs.

THE EURO-MEDITERRANEAN SETTING

The terrorist attacks on 11 September 2001, have ushered in a new era in international politics. The priorities in international politics, the nature of regional politics, the shape of political alliances, the driving purpose of US foreign policy, the nature of international cleavages, the evolving role of military forces and the risks of weapons of mass destruction have all been affected by the epoch-making events. Against a turbulent and unpredictable international environment, clear manifestations of which have been the wars in Afghanistan and, more recently, in Iraq, analysts were quick to point out that the Mediterranean region is particularly vulnerable to the emerging global security setting. The majority of security analyses suggest that the Euro-Mediterranean space constitutes a zone of strategic and socio-economic instability, migration flows, violent religious and cultural conflicts, varying forms of political and economic institutions, differing perceptions of security and above all differing worldviews. The Mediterranean security agenda includes *inter alia* Algeria's civil war, Turkey's question, Lebanon's struggles, the Cyprus question, the Palestinian issue, Israel's relations with Arab world, terrorist groups, pervasive economic backwardness and demographic growth throughout the southern shore, the use of the region as an area of rising transnational crime including narcotics trafficking, proliferation of weapons of mass destruction, and the activities of the great powers in areas of long-standing rivalry and intervention.

Issues of Mediterranean security are not new, and yet they still rest on considerable variation in the EU's foreign policy. The extent to which the Mediterranean can be seen as a distinct region complicates further the discussion about the appropriate scope and level of a common European policy towards this part of the world. Partly as a result of the Community's Mediterranean enlargements in the 1980s, and partly due to the changing conditions post-1989, Mediterranean affairs have come to occupy a significant amount of Europe's external relations. Since the mid - 1990s, the EU's Mediterranean policy has gained a significant degree of multilateralisation, as compared with previous, generally incoherent, European approaches to the Mediterranean.

The 1995 Barcelona Declaration set a framework of cooperation between the EU and its 15 member states, and on the other hand, 12 southern Mediterranean countries (Turkey, Malta, Cyprus, Syria, Lebanon, Jordan, Israel, Egypt, Tunisia, Morocco, Algeria and Palestine).[1] The main objectives were to establish a common Euro-Mediterranean area of peace and stability;

---

[1] Libya has been attending all ministerial meetings since 1999 as an observer of the EU Council Presidency following the lifting of UN sanctions, which had been imposed over the Lockerbie affair. See further in Pargeter (2002).

create an area of shared prosperity through the progressive establishment of a free-trade area between the EU and its Mediterranean Partners and cooperation and policy dialogue in several areas. It also aims at helping improve mutual understanding and tolerance among peoples of different cultures and traditions (for more details see Panebianco, 2003).

Although 'hard' security plays a highly important role in Euro-Mediterranean relations, the EMP is essentially a soft-power projection of the EU in the region (Tanner, 2003). Therefore, it has infused a degree of political bias to Euro-Mediterranean relations, whilst encompassing an ambitious economic plan for an (industrially inspired) Euro-Mediterranean Free Trade Area by the year 2010, and a 'human dimension' similar to the one introduced by the Helsinki Process in 1975 (Xenakis, 1998). It has been argued that the concept of the Barcelona project is the careful 'westernisation' of the Mediterranean in terms of requiring a convergence of principles and methods in dealing with pressing issues such as democracy and human rights. Although the political conditionality principle allows the EU to suspend its commitments in cases of regime failure, it exposes the Mediterranean partners to the good will of the EU, thus offending their demand for equal partnership (Jünemann, 1998: 373–83). From this view, the charge of 'westernising' looks like a shady political stratagem aimed at discrediting forces that are pressing for change.

The EMP may prove instrumental in fostering a new co-operative ethos among its members. Interest-convergence around economic tasks could contribute to a relaxation of tensions in areas where controversy is more likely to arise – i.e., military security and human rights. It is on this premise that a more easily discernible Euro-Mediterranean regime may come into being (Xenakis, 1999). The composite nature of the regional process offers a wide range of opportunities for the functionalist expectations of the countries involved to form the basis of a consensually pre-determined set of policies, which are beneficial to overall systemic stability. In practice, however, the EMP has moved forward to a large extent through the new Association Agreements that updated and enhanced the previous individual agreements between the EU and its Mediterranean partners. They focus mainly on trade liberalisation, foreign direct investment and economic co-operation, and the strengthening of interregional socio-cultural ties.

In its almost nine years of function it is fair to say that the Barcelona Process has not yet fulfilled its rather high ambitions. The process has experienced significant constrains for two main reasons. First, because the Barcelona Process has not helped in the resolution of any major security problem in the region. All three of its baskets of co-operation have suffered from problems such as the proliferation of conventional weapons and weapons of mass destruction, low level of investment and infrastructure, illegal migration, violation of human rights, and above all the regional 'ticking bomb' called demography.

Second, all the initial optimism that the Oslo Process produced in the early 1990s has evaporated in a mutually reinforcing violent cycle of suicidal terrorist attacks and excessive use of military force. It is lamentable that since the beginning of the second *Intifada* in 2000, the EMP has failed continuously to free itself from the Middle East Peace Process. When the EMP was conceived, it was based on the assumption that the Middle East Peace Process, whatever its problems, was to be a permanent cornerstone of collective security in the Mediterranean. More than that, it was also to signal the final Arab–Israeli reconciliation. Although these hopes were to be dented by extra-regional development changes in subsequent years, as well as by tensions between Israel and the Palestinian Authority, Middle East peace has continued to be an integral part of the underlying assumptions of the EMP. Now, however, these assumptions can no longer be sustained. We face a real war between two members of the Barcelona Process. The implications of this for the EMP are particularly gloomy after Arafat's death.

The post-September 11th counter-terrorism campaign and the wars in Afghanistan and Iraq have complicated the development of the Barcelona project. Moreover, there has been little progress on regional conflicts where some relief was expected, such as in Cyprus, or Western Sahara. As a result, the long awaited *Charter on Peace and Stability* has been stalled. The talks on the Euro-Mediterranean Charter for Peace and Stability, first initiated by the southern partners, aimed to contain European desires to implement a fully-fledged regional security regime along the lines of the Helsinki Process, but gradually shifted towards democratisation, respect of human rights and the rule of law in the Southern partner countries. Given this impasse, the 'Charter' talks failed and were suspended, but since Marseilles the EU has sustained its efforts to advance democracy and good governance proposals within the EMP framework, and more recently in the context of the enlargement to Eastern Europe (Aliboni, 2004).

There is no doubt that the EU exhibits difficulties in dealing with Middle East security. But the EU also faces significant challenges as a result of the presence of the US and the continuing reluctance of the latter to share its 'co-operative hegemony' in the Middle East. The US sponsored counter-terrorism campaign in the Arab world and the crisis over Iraq have also highlighted the existence of profound divergences not only within the international community, the transatlantic alliance and the EU, but also within the EMP partners themselves. Moreover, the inadequacy of the EU's intervention in the 2002 Middle East crisis seriously affected the status of the EMP, not only regarding security co-operation but also its multilateral nature. It is no secret that the EU has to make considerable efforts to keep Israel in the process, whilst continuing to co-operate with the Arab countries. Europeans have to contribute something concretely positive to the Peace Process in accordance with the reasonable demands of their Arab states, whilst dealing with Israel's hostile attitude towards any EU-led intervention.

The Barcelona Process has been an ambitious and innovative initiative, and although today is not in its best shape, it is still alive. The follow up implementation has proved to be much more complex than expected. Based on tremendous results achieved by the Helsinki Process and, later, on the multifaceted EU involvement in the transition of the former communist countries to pluralistic democracy and market economy, the Barcelona project was primarily meant to extend that assistance in the Mediterranean (Xenakis, 2004). Of importance in the years to come will be the chosen institutional format to transcend the peculiarities of Euro-Mediterranean relations. But the institutionalisation of the Barcelona Process alone will not be sufficient to manage a rather complex regional security agenda. The question is twofold: whether the EMP can meet its prescribed ends without first transforming itself into a system of patterned behaviour, and whether the co-operative ethos embedded in the new regional institutional setting can go beyond the level of contractual interstate obligations and closer to a genuine or, at least, meaningful partnership.[2] New rules and norms will have to be created, given that behaviour, not just proclamations, will determine the outcome of this European regional order-building project.

EUROPEAN SECURITY AND DEFENCE POLICY: A NEW REGIONAL STRATEGIC VARIABLE

Euro-Mediterranean relations are as full of misunderstandings about distorted perceptions and images of Islam, as they are about the threat of terrorism used by transnational extremist groups, especially post-September 11th. The broader redefinition of Europe's relations with the Arab world is ever more necessary, including the power deficit between the two shores which has been escalating since the signing of the Schengen Treaty, which has been conceived by some as the forerunner of a 'fortress' Europe. Euro-

---

[2] In this framework, the EU's strategic choices will be of great importance, together with the promotion of norms of good governance, given the tensions arising from different conceptions of democracy and modernisation. Equally crucial are the socio-cultural barriers in furthering the prospects of an open inter-civilisational dialogue, keeping in mind the recent re-embrace of religious fundamentalism. Whatever the legitimising ethos of the prevailing views, a structured dialogue based on the principles of transparency and symbiotic association is central to the cross-fertilisation among distinct politically organised and culturally defined units. Such a dialogue, could not only alleviate historically rooted prejudices, but can also endow the EMP with a new sense of process. See the analysis in Xenakis and Chryssochoou (2001, chapters 2 and 3).

Mediterranean strategic affairs are clearly affected by the formation of the common European Security and Defence Policy (ESDP). Its formation suggests a new regional strategic variable that enhances the European role in Mediterranean security affairs. The ESDP was formally launched by the conclusions of the Cologne European Council (June 1999). Since then, ESDP has passed through decisions taken in Helsinki (December 1999), Feira (June 2000), Nice (December 2000), Goteborg (June 2001), Laeken (December 2001), Seville (June 2002), Brussels (October 2002), Copenhagen (December 2002), Thessaloniki (June 2003), Brussels (December 2003) and more recently. Each of these successive European Councils has gradually given substance to this desire to give to the EU the capacity for autonomous international action.[3]

The EU's official documents such as the Common Strategy for the Mediterranean are general descriptions lacking prioritisation over the EU's strategic intentions.[4] In the process of consolidating a common European defence identity with operational capabilities, the conceptions, intentions, planning, political goals, individual national interests of EU states and their attempt to maintain a relative diplomatic freedom in the region remain vague. 'In the absence of a clear range of goals, deriving from a joint strategic plan for the Mediterranean', the EuroMeSCo's report argues that 'a certain level of vagueness is inevitable' (EuroMeSCo, 2002: 14). However, most analysts, in the light of the negative experience with *Eurofor* and *Euromarfor*, have underlined the need for complementary measures to support the ESDP. Given the low level of information about the ESDP in the Arab world, the EU decided to pay greater attention to the misperceptions and fears of its Mediterranean partners regarding the strengthening of its military capabilities. Thus the ESDP acquired its own Mediterranean dimension, courtesy of the initiative taken by the Spanish Presidency during the first half of 2002. The Hellenic Presidency that followed played a decisive role to that end (Xenakis and Chryssochoou, 2003). Proposals on transparency, trust-building and the institutionalisation of security dialogue allow Mediterranean partners to gain better access in the making of a co-operative regional security space and to reduce the existing levels of regional power deficit.

---

[3] In the military aspects of ESDP, the EU has committed itself to setting up a force of 60,000 men, deployable within two months and sustained on the ground for 12 months. But this embryonic military structure is not meant to be a standing force. Hence, the term 'Euro-Army', which has been in increasing use for some time now, does not describe accurately, at least for the time being, the nature of the EU's crisis-management apparatus.

[4] The *Common Strategy for the Mediterranean* was adopted by the Feira European Council and constitutes a means for accommodating Mediterranean issues to European foreign policy aspirations, as well as a mechanism for implementing CFSP objectives according to the provisions of the Amsterdam Treaty.

There is no doubt that the creation of a united and military autonomous EU should not lead to a 'fortress' Europe, and therefore it should not obstruct the regional transformation process and the creation of a stable and prosperous Euro-Mediterranean free trade area. In this framework it is important for the Euro-Mediterranean partners to arrive at common definitions and responses to common security anxieties related to terrorism, information-flow, human security, civilian engagement and trust-building. All strategic intentions and perceptions in the Euro-Mediterranean space should be reconsidered and clarified, so that the open character of both projects (the EMP and the ESDP) is safeguarded.

Another issue of concern refers to the development of ESDP. Although the development of an ESDP is positive for Europe, in that it will lead to a degree of independence from the US for security, southern neighbours have become suspicious. The ESDP produces, in the same way as the enlargement, contradictory feelings: it is desired and yet feared. In the Mediterranean, although some sectors would wish the ESDP to represent an assertion of Europe's power to provide peace enforcement forces in the Mediterranean area under a UN mandate, the ESDP is at the same time feared among the EU's southern Mediterranean neighbours in that their particular country might become the involuntary target of a EU military intervention some day in the future. To remove the existing lack of information, or even outright misinformation, among EU neighbours regarding the ESDP, there was a large scale information campaign explaining the ESDP to the EU's neighbours during the Spanish and the Greek Presidencies of the EU (2002–3) and beyond (see more analytically in Tsinisizelis *et. al.*, 2003). This has been going on to reassure southern Mediterranean countries through regular Euro-Mediterranean defence and security dialogue within the framework of the Barcelona Process.

Most of the southern partners of the EU see a positive side to the strengthening of regional defence co-operation and their involvement in joint military exercises. It is essential to promote the positive expectations for a more active EU in Mediterranean security affairs, by encouraging its partners to participate in joint strategic activities. The participation of southern EMP partners in future ESDP exercises in the region is a confidence-building measure that needs to be encouraged (Papantoniou, 2002). The reinforcement of scientific co-operation in joint military exercises like emergency rescue missions and the handling of natural disasters is a good case in point (Tanner, 1999). It is also suggested that co-ordination mechanisms for bilateral security and defence co-operation should not be excluded from the agenda, initially at the level of exchange of information in sub-regional initiatives where security is a clear issue, such as the Mediterranean Forum.[5] This could then be extended to the EMP. This will promote regional co-operation in the fields of security and defence through immediate upgrade of the intelligence level in ESDP matters.

THE VIEW FROM THE SOUTH

Southern Mediterranean responses to the EU's enlargement process have so far been moderate and not very articulate – which is not so strange if one takes into account that during the last years these countries have had other, more immediate concerns stemming from the Middle East crisis and its assorted zones of conflict. In looking deeper though, there is a degree of uncertainty among southern Mediterranean partners about the situation beyond the accession day, for the most vital decisions about the region are normally taken by Europeans outside the Barcelona framework, usually within the EU, and sometimes at the other side of the Atlantic. At the same time, the lengthy procedures in several EU bodies for taking decisions, programming and implementing capacities that keep Euro-Mediterranean co-operation at low levels are expected to become more acute after the enlargement.

A concern in some southern Mediterranean countries is the inevitable feeling of exclusion from the EU. Some of these countries (Morocco and perhaps Israel) would also like to join the EU in that they feel that this could be a panacea to a majority of their socio-economic problems. Although not being accepted as eligible for EU membership causes frustration, exclusion is even more hurtful when such refusal is based on the fact of being located on the 'wrong' side of the Mediterranean. This feeling of exclusion is dangerous in that it produces hostility and alternative explanations for being left outside (religion, culture, race, etc.). Such feelings are unfortunate for the new Europe in that they generate a lot of friction in regional relations and fuel social discontent and radical groups in Arab societies.

Mediterranean partners do not perceive the EU's eastward enlargement as equal to the Euro-Med project and regional co-operation. They do not claim EU membership, nor do they expect, for instance, equal financial aid packages or appropriations to MEDA as to PHARE and TACIS programmes. Although the Mediterranean partners have a clear understanding of the

---

[5] While conceived as a sub-regional 'proximity' circle within the wider Euro-Mediterranean space, the Mediterranean Forum could have a very active and specific role in promoting a multilateral co-operation agenda in the Mediterranean concerning particularly security and defence issues. Its membership makes it easier to tackle co-operation on such issues, which would be a harder task, due to current circumstances, to address at the EMP level (IAI, 2002).

privileged treatment of the new member states, they do not expect the EU to present them with lists of criteria identical or even similar to those agreed in Copenhagen. Occasionally, however, they have come to meet some of these criteria in their interactions with the EU (Schmid, 2003).

There is a frequently expressed expectation among EU neighbours that once the enlargement was finalised, the EU would pay more attention to the Mediterranean security anxieties. Although the Barcelona Process and several other minor Mediterranean projects (Mediterranean Forum, CSCM, Five + Five Initiative, etc.) have been undertaken post-1989, these cannot compare to the political attention and the unparallel quantities of technical and financial aid devoted to the enlargement process. This is natural, for the new members have to undertake domestic reforms and hence are badly in need of EU help. Yet, most of these countries compete with others in the EU's periphery that are also in need of economic and social reforms. Many Mediterranean countries also need urgent reform, and perhaps the EU will now be able to dedicate more attention and resources towards helping its non-candidate neighbours, the same way that it has assisted its recently accessed members, in terms of financial and technical assistance.

There is no doubt that regional economic relations will be affected by the EU's enlargement. On the one hand the southern Mediterranean economies will be able to grow and prosper, as a result of expanding their potential markets to some 700 million people. The 'Wider Europe-Neighbourhood' initiative can also reinforce the trade dimension of the Barcelona project by further encouraging Mediterranean partners to engage in trade liberalisation, sub-regional economic integration and regulatory convergence. On the other hand, it raises challenges in terms of the capacity of different groups of countries to integrate into more developed markets and face increased competition, particularly between the southern partners and the newly accepted EU member states.

The enlargement of the Union is a development of truly historic proportions and its long-term effects form the basis for a stronger EU in international affairs. The enlarged Union will develop into a much more important international actor, being one of the largest regional economic blocs in the world. This growing international importance might be used in various ways, which directly or indirectly will benefit southern Mediterranean countries, i.e. the need to find a permanent solution in Palestine – the caucus of the problem in the Middle East. The Bush administration's focus on the 'anti-terrorist' campaigns in Afghanistan and Iraq has opened a vacuum in the Middle East conflict, which noone so far has managed to fill. It is highly expected that the EU will press for the announcement and implementation of the Road Map, shelved since December 2002. It is important, however, to mention here that the Arab partners generally doubt the international role of the EU, since the favourable European attitude towards the right of existence of the Palestinian Authority is counterbalanced by its ineffective action in Palestine. Rather naturally, public opinion in the Arab populations of Mediterranean societies considers the EU's stance fairer than that of the US, but the Israeli perception over the European presence in the area is opposite. In Israel there is a dominant 'hopeful pessimism' over the international role of the EU *vis-à-vis* the 'obvious' hostility towards Israeli interests in the Palestinian issue. On the other hand, the Arabs are in favour of a more active EU role in the Middle East (see more analytically in EuroMeSCo, 2002: 11–12).

An important issue here is the EU's ability and willingness to be an active and efficient party in regional conflict resolution or, on the contrary, to choose to protect itself, to isolate itself from the overflow of violence related to these conflicts. This is a very important issue because political and security dialogue is the most underdeveloped pillar of the EMP. And it will continue to be so until the EU becomes more clearly involved in the resolution of urgent conflicts, which have prevented, to date, the approval of the Euro-Mediterranean Charter for Peace and Stability.

A final expectation refers to a role that the EU is expected to play for a viable solution, in line with its own *acquis communautaire*, in the Cyprus issue. Although the EU ideally preferred a solution before opening its membership to the Republic of Cyprus, the situation today suggests that the whole of Cyprus should benefit from EU membership. Apart from the urgent need to address the implications of the many new and foreseen developments in the EU's *acquis*, the Euro–Med *acquis* included, in the context of enlargement, and even within the new Constitution Treaty, the shifting geo-political, geo-economic and legal scenarios on the variegation (or otherwise of 'EU–Med' and 'Med–Med' relations) should also be of primary concern.

The peaceful resolution of the Cyprus question may also further improve regional relations. The easing of tensions in the Aegean will relieve subsequently some congestion from the wider Mediterranean security complex. At the same time, and considering that all past efforts towards a settlement of the Cyprus question have failed, the EU will have made a great step to adopting a new role in international affairs if it is successful in contributing towards a peaceful solution. In this context, the solution of the historical problem would also affirm European commitment to be decisively involved in regional high politics. However, if the EU fails to follow an assertive policy based on its own declarations for the preservation of peace and prosperity in the wider Mediterranean, it will further expose the difficulties involved in the making of the new Europe.

THE MEDITERRANEAN DIMENSION OF AN ENLARGED UNION

The enlargement of the EU brought new neighbours from the East, and decreased the distance to the other side of the Mediterranean. The accession of Cyprus and Malta expanded the EU's geographical borders very close to North African and Middle Eastern shores. This does not however suggest that a renewed interest on the part of the enlarged Union is guaranteed. This is because today, the EU is a much wider institution, composed of 25 members, whose characteristic is the non-uniformity of economic, political and legal systems, let alone defence and foreign policy orientations and priorities. In other words, today the EU is approximating more closely a regional regime, where the dominant logic is that of differentiation or, in recent EU parlance, flexibility.

The analytical validity of these presuppositions is further justified when trying to establish a link between continuity and change within a system of multinational shared rule; when attempting to identify the common values of distinct polities and the prospects for the emergence of new ones; when aiming at shedding some additional light on the dialectical union between a highly interactive society of independent nations and new sources of political authority; or even when engaging in a process of investigating the allegedly 'part-formed' and/or *sui generis* physiognomy of a Union composed of distinct culturally defined and politically organised units, where the dynamics of intrastate policy-making intermesh with those of large-scale polity formation with enormous complexity, producing a new type of collective entity characterised by interlocking structures of political authority: a transnational polity which lacks a single locus of decision-making (Chryssochoou *et al.*, 2003).

There is no doubt that the EU is a polity with no historical precedent. Hence our expectations of elevating its current status to the level of a global actor with enhanced military capabilities are difficult to put in context. Even though the transformation of the EU into a collective security system is inadequately addressed, it is clear that, today, extraordinary opportunities arise for a redefinition of its future, given that the EU represents a global symbol of political stability and economic prosperity. The EU has been actively involved in the process of democratising the countries in Central and Eastern Europe and of promoting political and economic change in the Mediterranean countries. The vision of an EU that plays an important part in global security management entails more than the consolidation of economic might; it requires the emergence of a commonality of interests leading to a single European voice in world affairs. This, however, implies that EU members will have to sacrifice their gains from diplomatic manoeuvres in their national foreign policy for the achievement of a defence-oriented CFSP.

The EMP is also a means of co-ordinating the different national policies of EU members. The CFSP Common Strategy on the Mediterranean (2000) is a way of making sure that the EMP's main role is one of co-ordinating better the EU policy and then imposing any given decision on the southern Mediterranean partners who are neither united, nor co-ordinated. Thus, the EMP depends very much on intra-EU coordination (Attina, 2001).

Gillespie suggests that the North/South European dimension must be considered in any analysis of EU Mediterranean policy, for it provides a potential fault-line along which European disunity could develop (Gillespie, 1997). Today, developments in the region receive special attention mainly from the southern EU members, while they are hardly recognised in the North, let alone the new members from eastern Europe. Moreover, pre-1989 European ambitions for a stable and prosperous Mediterranean have been mainly promoted outside the framework of the EU, in the form of different state-led initiatives for regional co-operation like the CSCM, the Mediterranean Forum, etc. Mediterranean anxieties are clearly reflected in demands by southern EU members for increased financial and political support to southern Mediterranean countries. Such interest has resulted in a substantial increase in financial assistance from France, Spain and Italy (Marks, 1996: 11).

The intergovernmental nature of the Union itself ensures that the pursuit of national interests in the region will remain dominant in the foreseeable future. Therefore, the increased diversity within the Union after the enlargement will no doubt influence the future of the EMP. Turning the balance within the enlarged EU will thus be a difficult task, given that almost all are convinced that economic assistance should be aiming to support the newly accessed economies. The main challenge for the new EU's Mediterranean members Malta, Cyprus (and maybe Turkey tomorrow) is to redress the imbalance within the eastward enlarged Union. This could only be achieved though coalition-building and alliance-formation not only with the rest of the EU Mediterranean states – something that is the staple approach in EU decision-making – but also with the rest of the littoral countries, as they are supposed to share the concerns of the increasing challenges the region is facing in the new era.

Yet, differences of perceptions and interests also exist with regard to the EU's relations with its Mediterranean partners among the southern EU members. In particular, France, Spain and Italy bring Mediterranean issues to the forefront of the EU's agenda, since they traditionally maintain a plethora of economic and political interests in the region. France, however, has displayed a distinctive and rather inchoate policy towards some

Mediterranean states, thus making it hard for the Union to accept French leadership in the formulation of its Mediterranean policy. The problem is further compounded by the fact that other EU members have also expressed their own preferences in the EU's Mediterranean policy, most notably Italy and Spain.[6] It should be considered yet another 'Mediterranean paradox' that, while those three southern European countries play a more essential role in setting the Union's Mediterranean agenda, smaller countries like Greece, Portugal, Malta and Cyprus receive the challenges and constraints confronting peripheral but relatively less-developed regions in southern Europe.[7]

Differences in their priorities illustrate that the EU's Mediterranean members have not yet found a *modus operandi* for utilising their common membership to promote their interests in the EU's agenda. It is almost certain that in the enlarged and ever more diverse Union, the differences involved in the making of a genuine Mediterranean policy are even more acute. Co-ordinated pressure by all European Mediterranean countries will prove necessary if peace and prosperity of the Mediterranean region is to remain one of the EU's policy priorities.

PROSPECTS

There is no doubt that a different political status is attached to enlargement than to Euro-Mediterranean co-operation. Enlargement is about the complete integration of the established laws and practices of the EU's *acquis*. The Barcelona project is about developing and intensifying regional co-operation. The full integration of ten new members makes quite different demands of all parties than the creation of a free trade area. However, it is important for old and new EU members to send signals to the South that the Mediterranean remains important for Europe, also after the enlargement. Both old and new member states have ambitions of playing a more important role in the Middle East Peace Process; and of supporting national processes towards good

---

[6] These differences stem from the geographical position of the southern EU members and their different historical pasts: while Spain tends to concentrate on north-western Africa, Italy's main focus is Libya and the Eastern Mediterranean; the attention of France is divided between Algeria and Lebanon; and the main preoccupation of Greece is Cyprus and Turkey. For comprehensive analyses of Spain's role in the Mediterranean see Gillespie (1999). Respectively for Italy see Holmes (1996). For an overall account see Stavridis *et al.* (1999).

[7] Over the past two decades, international migration patterns have undergone considerable changes. These are basically due to the changing role of some southern European countries (Italy, Spain, Greece and Portugal) – transformed from sending to receiving countries – to the decline of migrations within the European Union, to the increase of immigration coming from less developed countries and, more recently, to the emerging of significant migration flows from southern Mediterranean countries.

governance, democratisation, rule of law and respect for human rights without trying to impose the western model, parts of which do not fit in with cultural, social and political specificities.

The EU's enlargement is bound to have a significant impact in and beyond the Old Continent. Recently, the European Commission issued a Communication entitled 'Wider Europe-Neighbourhood' proposing a new framework for relations with the EU's eastern and southern neighbours. It is thus imperative for the Union and its new members that they meet neighbouring non-candidate countries, listen to their concerns, and inform them fully and frankly about its security motives. Transparency is particularly important where the Mediterranean is concerned since one of the specific purposes of the Barcelona Process is to promote mutual trust. Indeed, security building in the Mediterranean cannot be properly handled without the involvement of all parties concerned. It is necessary to devise ways to give southern partners a greater voice in correcting the asymmetry amongst the partners. Indeed, since this asymmetry does not go unnoticed in the South, the partners' perceptions, concerns and suggestions regarding these matters should be given as much consideration as possible.

With an EU of 25, financial assistance to 'outsiders' risks becoming a residual after distribution of costs and benefits among 'insiders'. However, in five years time, we would be approaching the ultimate objective of establishing a Euro-Mediterranean Free Trade Area to form, together with EFTA and Central and Eastern European countries, a zone including some 40 states and about 800 million consumers, i.e. one of the world's most important trade entities. That is why the EU's enlargement and the EMP can be mutually reinforcing and complementary projects.

REFERENCES

Aliboni, R. (2004), 'Promoting democracy in the EMP: which political strategy', EuroMeSCo, Third Year Report, unpublished manuscript, Rome.

Attina, F. (2001), 'Conclusions: partnership-building', in F. Attina and S. Stavridis (eds), *The Euro-Mediterranean Partnership from Stuttgart to Marseilles*, Giuffre, Naples: 269–88.

Chryssochoou, D. N., Tsinisizelis, M. J., Stavridis, S. and Ifantis K. (2003), *Theory and Reform in the European Union*, 2nd revised edition, Manchester University Press, Manchester and New York.

EuroMeSCo (2002), 'European defense: perceptions vs. realities', Working Group III, *EuroMeSCo Papers*, No. 16, Lisboa.

Gillespie, R. (1997), 'Northern European perceptions of the Barcelona Process', *Revista CIDOB d'Afers Internacionals*, No. 37, CIDOB, Barcelona.

Gillespie, R. (1999), *Spain and the Mediterranean: Developing a European Policy towards the South*, Macmillan, London.

Holmes, J. W. (1996), 'Italy: in the Mediterranean, but *of* it?', *Mediterranean Politics*, 1 (2): 176–92.

Istituto Affari Internazionali (2002), *Summary of Deliberations*, workshop on 'Measures for conflict prevention in the Med forum countries' Framework', Ministry of Foreign Affairs, Rome 21–22 June.

Jünemann, A. (1998), 'Europe's interrelations with North Africa in the new framework of Euro-Mediterranean partnership – A provisional assessment of the Barcelona concept', *The European Union in a Changing World*, Third ECSA-World Conference, 19–20 Sept. 1996, Brussels.

Marks, J. (1996), 'High hopes and low motives: the new Euro-Mediterranean Partnership Initiative', *Mediterranean Politics*, 1 (1): 10–35.

Panebianco, S. (ed.) (2003), *A New Euro-Mediterranean Cultural Identity*, Frank Cass, London.

Papantoniou, Y. (2002), 'The Mediterranean dimension of the European Union's security and defense policy and the Hellenic Presidency', Inaugural speech at the Seminar on *The Mediterranean Dimension of the ESDP and the Hellenic Presidency*, Hellenic Ministry of National Defense, Rhodes, 2 November.

Pargeter, A. (2002), 'Libya – pariah no more', *The World Today*, 58 (6): 25–26.

Schmid, D. (2003), 'Linking economic, institutional and political reform: conditionality within the Euro-Mediterranean Partnership', *EuroMeSCo Papers*, No. 27, Lisboa.

Stavridis, S. *et. al.* (eds) (1999), *The Foreign Policies of the European Union's Mediterranean States and Applicant Countries in the 1990s*, Macmillan, London.

Tanner, F. (1999), 'Joint actions for peace-building in the Mediterranean', *The International Spectator*, XXXIIV (4).

Tanner, F. (ed.) (2003), *The European Union as a Security Actor in the Mediterranean: ESDP, Soft Power and Peacemaking in EuroMediterranean Relations*, Zürcher Beiträge, ETH Zurich.

Tsinisizelis, M. J., Xenakis, D. K. and Chryssochoou, D. N. (2003), 'Promoting security dialogue in the Mediterranean: the Hellenic Presidency and beyond', *Hellenic Studies*, 11 (2): 119–36.

Xenakis, D. K. (1998), 'The Barcelona Process: some lessons from Helsinki', *Jean Monnet Working Papers in Comparative and International Politics*, Special Euro Med Edition No. 17, Department of Political Science, University of Catania.

Xenakis, D. K. (1999), 'From policy to regime: trends in Euro-Mediterranean governance', *Cambridge Review of International Affairs*, 13 (1): 254–70.

Xenakis, D. K. (2004), *The Politics of Order-Building in Europe and the Mediterranean*, Defence Analysis Institute, Athens.

Xenakis, D. K. and Chryssochoou, D. N. (2001), *The emerging Euro-Mediterranean System*, Manchester University Press, Manchester and New York.

Xenakis, D. K. and Chryssochoou, D. N. (2003), 'The 2003 Hellenic Presidency of the European Union: Mediterranean perspectives on the ESDP', *ZEI Discussion Papers*, C. 128, Zentrum für Europäische Integrationsforschung, University of Bonn.

11. EU Energy Dependence and Co-operation with CIS Countries after EU Enlargement[*]

Yelena Kalyuzhnova and Maria Vagliasindi

INTRODUCTION

This chapter explores the scope to foster EU energy security through stable long-run economic relations with the CIS countries. It is part of a longer-run research programme focusing on the following issues:

1. What are the determinants of the EU long-term energy interests in the CIS region – and how far does genuine security depend not only on diversifying energy sources geographically but on stable political and economic structures in the energy-exporting states?
2. What have been the distributional impacts of the hydrocarbon development of the CIS, and how far does this provide insights into these potential energy sources?

An important motivation of this research is to identify factors relevant to internal and external stability in the CIS; to assess the impact of current policies; and to elucidate policy options that can help increase EU energy security. Such research needs to take into account traditional economic relations but also a complex system of global governance that involves NGOs, private companies, security forces and UN agencies – and to assess its impact on sources of instability in the region.

The governments of all resource rich countries face a challenge of adopting the optimal macro- and microeconomic policies for their countries which could channel productively 'income transfers to governments and

---

[*] The views expressed in this chapter are those of the authors and do not reflect the official position of the EBRD.

inflows of foreign exchange from foreign investments' (Kalyuzhnova, 2002: 79).

The aim of this chapter is to test the relevance of theoretical approaches that link economic development with the containment of instability and conflict – issues that have direct policy relevance as this region becomes increasingly important to EU energy security.

The following sections of the chapter discuss in turn the dependence of the EU on energy imports; some economic myths and realities in the Caspian Sea Region; and the challenge in fostering broadly-based economic growth in a setting of natural resource abundance.

EUROPEAN UNION: NEW ENERGY LANDSCAPE

The arrival of the 10 new members acceding to the EU, in May 2004, changed the energy landscape of the European continent. This change no doubt will have significant implications for EU energy markets and will provide investment opportunities to the EU energy system. The EU is already the largest energy importer in the world and the second-largest consumer. Around two thirds of the EU demand for oil and natural gas is presently imported from outside of EU (see Figure 11.1).

Figure 11.1
Imports of gas to the EU from non-EU countries, share per cent 2001

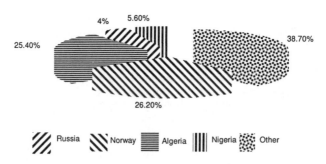

Source: Organisation for Economic Co-operation and Development.

A substantial proportion of these imports is coming from producer countries characterised by political instability (e.g. Libya, Iran, Syria, Iraq, Algeria, etc.) According to the IEA in 2000, the EU accounted for 16 per cent of world energy demand. This demand in absolute terms is expected to increase in the years ahead, particularly after the EU enlargement in May 2004. Oil is and will remain the dominant fuel in the EU, although gas is assuming a more important role (see Table 11.1).

Table 11.1
Reference scenario: EU, Mtoe

	1971	2000	2010	2020	2030
Coal	307	212	191	186	180
Oil	606	593	635	659	670
Gas	82	339	453	556	620
Nuclear	13	225	232	179	153
Hydro	19	27	28	30	31
Other Renewables	16	60	87	120	157

Source: IEA, *World Energy Outlook* 2002.

There are several features which should be highlighted with regard to these scenarios. First of all is the growing energy consumption in Europe, which leads ultimately to the point that the first component of the EU approach to energy supply should be tackling energy demand. It makes European economies more vulnerable to price and disruption risks with potential sources of conflict among EU countries and between EU and exporter countries.

That raises the second issue related to the increasing dependency of EU economies on external supplies. The EU is the largest net energy-importing region in the world. EU energy dependence will grow from 50 per cent at present up to 70 per cent in 2030 if nothing is done. The eight new Eastern European arrivals, which used to rely on the Soviet Union for imports of oil and other fuels are not going to improve the situation (see Table 11.2).

While energy pricing disagreement between the EU and Russia is not an enlargement-related issue as such, it is bound to come up in one way or another in the discussions. In this respect we may want to emphasise that the EU (contrary to its initial stance) does not require from Russia an increase in energy prices to the level of international/export prices but an increase (and a credible schedule for doing that) in the economic price for energy (gas and electricity). The preferred way of doing this would be a transition to a deregulated market-based pricing system.

Table 11.2
European oil import dependence, per cent, 2002

	Import Dependence
EU-15	77
Czech Republic	95
Hungary	77
Poland	96
Others (Estonia, Latvia, Lithuania, Slovakia and Slovenia)	98
Bulgaria	99
Romania	39

Source: World Oil Trade, Blackwell Publishing, 2003; Oil and Energy Trends Annual Statistical Review, 2003, Eurostat.

To summarise, the problems of the EU in relation to the security of energy supply are mainly concerned with:

• Decreasing indigenous supplies
• Increasing imports
• Fragile transit routes
• Competition with other importer countries
• Eastern European enlargement.

The security of energy supply is a vital interest of the EU member states. It would not be prudent to allow the situation of uncertainty to persist. A national energy policy of any EU state should be co-ordinated with the overall EU energy policy. The governments need to realise that EU energy policy will be an integral part of other policies. It is logical that the EU has to diversify energy supply among current exporters. The EU is expanding eastwards – and this will increase the linkage between the EU and Russia and the Caspian Sea region. The EU is interested in energy supplies from everywhere and Russia and the Caspian Sea region could be considered as major alternatives for the near future. The EU interest is a network of treaties and institutions supporting a commercial, rather than a political dimension among all countries involved; it could arbitrate – but has no political muscle. Tacis, Phare, Synergy and Inogate are the main programmes; in the long term, its geographical proximity will assert itself.

It is also important to keep in mind that Russia has traditionally close economic and political relationships with most of the new EU member countries. The EU–Russia integration might have also major implications in the area of FDI flows. Major commodity-based companies (Gazprom, Lukoil,

Yukos, TNK, etc.) have already made substantial investment in anticipation of the EU enlargement. Gazprom's recent acquisition of a 34 per cent stake in the Lithuanian national gas company is the latest example of this trend. It is obviously the EU which will be the key source of FDI inflows into Russia (and contributor to Russia's technological modernisation) once it picks up. In 2004 over 70 per cent of the FDI originated from the 'enlarged EU', importantly including Cyprus.

This process poses major challenges not only for Russia but also for the EU. Integrating the new entrant will test the EU's capacity for cohesion and compromise. In addition, enlargement takes place at a time when the general EU–Russia relationship itself faces major difficulties. The November 2003 EU–Russia summit in Rome (the last before enlargement) revealed a stagnating relationship. The Common European Economic Space seems to be a theoretical rather than a practical objective. Even where the greatest mutual interests are at stake (as in the case of the Energy Partnership) implementation is lagging behind. There are still disagreements on major issues such as energy pricing, creation of a visa-free regime, etc. Russia is opposed to the automatic extension of the Partnership and Co-operation Agreement to the new members and wants prior bilateral negotiations on its own concerns. Russia would also like to be compensated for the adverse consequences of EU enlargement (especially regarding trade in sensitive goods).

What is beneficial for Russia is that the common external tariff (simple average 6.4 per cent in 2001) is much lower than current tariff levels in many of the accession countries, especially Poland and Hungary. The new members will also apply the EU's Generalised System of Preferences with some additional advantages for Russia. The biggest advantages will come over the longer run with the diversification of Russian exports and rapid expansion of the trade flows. The negative trade consequences for Russia are primarily related to the relatively high share of sensitive goods in Russian exports (mainly metals and chemicals) which are subject to higher tariff protection, quantitative restrictions and/or antidumping procedures. And that is where Russia (apart from energy) has its main comparative advantages.

Enlargement also provides incentives for Russia to accelerate its integration with the EU, including the potential application of relevant parts of the Acquis Communautaire. This is expected not only to facilitate cooperation with both old and new members, but to provide guidance for the forthcoming difficult institutional reforms and ultimately to increase Russia's competitiveness.

In terms of application of the Acquis Communautaire in the power sector the new EU Directives on the internal market in electricity (Directive 2003/54/EC of 26 June 2003) and in gas (Directive 2003/55/EC of 26 June

2003), together with the Regulation on cross-border electricity exchanges (Regulation 2003/1228/EC) have now become part of Community law with the main provisions entering into force in July 2004. This event, combined with the EU enlargement, means that the electricity and gas markets have begun a new stage of development.

These two directives are essential to guarantee the opening of the electricity and gas markets in the EU. In practice, they have provided freedom of choice of supplier for industrial customers since 1 July 2004 and provide this for domestic customers as from 1 July 2007. The directives combine opening competition with maintaining service quality, universal service, the protection of vulnerable customers and the objectives of security of supply. These directives will determine the shape of the EU energy market for years to come and will serve as a basis for the development of energy partnerships with the EU's neighbours, in particular in the Western Balkans (see Broadman *et al.*, 2004). These reforms are designed to create a more efficient and dynamic energy sector providing high standards of public service by extending competition and encouraging cross-border transactions.

The *effective* opening up to competition is not something that can be easily implemented right from the moment the directives are nominally transposed. To measure the extent of opening of the market the Commission is using some relevant proxies, such as the number of changes of suppliers. For this reason, the Commission is closely monitoring the integration and degree of opening up of the energy markets to competition and, each year, will therefore publish, as requested by the Barcelona European Council in 2002, a benchmarking report, the next of which was published in December 2004. Today, only an average of one quarter of major users have changed electricity suppliers in the EU since the market started to be opened up (at the end of the 1990s). The Commission has decided to send letters of formal notice to 18 Member States for failure to communicate national measures for the transposition of the two EU directives.

The Commission is issuing regular reports on an annual basis using the very powerful tool of benchmarking. Through this exercise, it is possible to compare and evaluate the performance of the Member States for electricity and gas. In the last year, market opening has been extended and the unbundling strengthened in many Member States, for example, Belgium and the Netherlands. Some obstacles still remain to competition. In particular, Member States which have not yet opened their markets, mainly the acceding countries, must adhere to the agreed timetable for market opening. Regulators must continue to ensure effective regulation of network businesses in particular preventing cross-subsidies. However with the forthcoming general application of regulated Third Party Access (TPA) no judgment, will now be made on the suitability or otherwise of network tariffs since this is the responsibility of national regulators rather than the European Commission. The high levels of market power among existing generating companies, lack of interconnection including vital transmission lines creating bottlenecks within Member States, and the continued use of uncoordinated and discriminatory methods to manage congestion continue to impede new entrants.

As for electricity, there is an agreed timetable for gas market opening with which Member States must comply. Improvement to tariff structures has been recorded with the removal or modification of a number of crude distance-related tariff regimes. Greater consistency for transactions between different Transmission System Operator (TSO) areas is, however, still needed. Some improvements have been made in transparency regarding the availability of infrastructure capacity with most TSOs now publishing this information. However a harmonised methodology to calculate and compare the available capacities still needs to be established. The lack of harmonisation is causing an obstacle to new entrants in obtaining capacity and in managing transportation of the same flow through different countries.

In sum competition in the gas sector remains somewhat behind that for electricity. A key barrier is the continuing dominance of the existing companies in their Member State or, in some cases, specific region. The only way to resolve this issue is to create a smoothly functioning single market at European level. The agreement of new guidelines for good practice at the latest Madrid Forum will lead to some improvement on the issues above. The Commission has therefore proposed a Regulation, analogous to that for electricity, in order to establish a more formal framework. Better management of EU networks will reduce problems of concentration of gas production and import in a few companies and permit more competition. Due to its strong dependency on gas imports and transits, the gas market requires harmonised solutions on cross-border issues in order to efficiently satisfy the national demand in EU countries. Indeed, the way the directive is implemented on crucial topics such as network access and tariffs and on management of day by day operation in any single country will influence the gas market in the other countries.

What about Russia? The power sector reform is implemented in three stages. During the first stage, RAO UES, an industry monopoly that directly owns the majority of the Russian transmission grid and its largest power stations as well as controlling stakes in most of the regional vertically integrated power companies (energos) has created independent, wholly owned subsidiaries for its transmission assets and the system operation/dispatch services. In parallel, key industry participants including RAO UES itself, have created a market operator (the Administrator of the Trade System) that has been administering free trading of power since the end of 2003 within the competitive segment of the market, which is limited to 15 per cent during the first stage of reform. The government is counting on the privatisation of power-generating assets to bring in significant investment for modernisation, with the overall goal of preventing the sort of power shortages and outages that plagued the country's far east in 2000 and 2001. In addition to providing for maintenance of current levels of electricity production, the Russian government is looking to private investment to allow the country to export additional quantities of power and thereby increase state revenues from the sale of electricity outside Russia.

Russia's policy towards the gas sector is somewhat less clear, with talk of restructuring Gazprom, the majority state-owned gas company, which has been put on and off the agenda over the past few recent years. Proposals to split Gazprom's transportation and production functions (or at least into separate units) have been floated. Currently, restructuring Gazprom looks to be stalled, after the announcement in September 2004 that the company will merge with Rosneft, with the state gaining direct control of the combined company and the government then liberalising Gazprom's ownership structure. The dismantling of the 'ring fence', two-tier system of Gazprom's shares will allow foreign investors to own Gazprom stock directly, likely boosting the company's market valuation substantially and removing much of the impetus for company restructuring. Gas market reform – mainly taking the shape of a removal of price caps for gas supplied to Russian consumers – as reported earlier – are also moving slowly, although the government has pledged to significantly raise domestic prices by 2010 under a May 2004 deal with the EU.

The government's key objectives appear to be maintaining Gazprom's export monopoly (while earning additional monies from the sale of Russian gas abroad for the federal government), providing gas to Russian consumers at an affordable price, and maintaining state control of Gazprom. A central element of these goals is to ensure Gazprom's gas production potential. However, in order to invest in new upstream developments, Gazprom continues to seek higher ceilings for Russian domestic gas prices. The government is faced with these competing policy goals as it attempts to keep a lid on gas price increases so that consumers continue to pay their bills; gas supply cut-offs for consumer non-payment is politically unpopular and can be deadly, especially in winter when Russians use gas for heating.

THE CIS REGION: POTENTIAL, MYTHS, AND REALITY

As highlighted in the Commission's green Paper in the Security Energy Supply, the EU has a specific interest in the extensive oil and gas reserves of the Caspian Basin and Russia, which will, in the future, contribute to security of supply in Europe.

The role of the countries of the former Soviet Union may also prove to be particularly important for the EU since, in 1989, they were still the world's leading oil producers with production of more than 11 million. barrels a day. Production in this region could be double over the next 20 years, reaching 14 million. barrels a day in 2020.

The known oil reserves in the Caspian Sea basin (25 billion barrels) are about equivalent to those in the North Sea and the USA. Kazakhstan and Azerbaijan are both leaders in this respect, they have significant proven oil reserves (9 and 7 billion barrels respectively). 'Kazakhstan has the most potential [50–80 billion barrels], much of which is related to the size of the recent supergiant Kashagan discovery'. (Belopolsky and Talwani, 2002: 24).

Both Kazakhstan and Azerbaijan have expressed their interest in intensified energy co-operation in the framework of their Partnership and Co-operation Agreements with the EU. Expert discussions are being conducted to define prospects and conditions for an increased participation of these countries in the EU's internal gas markets.

To date the Caspian Sea region has over 11,623 billion cubic meters proven gas reserves. The major European oil and gas companies are well represented in exploration and production projects in the Caspian Sea region. BP has the leading role in the two biggest projects in Azerbaijan – the only successful projects to date in that country – while the company's decision to sell its stake in Kazakhstan's Kashagan field reflected its very small share in the project and its heavy exposure in Azerbaijan, which has become the company's focus in the Caspian Sea region. The Kashagan project is led by a European company, though, with Eni being partnered by Shell and TotalFinaElf among others. Eni and BP are jointly operating one of the other big three projects in Kazakhstan, the Karachaganak gas/condensate project. BP has a stake in Tengiz through its LukArco joint-venture.

However, without appropriate transport routes the whole business would be impossible. At the present time the transit routes are fragile, where security remains a substantial problem. The major European energy companies are also well represented in pipeline projects in the Caspian Sea region. For example, BP has the leading role in the The Baku-Tbilisi-Ceyhan (BTC) project, which is a $3 billion investment to unlock a vast store of energy from the Caspian Sea by providing a new crude oil pipeline from Azerbaijan, through Georgia, to Turkey for onward delivery to world markets, where Eni, Statoil and TotalFinaElf are partners (with a combined share of 58 per cent). European companies are involved in the Caspian Pipeline Consortium (CPC) crude pipeline system, which is the largest operating investment project with foreign participation on the territory of the former USSR. The cost of the first phase of construction amounted to $2.6 billion. The length of the main pipeline that connects the oil fields in Western Kazakhstan with the new Marine Terminal in Russia is 1,510 km – Agip, BG, BP (Lukarco), Shell. TotalFinaElf is studying a possible oil export pipeline from Kazakhstan across Iran, a project in which US companies would not be able to participate.

An analysis of existing legislation within the EU has shown that there is a large variation in the degree to which Members States cover the control of major-accident hazards arising from pipelines.

Geographically and politically, Europe remains the most natural export market for the Caspian region. Exports southwards via Iran remain unlikely due to US embargoes on Iran. Exports via Afghanistan to Pakistan and India face huge economic hurdles despite recent political changes. Pakistan's gas market is not large enough to support an import pipeline from Turkmenistan, while India will not allow itself to become dependent on gas that first has to cross Pakistan. Exports to China are made prohibitively expensive by the vast distances involved in reaching the market in the east of the country and the need to cross high mountain ranges. Westward routes are really the only ones open to the Caspian Sea's oil and gas producers.

RUSSIAN AND CASPIAN GAS AND THE EU

Russian and Caspian gas is, no doubt, a new concept for the EU. There are several key features of this new supply which should be noted: increasing cost, required massive investment in long lead times as well as transnational issues. Therefore in order to think about Caspian gas as an alternative supply, the EU should recognise the following key requirements to unlock this new supply. With respect to security of supply, the main issue for Europe concerns ensuring that appropriate market conditions, and where necessary incentives, exit to ensure the construction of new gas production capacity and pipelines to supply the increasing gas requirements. Minimising supply costs would be one of the first keys to unlocking the Caspian gas supply. Attention should be also given to timely investment and the availability of financing, in this situation the certainty of the revenue (in terms of volume and price) is essential. Security of gas flow is the basis for the rest of the activities and this particular angle should be protected by the producers (Caspian region) and consumers (EU). Appropriate risk allocations and payback to investors would complete the list of the key requirements of the new Caspian gas supply.

As already mentioned, EU gas consumption is expected to increase considerably in coming decades, whereas internal EU production will decline. Gas trade tends to be regional, with producers and consumers usually linked by pipeline. At present, almost all the gas exported from the Caspian region goes to Russia, with a very small amount sold to Iran by Turkmenistan. Europe imports around 130 bcm of gas from Russia through pipelines, 60 bcm from North Africa, (more than 50 bcm of which is piped) and a further 5 bcm in the form of LNG from Nigeria, but as Europe's indigenous gas reserves are depleted, the region will increasingly turn to the states of the former Soviet Union for additional supplies. While Russia will remain the region's biggest gas supplier to Europe, the Caspian region will have a growing role to play, exporting gas into both northern and southern Europe.

NATURAL RESOURCES AND SUSTAINABLE ECONOMIC GROWTH OF THE EXPORTER COUNTRIES (CIS): SHOULD THE EU BE CONCERNED?

The Caspian region possesses certain natural advantages for economic growth due to its abundant reserves of natural resources. Provided they are carefully harnessed and their benefits are thoughtfully distributed, this growth is also likely to lead to development. Such development and the improvement in living standards that it will bring about could well help to improve domestic security and reduce the influence of militant elements in the region. This, in turn, is likely to help preserve a suitable and reliable energy supply for the EU. This is why the question of the sustainability of the economic development in the Caspian Sea region should be a matter of importance for the various EU policies towards the Caspian region.

As an investor in the Caspian region the EU should clearly depict the reserves and production potential, capital investment and key risks and challenges ahead. However, that would only be the key condition, but to complete the picture the EU should spell out the following crucial points:

- Profit and returns: consortium / government
- Business development potential
- Impacts and sustainability.

The latter is bringing a new perception of a broader concept of economic governance and an understanding of the deep link in economic partnership between EU and the Caspian region. It must be translated in terms of the specific economic challenges which the Caspian region's economies are now experiencing. On that basis, the framework of this economic partnership should be created, which no doubt will help to shape the relations and to improve the economic governance of the Caspian region's economies.

Natural resources are good for economic growth if they are accompanied by sound economic policies, which should be very individual for every given country.

There is some significant evidence (e.g. Gylfason and Zoega, 2003; Paldam, 1997) of the poor performance of the resource rich countries. A natural resource boom makes a country better off at least for while, however if it reduces growth, then, after a time, the country will be worse off than it would have been without the boom, other things being equal. The large concentration on natural resources may harm education, investment and export.[1]

CONCLUSION

Geographically and politically, Europe remains the most natural market for Caspian energy. This is indicated by the fact the obvious export routes lie to the north and west, into Europe, and the European Union, which has itself become concerned about the future security of the region's energy supplies.

The May 2004 EU enlargement has changed the energy landscape of the European continent and will have significant implications for EU energy markets. The opening of new EU gas and power markets to the east will produce major challenges as well as wide opportunities for investment and trade. European energy interests in the Caspian region include the involvement of European energy companies in the region and a growing interest in the Caspian region as a current and future source of energy for use in Europe itself.

REFERENCES

Belopolsky, A.V. and Talwani, M. (2002), 'Geological basins and oil and gas reserves of the Greater Caspian region', Chapter 1 in Yelena Kalyuzhnova, Amy Myers Jaffe, Dov Lynch and Robin Sickles (eds), *Energy in the Caspian Region: Present and Future*, Palgrave.
Broadman, H. G., Anderson, J., Claessen, C., Ryterman, R., Slavova, S., Vagliasindi, M. and Vincelette, G. (2004), *Building Market Institutions in South Eastern Europe: Comparative Prospects for Investment and Private Sector Development*, World Bank, in cooperation with the EBRD.
Gylfason, Thorvaldur and Zoega, Gylfi, (2003), 'Inequality theory and policy implications', in Theo Eicher and Stephen Turnovsky (eds), *Inequality and Growth: Theory and Policy Implications*, MIT Press.
International Energy Agency, *World Energy Outlook* 2002.

---

[1] For details on Caspian Economic Development please see Kalyuzhnova (2002). For details on the Oil Funds please see Kalyuzhnova (2004).

Kalyuzhnova, Y. (2002), 'Economies and energy', Chapter 3 in Yelena Kalyuzhnova, Amy Myers Jaffe, Dov Lynch and Robin Sickles (eds), *Energy in the Caspian Region: Present and Future*, Palgrave.
Kalyuzhnova, Y. (2004), 'The Curse of Hydrocarbon: Development of the Oil Funds in Kazakhstan and Azerbaijan', *Comparative Economic Studies* (submitted).
Organisation for Economic Co-operation and Development, Statistical Data.
Paldam, M. (1997), 'Dutch disease and rent seeking: the Greenland model', *European Journal of Political Economy* 13, August, 591–614.
World Oil Trade, Blackwell Publishing, 2003; Oil and Energy Trends Annual Statistical Review, 2003, Eurostat.

12. Impact of EU Enlargement to CEE Countries on Transatlantic Relations

René Schwok

INTRODUCTION

On 1 May 2004, ten new countries joined the EU as fully-fledged members. From the Baltic to the Mediterranean, the eight Central European countries (Estonia, Latvia, Lithuania, Poland, Czech Republic, Slovakia, Hungary and Slovenia)[1] and two Mediterranean island states (Cyprus and Malta) increased the EU's population by more than 80 million, from 370 million to over 450 million. The new members represent some 20 per cent of the existing EU population, with only 5 per cent of the actual GDP of those already there.

In order to analyse and conceptualise the debate, we will use in this article the dichotomy between *dissociative and associative* schools (Schwok, 2001). *Dissociative* means that analysts belonging to this framework diagnose a deterioration of the transatlantic link. For those researchers, relations between the European Union and the United States – always tense – have been recently aggravated.

To be sure, this approach does not overlook the fact that some relations between the two rims of the Atlantic Ocean can be positive, but the few positive aspects are minimised. For *dissociative* analysts, today's situation is characterised by the disappearance of the common communist enemy and by a growth of conflicts between the commercial blocs. According to this view, numerous developments are pushing the world back to transatlantic rifts. One is the rise of Europe, which is acquiring both the economic and political heft necessary to challenge American leadership. The other is the decline of American public support for internationalism that makes it increasingly difficult for the United States to honour commitments and bear the burdens of sustaining the existing order. In such circumstances, the relations between the

---

[1] The eight Central and Eastern European Countries are labelled here the CEECs-8.

United States and the European Union can only deteriorate even more, towards a kind of dissociation.

In 2002–2004, endless series of books and articles have been published about the 'near-death of the transatlantic alliance' (Pond, 2004), about the irreconcilable natures of the Americans and the Europeans,[2] about the American decline (Kupchan, 2002), about the 'breakdown of the American order',[3] about the arrogance of the American 'hyper-power' (Védrine with Moïsi, 2001), etc.

The *associative* approach, on the other hand, underlines the depth of the transatlantic link. Researchers belonging to this framework point out the numerous elements of convergence between Europe and America. Contrary to accepted wisdom, they argue that the end of the Cold War actually enhanced the prospects for partnership between the United States and the European Union (Peterson, 1996). Relations between the European Union and the United States are going not so badly and there is so far no indication that this may change (Ginsberg, 2002). To be sure, the associative approach does not ignore that there have been some clashes between the two actors, but it rejects as an exaggeration claims of a steadfast societal separation between either side of the Atlantic (Serfaty, quoted in Grabbe, 2004). For *associative* analysts, the relations between the EU and the US have not been radically altered by the George W. Bush administration and wars in Afghanistan and in Iraq (Peterson and Pollack, 2003).

The main objective of this chapter is precisely to assess if the 2004 EU enlargement will strengthen the *dissociative* approach or the *associative* approach. In the first part, we deal with the political and strategic dimension. In the second part, we assess the economic sphere. For both parts, we introduce first the arguments that strengthen the *dissociative* approach, and then the ones that corroborate the *associative* view.

---

[2] For instance, the well-known thesis by Robert Kagan (2002): 'On the all-important question of power – the efficacy of power, the morality of power, the desirability of power – American and European perspectives are diverging. Europe is turning away from power, or to put it a little differently, it is moving beyond power into a self-contained world of laws and rules and transnational negotiation and cooperation. It is entering a post-historical paradise of peace and relative prosperity, the realization of Kant's "Perpetual Peace". The United States, meanwhile, remains mired in history, exercising power in the anarchic Hobbesian world where international laws and rules are unreliable and where true security and the defense and promotion of a liberal order still depend on the possession and use of military might. That is why on major strategic and international questions today, Americans are from Mars and Europeans are from Venus: They agree on little and understand one another less and less. And this state of affairs is not transitory – the product of one American election or one catastrophic event. The reasons for the transatlantic divide are deep, long in development, and likely to endure'. See also, Kagan (2003).

[3] Emmanuel Todd, *After the Empire: The Breakdown of the American Order*, New York, Columbia University Press, 2003.

POLITICAL AND SECURITY DIMENSION

'Dissociative' Approach

First, researchers belonging to the school often argue that one should not exaggerate the *Atlanticism* of the new members. They will be no simple-minded *groupies* (Cernoch, 2003). Emotional bonds to the United States in Poland, the Czech Republic and the Baltic countries are strong, but other central European countries have long traditions of left- and right-wing political extremism that include elements of anti-Americanism. It has already been noticed that Slovenia is much more cautious about the US than the other countries.

Moreover, it would be wrong to assume that the CEECs-8 will align themselves with Washington on every issue. The test of loyalty over Iraq in 2003 came at an awkward moment when the US Senate was considering ratification of the second enlargement of NATO. And public opinion in the Central and Eastern European countries was against the war, just as it was in the rest of Europe. Sometimes the actions of the Bush administration reminded of the behaviour of the Soviet Union that used its status of a superpower as a free ticket to use military force without limits.

One has also to keep in mind that EU membership means that the CEECs-8 will be caught up in processes of socialization or *Euroisation* (Meade, 2003) that will draw them closer to Brussels than to Washington (see theory of constructivism). This means pressures to side with the 'old' European countries on multilateral issues with security implications.

Finally, enlargement is increasing the size, relative weight, and cohesion of the EU voting bloc in the UN and other international forums (IMF, World Bank). One can already observe that the new countries generally side with the 'old' EU countries on most multilateral questions, with votes in the UN or support for multilateral treaties such as the Rome Statute of the ICC, the death penalty, non-proliferation and the Kyoto protocol on global warming (Grabbe, 2004). They also align themselves with the EU's common positions on CFSP.

'Associative' Approach

Researchers belonging to the 'associative' approach underline, on the contrary, the following arguments in support of their thesis:

First, EU enlargement is a historic step towards the long cherished goal of a Europe 'whole, free, at peace and growing in prosperity'. After generations in which internal conflict in Europe posed one of the most serious security threats to the United States, the Western alliance and world peace, the unification of Europe by consent is a major strategic prize for the US. EU enlargement ensures that the democratic transition in Central and Eastern Europe is irreversible. This serves US security and geopolitical interests.

Second, there is an emotional dimension that works in support of the US. Most leaders within the eight Central and Eastern European Countries (CEECs-8) share a so-called 'reflexive pro-Americanism'. This means that they feel that the US support was one of the key elements in their resistance against communism and in their quests for independence (Cernoch, 2003). Memory of the past still plays an important role. And many citizens from Central and Eastern Europe want to remember the actions of the US in their support, such as the Truman Doctrine, the creation of NATO, condemnations of various Soviet actions, support of dissidents, etc. One can find in those countries many intellectuals who broadly agree with the American statement, mostly put forward by 'Republicans' that the American arms race of the 1980s led to the failure of the Soviet Union.

Moreover, this emotional dimension works again a rather autonomous Europe led by Germany and France. There are still dark memories of Third Reich's imperialism and racism. And most people in countries such as Poland and the Czech Republic remain cautious about any German move. Recent claims by people from German descent about lost properties in Silesia, Dantzig/Gdansk and Sudetenland raised concerns about some kind of German 'revanchism'. At the same time, German pacifism is also considered in Central and Eastern Europe as a kind of danger vis-à-vis serious security challenges.

Feelings about France are also ambivalent. On the one hand, this country does not evoke the same kind of negative remarks as Germany. On the other hand, France is not considered as a credible protector in case of hard times. One can frequently hear negative assessments about traditional French 'cowardice'. French support for the 1938 Munich agreements are sometimes mentioned. Tacit French consent for Soviet moves against Hungary, Czechoslovakia and Poland is sometimes remembered. Attempts by the former French President François Mitterrand to slow down German reunification and Soviet departure from the CEECs also come readily to mind in some countries. Paris's coolness towards EU and NATO enlargements to the CEECs added to this cautious mood about France (Grabbe, 2004). Finally, Paris, has also damaged its popularity in Central and Eastern Europe by dealing condescendingly with the CEECs governments in condemning their support for the American war in Iraq.

The behaviour of the CEECs-8 over Iraq in 2003 confirmed their 'Atlanticism', especially when they supported the enforcement of UN Security Council Resolution 1441. They seemed to vindicate the idea that they would be Washington's loyal allies, opposed to the 'old Europe' of Germany and France (Rumsfeld's).

Finally, it is important to keep in mind that the CEECs-8 are mainly interested in getting protection from a possible Russian threat. And only the US can provide them with credible protection. EU enlargement means indeed keeping pace with NATO enlargement. Their socialization into western security structures is occurring through NATO rather than the EU or ESDP, as the first EU enlargement to CEECs-8 and the second enlargement of NATO are increasing by eight the number of countries that are members of both organizations.

The new EU member states have a strong interest in preserving the viability of the Atlantic alliance, and that the United States remains engaged in European security affairs. It is rather clear that the new members will serve as a brake on tendencies to decouple Europe from the United States.

ECONOMIC DIMENSION

'Dissociative' Approach

The *dissociative* approach is based on the assumption that the world is leaning towards the constitution of protectionist commercial blocs. In one part of the world, the European Union is becoming stronger through the objectives of an internal market and a single currency, and its ramifications are spreading to Central and Eastern Europe, to the EFTA states through the European Economic Area (EEA), to the Eastern and Mediterranean countries through all kinds of association agreements. In the meantime, one finds the United States that has established NAFTA and is active in APEC and other free-trade areas in Central and South America. With so many commercial blocs in the world, there will be, according to this approach, a series of trade clashes.

Neomercantilism is the theory that has the most influenced the *dissociative*' approach. *Neomercantilist* researchers point to the growth of protectionist barriers. They also show that the end of the Cold War, with the disappearance of the military, political and ideological competition between the two Blocs, constitutes a fertile field for numerous hidden economic protectionist conflicts. They particularly insist on the constitution of economic blocs (enlarged and deepened EU, EEA, FTA, NAFTA, APEC) as the most manifest illustrations of the transformation of national protectionism in bloc protectionism.

The *Theory of Hegemonic Stability* (Gilpin, 1987) has grown within this neomercantilist theoretical framework. This theory's key element is the view that stability in international relations stems from the presence of hegemony or dominance. The absence of hegemony implies a lack of order in the relations between states whether in commercial activities (trade, money), social issues, or security concerns. Its main axiom is to establish a correlation between hegemonic power and stability of international regimes, such as WTO (Petersmann and Pollack, 2003).

As long as a country such the United Kingdom in the 19th century or the United States after the Second World War were capable of assuming power, international regimes remained credible. With their decline[4] or their lack of responsibility (i.e. isolationism), other states (Japan, Europe etc.) will defect more. Applied to international trade, the logical conclusion of the *Theory of Hegemonic Stability* is that we are going towards a reorganisation of the system towards insular and conflictual trade blocs.

According to the *dissociative* school, the 2004 enlargement will mean the new members accepting some rules and standards that the United States regards as unfair barriers to trade (genetically modified organisms, GMOs).

Accession of the CEECs-8 could also exacerbate US–EU trade tensions in a few specific industrial sectors, notably steel. The United States might continue to bargain with the Commission over compensation for market losses under GATT 24(6) and the changes in its bilateral investment treaties with the accession countries that the Commission is demanding.

There are also problems that could arise in connection with the fate of the treaties the United States concluded with the Central and Eastern European countries in the early 1990s. In some cases these countries have granted US firms particular tax breaks to encourage large investment projects. For instance, the Commission is insisting that these treaties be abrogated or renegotiated to conform to EU norms.

Enlargement to Central and Eastern Europe could also be negative for US agricultural interests (Cochrane and Seeley, 2004). Analysts belonging to the *dissociative* school always attack the Common Agricultural Policy (which is on purpose a system of protectionist and planned economy) as being the archetype of the whole European commercial policy.

Previous enlargements had resulted in losses of markets for US agricultural exporters and disputes in the GATT. And an enlarged EU, which includes Poland and other poorer and more heavily agricultural Central and Eastern European states, could find it more difficult to reform the CAP in ways which reduce trade conflicts with the United States and other large agricultural producers.

---

[4] One can also observe that the *Theory of Hegemonic Stability* is underlined by a fundamental assumption: of the *decline* of the United States. This theme was one of the most popular in the American scientific literature in the late 1980s.

The most dramatic changes after accession are likely to be significant increases in output of beef and coarse grains by the Central and Eastern European countries and a small decline in wheat output by the enlarged EU. The United States stands to lose its poultry market in the new member states, but could see slightly larger wheat exports (Cochrane, 2004, p. 78).

'Associative' Approach

For their part, researchers belonging to the *associative* school consider the 2004 enlargement as positive for transatlantic relations. First, they criticise the *Theory of Hegemonic Stability* on two fundamental points: (1) they argue that the *Theory of Hegemonic Stability* is wrong on the conditions which motivate a state to exercise its leadership and (2), that it ignores the true motivations of the followers (Japan, Europe) towards the leader (USA).

In other words, the *Theory of Hegemonic Stability* underestimates the fact that both Japan and the European Union also have their own interest in keeping, developing and guaranteeing free trade through international regimes, that they are trying to diminish the costs of transaction and of diffusion of information, and they are pressed by their own myopic interest to cooperate and to dismantle their protectionist barriers.

More empirically, *associative* researchers remark that, despite the perennial hype about the 'rise of Asia' and the significance of NAFTA, Europe and the United States remain by far each other's most important commercial partners. Contrary to a widespread myth, European and American economies and societies have not drifted apart since the end the Cold War; on the contrary they have become even more interdependent. For instance, the combined US GDP and EU GDP is around 60 per cent of the world total on a market exchange rate basis. Together, they command 40 per cent of world trade, and their bilateral economic relationship is worth just short of $3 billion per day in trade of goods, services and foreign direct investment.

Even more interesting is their cumulative mutual investment stake in each other's economy. In 2000, Europe's investment stake in the US represented 75 per cent of all European investment abroad and roughly 60 per cent of all foreign direct investment in the United States (Hamilton and Quinlan, 2003). Meanwhile, the US investment stake in Europe grew to roughly half of all US investment abroad. In 2001, this investment yielded half of all foreign earnings for US companies.

Despite transatlantic tensions over Iraq, corporate America pumped nearly $87 billion in foreign direct investment (FDI) into Europe in 2003. That represents a jump of 30.5 per cent from 2002. Europe accounted for nearly 65 per cent of total US foreign direct investment in 2003. US investment in

Ireland alone in 2003 ($4.7 billion) was more than two-and-a-half times greater than US investment in China ($1.7 billion). The $19.2 billion of US investment in the Netherlands alone in 2003 was not far behind total US investment in all of Asia ($22.4 billion) (Hamilton and Quinlan, 2004).

As for the specific impact of the 2004 EU enlargement, *associative* researchers remind us that the new EU countries are clearly secondary markets for US firms. No CEEC ranks among the top 50 US overseas markets. US exports to the eight CEECs were approximately $3.12 billion in 2001, only 0.4 per cent of total US exports (Hamilton and Quinlan, 2004)! In other words, the US does not take many risks in this enlargement, as its trade in Central and Eastern Europe is so small.

The relatively modest share of the CEECs in US trade is a consequence of two factors: the higher tariffs that apply to US exports under pre-accession agreements with the EU countries, and the natural advantages of proximity and historic ties that EU exporters enjoy in the region.

Therefore, 'associative' researchers argue that enlargement will benefit US exporters for the following reasons:[5]

First, economic growth in the CEECs-8 will mean a larger and more affluent market with increased investment opportunities and export for US firms (Van Oudenaren, 2003, pp. 56–60). The accession countries have growth rates of between 5 per cent and 8 per cent of GDP, far outstripping those of the current EU-15, and are likely to do so for the next decade.

Second, the new members are adopting the Common External Tariff, which generally is lower than the current MFN tariffs applied to the US by the candidate countries. This will lead to a decrease of their current average tariff of 9 per cent to an average of 4 per cent (Burghardt, 2004).

Moreover, the enlarged EU has a single tariff system and a single set of customs and administrative procedures. Thus, the system whereby US exporters were faced with various import regimes has disappeared.

One has to add that the new Member States are applying the commitments undertaken by the EU in its trade relations with third countries such as the WTO, or directly with the US. This applies notably on the mutual recognition of standards and conformity assessment procedures, on co-operation on

---

[5] Eventual adoption of the euro by another eight countries will have some effects on US interests. The new member countries are not yet permitted to adopt the euro, but they are bound by the same convergence criteria that the old member states.

It will increase the demand for euros and accelerate somewhat the rebalancing of reserves from the dollar to the euro as these countries shift public foreign and private debt from dollars to euros (a process already well underway).

The added effect of CEECs-8 participation in the euro is however likely to be quite modest. Ultimately the relative performance of the dollar and the euro will be determined by other factors, above all the strength of the US and the major western European economies.

customs and competition issues, as well as the arrangement of regulatory co-operation.

The 2004 enlargement will be a net benefit for US investors. To the extent that investment requires more protection against corruption, well-established property rights, and impartial mechanisms for dispute resolution, EU enlargement is in the interest of US investors.

Nor is agriculture considered as a major difficulty for future EU–US relations. US agricultural trade with the CEECs is indeed very limited. American farmers export to the CEECs-8 is less than 4 per cent of their exports to the EU-15 and roughly **0.4 per cent** of their world exports! (Cochrane, 2004, pp. 78–85). There is a generally downward trend in US agricultural exports to the region since 1993 and this has to do with the fact that the CEECs-8 have adopted EU and national health and food safety regulations that exclude US products.

The positive point is that the American farm industry does not have a lot to lose from CAP's enlargement to the newcomers. The situation is very different from the mid-1990s when the US complained bitterly about Spain and Portugal's accessions to the EC as these countries were important agricultural markets.

CONCLUSION

We have tried to analyse the impact of the 2004 EU enlargement to the CEECs-8 using the theoretical framework *dissociative / associative*. This predicates a dichotomy in the way that different interpretations have been expressed about the relationship between the European Union and the United States. By pointing out the divergences between the two approaches, we hope to offer better concepts to the debate and to contribute to a better understanding of the most important issues of interpretation.

Our observations clearly support more the *associative* rather than the *dissociative* school. This may explain why opponents of the US and of the current transatlantic relationship expressed negative views about EU enlargement. As they anticipated a dissociation between Europe and the US and as they used for many years 'scientific' arguments to prove that it will happen, they are very frustrated by the 2004 enlargement because it goes in the other direction.

For instance many leftist anti-American intellectuals and scholars wrote very negative pieces about the CEECs' accession to the EU. Especially in France, this enlargement has been seen as an American plot because the Atlanticist Central and Eastern European countries might serve as a 'Trojan horse' for US interests in Europe. As Pascal Boniface wrote: 'l'élargissement le plus significatif, le plus réel, n'est donc pas celui de l'Europe, mais celui de la puissance américaine en Europe' (Boniface, 2004). Bernard Cassen, one of ATTACs's leaders, even claimed that Europe became less European by accepting the CEECs-8 (Cassen, 2003 and Schreiber, 2004).

We still lack distance from events to help us come to any definitive conclusions about the impact of the 2004 enlargement on transatlantic relations. One key question is the depth of the pro-US attitude of the new members. Is the collective memory of history a lasting factor or will it vanish relatively quickly with the change of generations? Do the new members see their pro-US attitude as an addition to their general commitment within the EU and an integrated CFSP? Another point to be followed is the impact of the EU process of socialisation on the CEECs-8. Will they be less pro-American or will they go into a kind of a British path?

Finally, to what extent will these countries be ready to follow any possible future American unilateralism? Is there a point where American unilateralism could push those countries to distance themselves from Washington? One can wonder if the 2003 Iraqi war was the most pro-Americanism that can be expected from them.

REFERENCES

Boniface, P. (2004), 'L'élargissement au prix de l'affaiblissement?', *Le Figaro*, 17–18 Avril 2004.

Burghardt, G. (2004), *EU Enlargement and the Transatlantic Relationship*, Chicago, The Executives' Club, 11 March 2004.
http://www.eurunion.org/News/speeches/2004/040311gb.htm.

Cassen, B. (2003), 'Une Europe de moins en moins européenne', *Le Monde Diplomatique*, Janvier 2003.

Cernoch, P. (2003), 'On March, Venus, and Czech mates from the "New" Europe', in J. Van Oudenaren (ed.), *The Changing Face of Europe: EU Enlargement and Implications for Transatlantic Relations*, Washington, DC, AICGS Policy Report No. 6, American Institute for Contemporary German Studies, Johns Hopkins University.

Cochrane, N. and Seeley, R. (2004), *EU Enlargement: Implications for New Member Countries, the United States, and World Trade*, Washington, United States Department of Agriculture, April 2004, WRS04-05-01.
http://www.ers.usda.gov/publications/WRS04/Apr04/WRS040501/WRS040501.pdf

Cochrane, N. (2004), *EU Enlargement: Implications for US–EU Agricultural Relations*, Washington, DC, Economic Research Service, USDA.

Gilpin, R. (1987), *The Political Economy of International Relations*, Princeton, Princeton University Press.

Ginsberg, R. H. (2002), *United States-European Union Political Relations in the Bush Administration*, Sixth ECSA-World Conference, Brussels, 5–6 December 2002, http://www.ecsanet.org/ecsaworld6/.

Grabbe, H. (2004), 'The newcomers', in F. Cameron (ed.), *The Future of Europe. Integration and Enlargement*, London, Routledge.

Hamilton, D. S. and Quinlan, J. J. (2003), 'Alors que les divergences stratégiques persistent de part et d'autre de l'Atlantique; Europe–Etats-Unis: les affaires tournent', *Le Figaro*, 3 Décembre 2003.

Hamilton, D. S. and Quinlan, J. J. (2004), *Conflict and Cooperation in Transatlantic Relations*, Washington, DC, Center for Transatlantic Relations, Johns Hopkins University — SAIS.

Kagan, R. (2002), 'Power and weakness', *Policy Review*, June–July 2002, No. 113, http://www.policyreview.org/JUN02/kagan.html.

Kagan, R. (2003), *Of Paradise and Power: America and Europe in the New World Order*, New York, Knopf.

Kupchan, C. (2002), *The End of the American Era: US Foreign Policy After the Cold War*, New York, Alfred Knopf.

Meade, E. E. (2003), 'Euroisation in EU Aaccession countries', in J. Van Oudenaren (ed.), *The Changing Face of Europe: EU Enlargement and Implications for Transatlantic Relations*, Washington, DC, AICGS Policy Report No. 6, American Institute for Contemporary German Studies, Johns Hopkins University.

Petersmann, E. U. and Pollack, M. A. (eds) (2003), *Transatlantic Economic Disputes. The EU, the US and the WTO*, Oxford, Oxford University Press.

Peterson, J. and Pollack, M. (2003), *Europe, America, Bush: Transatlantic Relations in the 21st Century*, London, Routledge.

Peterson, J. (1996), *Europe and America: The Prospects for Partnership*, London, Routledge, 2nd edition.

Pond, E. (2004), *Friendly Fire. The Near-Death of the Transatlantic Alliance*, Pittsburgh, Washington, DC, European Union Studies Association & Brookings Institution.

Schreiber, T. (2004), 'Le rêve américain de la "nouvelle Europe"', *Le Monde Diplomatique*, Mai 2004.

Schwok, R. (2001), 'Drifting apart? Disssociative and associative approaches', in P. Winand and E. Philippart (eds), *Ever Closer Parnership. Policy-Making in US–EU Relations*, Brussels, European Interuniversity Press/Peter Lang, pp. 363–85.

Serfaty, S. (2004), 'The Transatlantic dimension', in H. Grabbe, 'The newcomers', in F. Cameron (ed.), *The Future of Europe. Integration and Enlargement*, London, Routledge.

Todd, E. (2003), *After the Empire: The Breakdown of the American Order,* New York, Columbia University Press.

Van Oudenaren, J. (2003), *The Changing Face of Europe: EU Enlargement and Implications for Transatlantic Relations*, Washington, DC, AICGS Policy Report No. 6, American Institute for Contemporary German Studies, Johns Hopkins University.

Védrine, H. with Moïsi, D. (2001), *France in an Age of Globalization*, Washington, DC, Brookings Institution Press.

Conclusions

The question as to whether EU enlargement to 10 new countries will affect the effectiveness of the Union has dominated academic and political debate for quite some time. Various scenarios, based on statistical projections, evidence from previous enlargements and some degree of intuitive reasoning, arrived at conflicting evaluations. Positive evaluations underlined the fact that the Union would become a larger market and a stronger international player in the context of globalisation. Negative evaluations underlined the fact that, following enlargement, the Union would be incapable of taking decisions and would therefore become ungovernable and ineffective in the world scene.

The central question raised in this book is whether and to what extent the new member States, whose policy preferences are at variance with those of most old member States, are likely to affect the EU policy output, either by impeding decision-making or by changing the policy-mix. The answer to these questions requires a closer look at the new economic setting and the potential winners and losers. Moreover, an evaluation of the policy output has to be based on evidence regarding the perceptions and attitudes of new member States and, especially, their capacity to shift the balance between economic liberalism and interventionism, on the one hand, and, on the other, between pro-Atlantic and pro-European visions in the area of foreign policy.

THE NEW ECONOMIC SETTING

The findings about trade and investment flows (Curzon-Price) and investment decisions (Jovanovic) suggest that the economies of the 10 new EU member states underwent extensive modernisation during the pre-accession period and are now economically integrated with the rest of the EU. Some of them appear to be in a better position to benefit from the new economic setting than old members. In the agricultural sector producers' decisions will be driven by market considerations rather than the maximisation of direct payments (Baltas). As regards EMU, the perspective of an early extension of the eurozone to the new member States is not risk-free, bearing in mind the enhanced probability of asymmetric shocks following the rise in EMU heterogeneity and the problems that are likely to arise from the 'one man one vote' principle in ECB decision-making (Prausello).

GOVERNANCE AND COHESION

EU policies are constantly under review. Quarrels about the equitable distribution of gains and losses are likely to dominate EU politics in the near future, as they did in the past. The political dynamics of decision-making have not fundamentally changed as a result of recent institutional reforms and the preferences of the new member States. Enlargement has shown no signs of bringing completely new cleavages to the fore, though it has made existing ones more complex. Differentiated and new governance approaches, such as the Open Method of Coordination can facilitate enlargement by providing a way in which new member states can 'slide' into what may be difficult policy areas for them (Nugent). As regards, however, the policy output, the varying perceptions of new member States and new neighbours in respect of economic and social reforms associated with regulatory approximation are likely to impede regulatory convergence in the wider Europe area (Stephanou).

In the past 20 years structural policies have been substantially strengthened by demands of the so-called 'cohesion countries', essentially Spain, Portugal and Greece. These countries were in a position to affect the policy process because of the relevant decision-making rules, i.e. unanimity at the Council for decisions on the mid-term financial perspectives and for the reform of the structural funds. The question arises as to whether the new member States will be satisfied with the current policy-mix or will be willing to change it in their favour.

In the past, budgetary transfers from the structural funds were viewed by Southern countries as a form of compensation for opening-up their markets. The new member States have already opened their markets during the pre-accession periods and may actually be in a better position as regards structural reforms and competitiveness than some old member States. The latter will therefore oppose moves aimed at excluding them from budgetary transfers from the structural funds. Objective I based funding will probably continue to be allocated on the basis of GDP and population. Objective II based funding, focusing on competitiveness and employment, requires agreement on specific eligibility criteria. Moreover, agreement may prove difficult on the rates of co-financing (Liargovas).

EXTERNAL RELATIONS OF THE ENLARGED UNION

As far as EU–CIS relations are concerned, it is expected that if enlargement boosts the economic performance of the new member States it will have an expansionary effect on imports from, and hence on GDP of non-member States (Cosgrove-Sacks). Moreover, the new external borders gave new impetus to EU policies aimed at the stabilisation of its periphery by means of new institutional and financial instruments in the context of the 'European Neighbourhood Policy' (Franck). They have also led to demands for upgrading the structural relationships with the Mediterranean partners (Xenakis).

Dilemmas continuously emerge on how to accommodate the larger neighbours, namely Russia, Ukraine and Turkey. In the case of Russia, action plans were agreed in May 2005 on the implementation of the four common spaces decided in 2003. Such implementation is not seemingly affected by Russia's performance in the field of human rights. EU energy dependence on Russia increased significantly as a result of enlargement, and is likely to be accompanied by additional European investment in the oil sector, especially in the Caspian sea area (Kalyuzhnova and Vagliasindi).

Finally, the fight against terrorism has enhanced cooperation with the USA. In addition, new member States have demonstrated strong pro-Atlantic feelings before joining the EU. It is thus safe to predict that EU enlargement will shift EU foreign policy towards more cooperation with the United States (Schwok). The EU will remain, however, for the foreseeable future, a subordinate partner in its relations with the United States, not least because of the recent rejection of the draft constitutional treaty by two members of the original Community.

FINAL CONSIDERATIONS

Enlargement has in the past been accompanied by institutional reforms. The 2004 enlargement to 10 new member States has been preceded by the Nice Treaty reforms which aimed, essentially, at maintaining the influence of larger member States in the Council, while also upholding the principle of one Commissioner per member State. Enlargement continued, however, to lack public support in the EU-15. Large segments of public opinion remained convinced that it posed a threat to their economic well-being.

The idea that a constitutional treaty would help appease concerns about enlargement and mobilise public opinion in favour of the European project made its way through at the Laaken European Council in December 2001. Although enlargement became a fact on 1 May 2004, opposition did not subside. In France, Germany and Italy economic stagnation and job losses were attributed to unfair practices of the new entrants, rather than failure to introduce economic reforms. The French rejection of the constitutional treaty on 29 May 2005 may have been related to domestic factors but it also demonstrated dissatisfaction with the way integration was proceeding after the recent enlargement. The result may have been different if the vote on the constitutional treaty had preceded enlargement.

Although the potential negative effects of the French vote have been exaggerated, confidence in the European project has received a blow. Moreover, the conflict between supporters of economic liberalism and economic *dirigisme* is becoming more acrimonious. Determination to proceed with the reforms envisaged in the recently revised Lisbon strategy is likely to suffer and, in the long run, the competitive position of the EU, or rather that of member states which fail to adjust. Finally, further enlargement, beyond Bulgaria, Romania and possibly Croatia, lacks public support and may have to be approved by referendum in some countries. Instead of full membership, associate membership may have to be envisaged for countries such as Turkey, Ukraine and, in the more distant future, Russia. EU Treaty provisions would have to be amended accordingly. Associate membership could entail participation in the European Economic Area, but seemingly not in the Schengen travel area; it could also entail participation without voting rights in some EU institutions, such as the European Parliament, for the purpose of embedding democracy in the aforementioned countries. In doing so, however, the Union should be careful not to undermine further its own democratic legitimacy.

The Editor

Index